Discovering Shakespeare's Meaning

An Introduction to the Study of Shakespeare's Dramatic Structures

Leah Scragg

Longman
London and New York

Longman Group UK Limited,
Longman House, Burnt Mill,
Harlow, Essex CM20 2JE, England
and Associated Companies throughout the world.

*Published in the United States of America
by Longman Publishing, New York*

First published in hardback in 1988
by The Macmillan Press Ltd.

This edition first published by Longman Group UK Ltd. 1994

ISBN 0 582–22930–8 PPR

British Library Cataloguing-in-Publication Data

A catalogue record for this book is
available from the British Library

Library of Congress Cataloging-in-Publication Data

Scragg, Leah.
 Discovering Shakespeare's meaning : an introduction to the study
of Shakespeare's dramatic structures / Leah Scragg.
  p.   cm.
 Originally published: Totowa, N.J. : Barnes and Noble, 1987.
 Includes bibliographical references (p.) and index.
 ISBN 0–582–22930–8 (pbk.)
  1. Shakespeare, William, 1564–1616 – – Criticism and interpretation.
 2. Shakespeare, William, 1564–1616 – – Technique. 3. Meaning
(Philosophy) in literature.   4. Rhetoric – – 1500 1800.   5. Drama –
–Technique.   I. Title.
PR2976.S325   1994
822.3'3 – – dc20   93–5081/
                                                        CIP

Printed in Malaysia by TCP

Contents

Acknowledgements

The New Arden editions of Shakespeare's plays are quoted throughout, and I would like to thank Routledge, the publishers, for their
kind permission to use them.

For Tim

Introduction:
Story and Meaning

Plays enact stories from which a spectator derives meaning, and in the case of Shakespeare these stories are not usually difficult to understand. Some details of the plot may remain obscure on a first reading, and some passages of verse may be hard to follow in the playhouse, but the general progress of the story towards a marriage or a death, the acknowledgement of an error or the acquisition of a throne, is sufficiently straightforward to permit the enjoyment of the plays by a wide spectrum of spectators of different ages and from different social and cultural groups.

The problem that confronts the student or general reader embarking on a more detailed study of Shakespeare's work is the gulf that appears to exist between the readily comprehensible stories enacted by the plays and the vast body of critical commentary that surrounds them. While some difficulties of plot and language may require explanation, the products of the 'Shakespeare industry' appear disproportionate to the need to unravel the minor obscurities of a relatively straightforward tale. The very nature of the tales themselves, moreover, presents difficulties. Many appear banal, coincidental or far-fetched, and it is hard to reconcile Shakespeare's reputation as a 'serious' dramatist with the apparent triviality of his work. At the same time, a glance through a theatre programme or through the introductory material to any critical edition is enough to establish that Shakespeare did not (in the main) invent his plots, yet neither the sources from which he borrowed, nor the later works which draw in turn on him (e.g. Charles Lamb's *Tales from Shakespeare*) enjoy the same measure of critical respect. In short, the evidence suggests that the meaning of a Shakespearian play is not to be equated with the story that the inexperienced reader assumes must be the vehicle for it, and such a reader is at a loss to know whence this larger meaning derives.

In seeking to understand the distinction between the tale and the meaning of the drama the student turns naturally to critical works for guidance – only to be daunted by the sheer quantity of material available for study. A glance along the shelves of any bookshop or any school or university library is enough to confirm the impression that Shakespearian scholarship 'has no end, no limit, measure, bound' and that any selection from its offerings must be essentially arbitrary. The difficulty of knowing where or how to begin has been compounded, moreover, in recent years by an explosion of 'new approaches' to literary studies. Whereas students in the 1960s and 1970s were faced with an array of interpretations of the text, together with discussions of the nature of the Elizabethan playhouse and investigations into imagery and sources, those now seeking some initial understanding of the plays are confronted with feminism, new historicism and structural materialism, plus a textual revolution that questions the validity of the very editions upon which the study of the plays is based. In addition, the stance adopted by contemporary criticism is essentially polemic, requiring the reader to adopt and refute positions rather than simply to absorb the information presented on the printed page. For the student or general reader, the leap from enjoying an amusing or moving play in the theatre to engaging with modern literary theory is a gargantuan one, and the temptation for the former at least must be to shy away from it in favour of one of the many collections of 'key' essays thought to ensure examination success.

The purpose of the present book is not to offer a survey of critical opinion or an approach to current literary theory, but to supply a species of staging post between enjoyment of the play as a story and as an inexhaustible source of critical enquiry. Each chapter focuses upon one aspect of the dramatic composition and explores the ways in which the strategies employed by the playwright serve to expand the significance of the story that the play unfolds. By offering an insight into the areas from which the meaning of a play derives, it is hoped that the reader will gain access not to a single drama but to a wide spectrum of Shakespeare's plays, and will ultimately be in a better position to engage with other types of literary discourse and the issues that they raise. Though the question of whether the plays themselves mean, or whether meaning is imposed by the spectator upon them, is itself a matter of considerable debate, it is assumed throughout that the dramas under discussion are the product of a conscious design, and that though different aspects of that design may be foregrounded by different audiences and may acquire different meanings in different contexts (a point of which Shakespeare himself was keenly aware), the design itself may be thought of as Shakespeare's. It is not, however, the dramatist's 'intention' that the book is attempting to recover. The aim is to suggest how an interpretation may be arrived at, and hence to help the interested reader to discover meaning in the work that we call 'Shakespeare' for him/herself.

1

Verse and Prose

One of the major obstacles encountered by the student or inexperienced reader in studying the work of Shakespeare is the form in which it is principally composed – blank verse. Accustomed, through television, to a kind of dramatic language which appears to reflect contemporary speech, the twentieth-century reader finds it difficult to adjust to an art form which appears to have more in common with 'poetry' than with the art of the theatre. But, in fact, the distance between Renaissance and twentieth-century drama is not as great, in this respect, as at first appears. For all its seeming realism, the dialogue of a contemporary play does not reflect everyday speech – it creates an illusion of actuality by drawing upon the audience's assumptions about the kind of speech patterns the individuals concerned might be expected to employ. Stage cockneys, for example, use rhyming slang, civil servants favour long sentences and polysyllabic words, while academics deal in abstract ideas. When the dialogue assigned to such characters is analysed, however, it quickly becomes apparent how remote their language is from day-to-day usage. There are few of those long companionable silences that make up such a high proportion of human intercourse; people rarely repeat themselves or leave their sentences unfinished; while 'um', 'er', 'y'know', 'as I say', 'I mean', etc. are used much more sparingly than in daily conversation. Moreover, the implications of a scene rarely depend solely upon what the characters say. The atmosphere or emotional tempo is dictated by background music – a convention to which the twentieth-century spectator is so wholly accustomed he is generally unaware, while the drama is in progress, of its role in determining his responses. The excitement of a car chase between cops and robbers, for example, is not created by the sparse 'Look out!', 'There he goes', 'Turn right!' which go to make up the dialogue, but by the pounding rhythm and mounting pace of the music, which the viewer accepts as unquestioningly as if his own life were conducted to unseen orchestral accompaniment. Lighting, too, plays a significant part in determining the impact of the words that are

1

spoken. A single spotlight can suggest the isolation of the speaker from the rest of a group, while a deepening gloom can dictate the atmosphere of an entire scene, or lend a sense of foreboding to an otherwise banal exchange. In short, what the twentieth-century audience is conditioned to regard as naturalistic is often at a considerable remove from the unlit, unaccompanied, inarticulate actuality of human communication. It is the product of an agreed set of assumptions, or dramatic conventions, that are so familiar to the contemporary spectator that he or she is no longer aware that the playwright is operating within them.

Shakespeare's dramatic language, and, in particular, his blank verse, constitutes a kind of portmanteau of twentieth-century conventions. The resources of the sound mixer and the lighting engineer were not available to the Renaissance dramatist, and the sixteenth-century playwright had consequently to project, through language alone, what a modern producer achieves through a combination of lights, words, and music. The lines which Shakespeare's characters speak are designed, not merely to convey information between those on stage, and from the dramatis personae to the audience, but to suggest the atmosphere of a scene, the nature of the speakers, and the degree of excitement which the situation as a whole generates. Where a modern audience is conditioned to respond to the changing rhythms of background music, the Elizabethan theatre-goer was attuned to the aural effects produced by alternations between prose and verse, and by the disruption of the iambic pentameter. For this reason, some knowledge of the mechanics of the forms of expression which Shakespeare employs is essential for any student or interested reader seeking an understanding of the way in which meaning is generated in a Renaissance play.

The modes of communication Shakespeare uses are much more varied than is commonly supposed. Though he relies heavily on blank verse, he also employs rhyming couplets and song, together with formal and informal prose. A movement between literary forms frequently marks a shift from one class of speaker, or cast of mind, to another, or from one order of experience to a different level of apprehension. Since song, for example, is more obviously structured than blank verse or prose, and is usually performed to a musical accompaniment,[1] it is often used to suggest a distinct order

---

1. A song is recited in *Cymbeline* (IV.ii.258–81) over the body of the supposedly dead Fidele.

of reality in the play world, or an element of artifice within that of the play itself. The spirituality of Ariel in *The Tempest*, for instance, is conveyed, in part, by the songs which he is assigned; while the element of fancifulness in Orsino's love for Olivia in *Twelfth Night* is implied by the melancholy songs which Feste sings to him. Prose by contrast is frequently – though not always[2] – used to suggest earthiness as opposed to spirituality. Sir Toby, Sir Andrew and Maria in *Twelfth Night*, for example, reveal their opposition to the refinement of Olivia and her suitors as much by the language they employ as the actions which they perform; while Prince Hal's abrogation of the responsibilities of his rank in *1 Henry IV* is implicit in his adoption of the racy idiom of Eastcheap when he is in Falstaff's company. Couplets, by their recurring rhymes and insistent metres are, like song, more self-consciously 'poetic' than blank verse and can therefore denote the intrusion of romance into the day-to-day world, or point to dramatic stylization. Romeo falls into couplets in expressing his love for Rosaline before he meets Juliet, while Gower, in *Pericles*, is distinguished as Chorus from the remainder of the dramatis personae by his use of the rhymed iambic tetrameter.[3] Blank verse itself, the most dignified English metre, is generally assigned to upper class speakers with some measure of self-determination. King Lear uses blank verse when he is in control of himself and his kingdom – prose when his hold on both deserts him. By bringing together a variety of styles within a single structure, an entire microcosm may thus be implied. In *A Midsummer Night's Dream*, for example, the five groups into which the characters fall are clearly differentiated by metrical means. Theseus and Hippolyta, the dignified rulers of the human arena, communicate in blank verse; Hermia, Helena, Demetrius and Lysander, the nobly-born, volatile young lovers, speak in rhyming couplets; Bottom the weaver, and his working-class companions, use prose; the fairies, who belong to a different order of reality, sing songs and are assigned a dazzling variety of metres; while Pyramus and Thisbe, the hero and heroine of the play incompetently performed by Bottom and his friends, betray their fictional status within the play world through their absurdly emphatic alternate rhymes.

It will already be apparent that a hierarchy of artifice is at work in Shakespearian drama in the projection of meaning through form. Spirituality and earthiness are implied through the use of song on

2. See the discussion of the opening scene of *The Winter's Tale*, pp. 17ff. below.
3. For a definition of this term, see below p. 27.

the one hand and prose on the other, not because the first is inherently more elevated than the second, but because they represent departures, in contrary directions, from a norm – and that norm is supplied by blank verse. The principal characters of Shakespeare's plays are drawn, in the main, from the upper classes, and blank verse, with its connotations of dignity and weightiness is the natural vehicle for such figures. Any deviation from the code of conduct expected of such characters, or any social or temperamental disparity between them and those they encounter, is registered by an increase or decrease in formality, either in their own language, or in the language of others. It would be wrong to suggest, however, that blank verse itself constitutes one single, monolithic form of expression. Just as Shakespeare implies differences between or within individuals by moving up or down a register of metrical forms, so he suggests emotional or temperamental differences between or within his speakers by the kind of blank verse his characters are assigned.

Blank verse is the term conventionally employed to denote the unrhymed iambic pentameter. It differs from *free verse* in that the latter has no regular pattern of stressed and unstressed syllables, whereas the former consists of five units, or *feet*, each composed of one unstressed syllable followed by a stressed one, for example:

Dŭmaín | iš mine, | aš súre | aš bárk | oň trée.

(*Love's Labour's Lost*, V.ii.285)

A high proportion of English words form complete iambic feet (e.g. imply; suggest; mistake; within) and the iambic measure therefore lends itself naturally to drama since its rhythms correspond to those of everyday speech. A regular blank verse line has a pause in the middle (i.e. after the second foot), which is known as the *caesura*, and a pause at the end – those lines which conclude with a mark of punctuation being referred to as *end-stopped*. Thus the line quoted above:

Dŭmaín | iš mine, || aš súre | aš bárk | oň trée.

may be described as a regular blank verse line in that it is end-stopped, and consists of five iambic feet with a medial caesura.

On this basic pattern Shakespeare achieves almost infinite

variation to produce a wide range of effects. A high degree of
formality, approximating to ritual, may be implied, for example, by
accentuating the regularity of the poetic form, while, at the other
extreme, the emotional turmoil of a specific speaker may be
conveyed by the disruption of the dominant rhythm. Suffolk's curse
on those who have procured his banishment (*2 Henry VI*) provides
an example of the former:

> Would curses kill, as doth the mandrake's groan,
> I would invent as bitter searching terms,   310
> . . . .
> As lean-fac'd Envy in her loathsome cave.
> My tongue should stumble in mine earnest words;   315
> Mine eyes should sparkle like the beaten flint;
> My hair be fix'd on end, as one distract;
> Ay, every joint should seem to curse and ban:
> And even now my burden'd heart would break
> Should I not curse them. Poison be their drink!   320
> Gall, worse·than gall, the daintiest that they taste!
> Their sweetest shade a grove of cypress trees!
> Their chiefest prospect murd'ring basilisks!
> Their softest touch as smart as lizards' stings!
> Their music frightful as the serpent's hiss,   325
> And boding screech-owls make the consort full!

(III.ii.309–26)

Virtually every line here is end-stopped; a pause is marked, or
implied by the syntax, in the middle of almost every line; while the
relentless iambic beat is heightened by syntactic repetition. The total
effect is mesmeric, with the individuality of the speaker subsumed
into the process of cursing. A very different impact is produced by
Lear's curse upon his daughter in *King Lear*:

> Hear, Nature, hear! dear Goddess, hear!
> Suspend thy purpose, if thou didst intend   285
> To make this creature fruitful!
> Into her womb convey sterility!
> Dry up in her the organs of increase,
> And from her derogate body never spring
> A babe to honour her! If she must teem,   290

Create her child of spleen, that it may live
And be a thwart disnatur'd torment to her!
Let it stamp wrinkles in her brow of youth,
With cadent tears fret channels in her cheeks,
Turn all her mother's pains and benefits   295
To laughter and contempt, that she may feel
How sharper than a serpent's tooth it is
To have a thankless child!

(I.iv.284–98)

Here, though eight of the opening eleven lines of the passage are end-stopped, the concluding four lines are not – the sense sweeping onwards from 'Turn all her mother's pains and benefits' (295) to 'To have a thankless child' (298) with only one, medial, pause. The effect is to suggest a crescendo of emotion, with the violence of the speaker's feelings and the potency of his utterance bursting the bounds of the form that should, theoretically, contain them. This kind of departure from the regular pattern of blank verse is known as *enjambement*, while those lines that do not conclude with a mark of punctuation (or an implied pause) are referred to as *run-on*. Enjambement is almost always accompanied by some variation in the positioning of the caesura – the two devices combining to diminish the 'poetic' quality of a passage and to heighten its naturalism. Line 284, for example, has several pauses, not one, while line 286 has no caesura at all, and line 296, which is run-on, breaks after the third, rather than the second foot. Whereas in Suffolk's speech the unit of composition might be said to be the pentameter itself, since virtually every line consists of a complete clause, in Lear's curse there is a less pointed correlation between metrical and syntactic units, with statements ranging in length from a single line,

Dry up in her the organs of increase,

(288)

to the much longer:

that she may feel
How sharper than a serpent's tooth it is
To have a thankless child!

(296–8)

The same kind of variation from the expected pattern is evident in the handling of the metre. Though the iambic measure is dominant, cf.

Wĭth cá|dĕnt teárs

(294)

Ă bábe | tŏ hó|noŭr hér

(290)

every line of the passage exhibits some departure from the regular iambic rhythm. The opening line, for example, begins not with an unstressed syllable followed by a stressed one, but with two strong beats:

Heár, Ná|tŭre, heár.

This kind of foot in which both syllables are accented is known as a *spondee*, and it is employed to highlight particular words or phrases by the violence that it does to the listener's metrical sense. A similar technique is at work in the *reversed feet* with which many lines open, cf.

Drý ŭp | iň hér

(288)

Here, rather than the rhythm following the conventional pattern (‿ ⁄) the opening foot is inverted, accentuating the injunction with which the line begins. In line 293 both kinds of aberrant foot, the spondee and the reversed (or inverted) foot, are employed, the two combining to suggest the violence the speaker invokes (by the dislocation of the metrical pattern), and the perversion of nature his curse involves (by the departure from the metrical norm, representative of normality):

Lét ĭt | stámp wrín|klĕs . . .

A yet more radical movement away from blank verse occurs in line 286:

Tŏ máke | thís créa|tŭre frúit|fŭl.

Here, though the first and third feet are regular, the second is a
spondee, while the line over-all consists of only three and a half feet.
The effect is emphatic – particular stress falling upon the outrage
and contempt implied in 'this creature', and upon the pause with
which the line closes. The spectator lingers upon the magnitude of
the curse, and experiences the sense of unnatural curtailment which
it involves. At the same time, the illusion is created that the audience
is listening to natural speech, rather than to a recitation. The
construction of the line is dictated, not by the requirements of the
metre, but by the pressure of the speaker's emotions, with the
accent falling upon those elements of his utterance which are of
most significance to him. In short, where Suffok's curse implies the
enactment of ritual through its insistent regularity, Lear's enacts a
state of mind by its dislocation of the metrical pattern.

A third curse, that of Coriolanus upon the people of Rome,
illustrates the extent to which Shakespeare carries the disruption of
his dominant form as a means of projecting a mental state.
Coriolanus has been banished by the city for which he has fought
since his youth, and his response is both furious and outraged:

You common cry of curs! whose breath I hate	120
As reek o' th'rotten fens, whose loves I prize	
As the dead carcasses of unburied men	
That do corrupt my air: I banish you!	
And here remain with your uncertainty!	
Let every feeble rumour shake your hearts!	125
Your enemies, with nodding of their plumes,	
Fan you into despair! Have the power still	
To banish your defenders, till at length	
Your ignorance – which finds not till it feels,	
Making but reservation of yourselves,	130
Still your own foes – deliver you as most	
Abated captives to some nation	
That won you without blows! Despising	
For you the city, thus I turn my back.	
There is a world elsewhere!	135

(*Coriolanus*, III.iii.120–35)

This passage clearly has much in common with the lines from *Lear* quoted above. The situations of the two speakers are similar. Both have been rejected by those from whom they might have expected gratitude and respect, and both respond with an enraged desire for vengeance, in the form of some visitation of suffering, upon the wrong-doers. The devices Shakespeare employs to suggest the gathering wrath and social disorder implied in the responses of both speakers are similar. Enjambement occurs at lines 120, 121, 131, 132, etc., reaching a crescendo at the end of the passage, while the caesura varies in its position from its medial occurrence in the line

For you the city, ‖ thus I turn my back,

(134)

to the late:

That won you without blows! ‖ Despising.

(133)

Metrical variation, too, occurs in every line. Reversed feet again stress injunctions (cf. 'Háve thĕ | pówer' (127)); spondees accentuate powerfully-felt phrases (cf. 'Í bán|ĭsh yóu' (123)); while some lines do not exhibit the expected five stresses (cf. 'Abáted cáptives to sóme nátion' (132)). Where *Coriolanus* differs from *King Lear* is in the breakdown of control suggested by the much more systematic use of all these devices. Where Lear's speech opens with comparatively short statements, and a considerable measure of end-stopping, implying some degree of control by the speaker over his emotion, Coriolanus' lines run on from the outset. The subject of the first sentence is reached, for example, only at the end of the fourth line, while major syntactic breaks occur within, rather than at the end of, lines (e.g. after 'curs' (120), 'fens' (121), 'air' (123)). Lines 127 to 133 also constitute a single sentence which becomes increasingly tangential. The tumbling clauses, over-running the five foot line, together with strong medial pauses, make it hard for the listener to know where the lines begin and end, reducing the 'poetic' quality of the passage and heightening its naturalism. The same effect is achieved by the insistent undercutting of the iambic rhythm. Where the power and potency of Lear's utterance is suggested by functional departures from an established metrical pattern (as in the stressing of injunctions), Coriolanus' speech conveys a sense of hysteria by the tenuousness with which the underlying rhythm is maintained. Lines 127–33 are again the most striking in this respect. Five stresses (on 'fan', 'despáir', 'have', 'pówer', 'still') do occur in line 127, but their arrangement does not coincide with the expected pattern, while line 130 has only four stresses (on 'máking', 'réservátion', and 'yoursélves') and line 132 only three ('Abáted', 'cáptives', 'nátion') – with a partial stress on 'some'.

In each of these speeches it is evident that Shakespeare's rhythms are functioning very like the background music in a television drama. They are conveying the mood of the scene, or the speaker, to the audience, and they are doing so by auditory means. A reader unfamiliar with any of the passages quoted above does not need a stage direction in order to know that the first is a kind of chant, or that the second and third should be spoken in an excited voice. The degree of personal emotion each involves is communicated by the degree of tension that is set up between the metrical norm and the speaking voice, with emotional disorder projected, as it is today, by discordancy. It is not simply heightened emotion, however, that Shakespeare projects through the manipulation of rhythm. As noted above, any movement away from the kind of structure exemplified by:

Dŭmáin | iš míne, | aš súre | as bárk | ŏn trée

can be used to enhance the naturalism of a scene, and thus to encourage an audience to view those on stage as people like themselves rather than as stylized embodiments of an attribute or an attitude. Lysander's justification of his pursuit of Hermia in *A Midsummer Night's Dream* and Hermione's defence of her reputation in *The Winter's Tale* illustrate the point. The situations of the two characters have some similarities. Both speakers are of noble rank, have been accused of misconduct, and feel called upon to defend their behaviour in public. Nevertheless, the responses of a theatre audience to their predicaments are very different. Lysander remains a character observed:

> I am, my lord, as well deriv'd as he,
> As well possess'd; my love is more than his;   100
> My fortunes every way as fairly rank'd,

If not with vantage, as Demetrius';
And, which is more than all these boasts can be,
I am belov'd of beauteous Hermia.
Why should not I then prosecute my right?   105
Demetrius, I'll avouch it to his head,
Made love to Nedar's daughter, Helena,
And won her soul: and she, sweet lady, dotes,
Devoutly dotes, dotes in idolatry,
Upon this spotted and inconstant man.   110

(I.i.99–110)

Here, for all the superficial urgency of Lysander's appeal, the
spectator does not become involved in his situation. The heavily
end-stopped lines, and regular rhythm (cf. 'My̆ fór|tunĕs év|er̆y
wáy | ăs fáir|ly̆ rank'd' (101)), sustain, rather than diminish, the
audience's awareness of artifice, and hence frustrate dramatic
involvement. That is not to say, of course, that the execution is
flawed. The style is designed to promote dramatic distance, to allow
us to enjoy what happens to Lysander rather than becoming
implicated in his experience. It is a style perfectly adapted for the
kind of comedy in which we laugh at, rather than with, individuals.
Hermione's speech in *The Winter's Tale* has a very different effect,
and this difference is not merely a product of the gravity of her
situation (she has been accused of adultery):

Since what I am to say, must be but that
Which contradicts my accusation, and
The testimony on my part, no other
But what comes from myself, it shall scarce boot me   25
To say 'not guilty': mine integrity,
Being counted falsehood, shall, as I express it,
Be so receiv'd. But thus, if powers divine
Behold our human actions (as they do),
I doubt not then but innocence shall make   30
False accusation blush, and tyranny
Tremble at patience. You, my lord, best know
(Who least will seem to do so) my past life
Hath been as continent, as chaste, as true,
As I am now unhappy; which is more   35
Than history can pattern, though devis'd

And play'd to take spectators. For behold me,
A fellow of the royal bed, which owe
A moiety of the throne, a great king's daughter,
The mother to a hopeful prince, here standing   40
To prate and talk for life and honour 'fore
Who please to come and hear. For life, I prize it
As I weigh grief (which I would spare): for honour,
'Tis a derivative from me to mine,
And only that I stand for.   45

(III.ii.22–45)

Here, some very radical departures from conventional blank verse
are evident. Very few lines are end-stopped, while the caesura, far
from falling inexorably at a given point, occurs at any position
dictated by the sense, from after the second foot:

Be so receiv'd. ‖ But thus

(28)

to midway through the last:

Which contradicts my accusation, ‖ and

(23)

Moreover, in a number of instances the pause falls after an
unstressed, rather than a stressed, syllable (i.e. in the middle of a
foot), the resulting *feminine caesura* contributing to the disruption of
the conventional pattern, cf.

Aš Í | ăm nów | ŭnhá|pp̆y; ‖ whích | iš móre

(35)

The insistent enjambement, together with variation in the position
of the caesura, results in a considerable divorce between metrical
and syntactic units. Statements, rather than being completed within
the line, as in Lysander's

I am, my lord, as well deriv'd as he,

(99)

or

I am belov'd of beauteous Hermia,

(104)

now extend over several lines, beginning and ending in mid-pentameter, and even, as noted above, in mid-foot, cf.

You, my lord, best know
(Who least will seem to do so) my past life
Hath been as continent, as chaste, as true,
As I am now unhappy.

(32–5)

Whereas an audience, confronted with Lysander's speech, remains conscious throughout of the poetic medium that is being employed, a spectator (as opposed to a reader) listening to Hermione's defence, has much greater difficulty in determining where lines begin and end, and hence has considerably less awareness of the metrical structure underlying the passage. The flow of the speech from one line to the next is promoted, moreover, by a variety of other devices. A high proportion of lines close, for example, on an unstressed syllable that does not form part of the conventional metrical scheme, cf.

But what | comes from | myself, | it shall | scarce boot | me

(25)

And play'd | to take | specta|tors. For | behold | me,

(37)

Who please | to come | and hear. | For life, | I prize | it.

(42)

An unstressed syllable falling at the end of a blank verse line, outside the metrical pattern, is known as a *feminine ending*, and it is frequently used in conjunction with unstressed endings of other kinds to promote enjambement. Such endings are conventionally divided into two groups – *light* and *weak*. The first consists of lightly stressed monosyllables, usually pronouns and auxiliary verbs, exemplified here by:

It shall scarce boot *me*

(25)

as I express *it*

(27)

while the second is made up of prepositions and conjunctions that serve to hurry the listener from one line to the next, cf.

Which contradicts my accusation, *and*
The testimony on my part

(23–4)

To prate and talk for life and honour *'fore*
Who please to come and hear.

(41–2)

An analysis of the twenty-three and a half lines of the passage shows how extensive the use of such devices is. Over a third have feminine endings (e.g. 24, 25, 37, 39), while nearly a half close with an unaccented syllable of some kind (e.g. 23, 27, 41, 42). The effect is to create the illusion of natural speech. Whereas Lysander's end-stopped lines sustain the audience's awareness of artifice, Hermione's more flexible blank verse diminishes the distance between the play world and the spectator.

The logical extension of this progress away from metrical regularity would appear to be the total rejection of blank verse in favour of prose. A student or inexperienced reader approaching Shakespeare's work for the first time, might well wonder why the dramatist does not employ prose in those contexts in which a high degree of naturalism or audience/actor intimacy is appropriate. The answer lies in the role played by blank verse as the norm of communication on the Shakespearian stage. Whereas a movement away from that norm towards metrical freedom may imply turmoil, or natural speech, the total rejection of it is used to denote a more radical shift to an entirely different social class or mental state. In *Othello*, for example, the personal disintegration of the central figure is registered (in part) by his descent into prose. At the outset of the play, confident of his wife's affection for him, and secure in his role within the state, he defends himself against the charge of having obtained Desdemona's love by witchcraft in a dignified blank verse that is indicative of his simplicity and self-assurance:

> She lov'd me for the dangers I had pass'd,
> And I lov'd her that she did pity them.
> This only is the witchcraft I have us'd:
> Here comes the lady, let her witness it.

(I.iii.167–70)

As his suspicions concerning Desdemona's faithfulness grow, however, the lack of tension implied here by the straightforward correlation between clause and line disappears:

> By the world,
> I think my wife be honest, and think she is not,   390
> I think that thou [Iago] art just, and think thou art not;
> I'll have some proof: my name, that was as fresh
> As Dian's visage, is now begrim'd, and black
> As mine own face: if there be cords, or knives,
> Poison, or fire, or suffocating streams,   395
> I'll not endure it: would I were satisfied!

(III.iii.389–96)

Here, the antithetical see-saw across the caesura:

> I think my wife be honest, ‖ and think she is not,
> I think that thou art just, ‖ and think thou are not;

> (390–1)

the run-on lines:

> My name, that was as fresh
> As Dian's visage,

> (392–3)

the fragmentation of the line by internal pausing:

> if there be cords, or knives,
> Poison, or fire, or suffocating streams,
> I'll not endure it,

> (394–6)

and reversed feet:

> Póisŏn, | ŏr fíre,

> (395)

all suggest the tumult in the mind of the speaker. No reader confronted with these two speeches for the first time could deliver them in the same tone. The distraction of the second is implicit in its movement, with the blank verse line not merely carrying the sense but providing that discordant music which so often denotes acute mental stress on the modern stage. Nevertheless, for all the distance between the two utterances, the second is still recognizably that of a rational human being – albeit a tortured one. An underlying order is still present in his lines, and the dignity of blank verse lends authority to what he has to say. By Act IV, however, a much more radical development has taken place. Under the influence of Iago, Othello surrenders himself to jealousy, and the overthrow of his moral and intellectual nature is signalled by a shift in the vehicle of communication he is assigned:

Lie with her, lie on her? – We say lie on her, when 35
they belie her, – lie with her, zounds, that's fulsome!
Handkerchief – confessions – handkerchief! To confess, and be hanged for his labour. First, to be hanged,
and then to confess; I tremble at it. Nature would
not invest herself in such shadowing passion without 40
some instruction. It is not words that shake me thus.
Pish! Noses, ears and lips. Is't possible? – Confess?
– Handkerchief? – O devil!   [*He falls down.*]

(IV.i.35–43)

The shift from verse to prose here is clearly not designed to enhance the 'realism' of the scene, or to diminish the distance between play and spectator. It registers the speaker's descent from a meaningful world into a meaningless one, and from a position of mastery to one of subservience.

Prose does not always indicate a degenerate state, however, nor is it necessarily less complex in its organization than verse. Though it functions as a stylistic contrast, and frequently points social divisions, its use does not automatically involve the juxtaposition of a racy 'low language' against a more elevated idiom. The opening scenes of *The Winter's Tale* afford an example of the variety of styles Shakespeare employs, and the way in which the speech patterns he assigns his characters not only convey information, but help to control the responses of an audience to the stage spectacle. The play begins with an exchange between two courtiers – Camillo and Archidamus:

Arch. If you shall chance, Camillo, to visit Bohemia, on
the like occasion whereon my services are now on
foot, you shall see, as I have said, great difference
betwixt our Bohemia and your Sicilia.
Cam. I think, this coming summer, the King of Sicilia 5
means to pay Bohemia the visitation which he justly
owes him.
Arch. Wherein our entertainment shall shame us: we will
be justified in our loves: for indeed –
Cam. Beseech you – 10
Arch. Verily I speak it in the freedom of my knowledge:

> we cannot with such magnificence – in so rare – I
> know not what to say – We will give you sleepy
> drinks, that your senses (unintelligent of our insuf-
> ficience) may, though they cannot praise us, as little   15
> accuse us.
> *Cam.* You pay a great deal too dear for what's given
> freely.
> *Arch.* Believe me, I speak as my understanding instructs
> me, and as mine honesty puts it to utterance.   20
> *Cam.* Sicilia cannot show himself over-kind to Bohemia.
> They were trained together in their childhoods, and
> there rooted betwixt them then such an affection
> which cannot choose but branch now. Since their
> more mature dignities and royal necessities made   25
> separation of their society, their encounters, though
> not personal, have been royally attorneyed with in-
> terchange of gifts, letters, loving embassies, that they
> have seemed to be together, though absent; shook
> hands, as over a vast; and embraced, as it were, from   30
> the ends of opposed winds. The heavens continue
> their loves!   (I.i.1–32)

The kind of prose employed here could not be further removed from
the third speech from *Othello* quoted above. Whereas Othello's
speech is highly exclamatory, and is largely made up of a series of
short phrases with little grammatical coherence (cf. 'Handkerchief –
confessions – handkerchief' (37)), the exchange between
Archidamus and Camillo consists of a number of long, elaborately
constructed sentences, rich in dependent clauses, parenthetical
statements, and antithetical balance (cf., in particular, lines 24–31).
Whereas the former passage projects an image of a man inarticulate
with emotion, the latter implies the social poise of the speakers and
the highly cultured social milieu they represent. Where Othello's
speech invites concern by its ferocity, the interchange between
Archidamus and Camillo frustrates audience involvement, with
Latinate vocabulary (cf. 'visitation' (6), 'entertainment' (8),
'justified' (9), 'magnificence' (12), 'insufficience' (14–15), etc.) and
complex sentences combining to produce an idiom remote from
day-to-day usage. Far from sharing the experience of the speakers,
the audience is taxed intellectually by the struggle to comprehend
them, and is led to marvel at an environment so sophisticated that a

simple affirmation of truthfulness becomes 'I speak as my understanding instructs me, and as mine honesty puts it to utterance' (19–20).

Shakespeare's dramatic language is conveying much more here than some background information about the friendship between two kings. On the one hand it is implying the kind of setting in which the action takes place – courtly, sophisticated, remote from naturalness and spontaneity – while on the other manoeuvering the listener into the role of spectator, rather than concerned participant in events. A further function of the prose exchange becomes apparent, moreover, as the next group of characters enters:

Enter LEONTES, HERMIONE, MAMILLIUS,
POLIXENES, CAMILLO, [*and Attendants*].

Pol. Nine changes of the watery star hath been
    The shepherd's note since we have left our throne
    Without a burden. Time as long again
    Would be fill'd up, my brother, with our thanks;
    And yet we should, for perpetuity,   5
    Go hence in debt: and therefore, like a cipher
    (Yet standing in rich place) I multiply
    With one 'We thank you' many thousands more
    That go before it.
Leon.   Stay your thanks a while,
    And pay them when you part.
Pol.   Sir, that's to-morrow.   10
    I am question'd by my fears, of what may chance
    Or breed upon our absence; that may blow
    No sneaping winds at home, to make us say
    'This is put forth too truly'. Besides, I have stay'd
    To tire your royalty.
Leon.   We are tougher, brother,   15
    Than you can put us to't.
Pol.   No longer stay.
Leon. One seve'night longer.
Pol.   Very sooth, to-morrow.
Leon. We'll part the time between's then: and in that
    I'll no gainsaying.
Pol.   Press me not, beseech you, so.

                           (I.ii.1–19)

Here, the shift from prose to verse makes plain a movement up the social scale. Elegant and cultured as Camillo and Archidamus are, they are not of the same social stature as the two kings, and the change of idiom allows the dramatist to point a difference in rank between even the most sophisticated of people. The kind of blank verse he assigns Polixenes and Leontes is also significant. While on the one hand some metrical irregularity (e.g. 'Níne chán|gĕs' (1)), considerable variation in the position of the caesura (including the division of a number of lines between speakers), and insistent enjambement (cf. 1–3, and 11–13) all help to create the illusion of natural speech, on the other, the complex sentences and circumlocutory style (cf. 1–3) enforce the urbanity of the speakers and frustrate identification with them. In terms of content the exchange between the two kings has much in common with that between the two courtiers and the same could be said of their style of speech. Relative clauses, elliptical statements, and parenthetic remarks all pose problems for the listener, so that although the verse moves like informal speech it nevertheless makes considerable intellectual demands of the spectator. The result is an impression of refinement, and the creation of dramatic distance. Kings and courtiers alike speak fluently, and elegantly, but they do not speak like us, and their convoluted style ensures that we observe them as beings from another, possibly more gracious, world.

The style established in the opening hundred lines of this scene is not, however, maintained throughout. At line 109 the tone changes abruptly as the Queen, Hermione, who has joined Leontes in attempting to persuade Polixenes to prolong his stay, gives the visiting king her hand – producing the following response from her husband:

Leon.   [*Aside*] Too hot, too hot!
   To mingle friendship far, is mingling bloods.
   I have *tremor cordis* on me: my heart dances,   110
   But not for joy – not joy. This entertainment
   May a free face put on, derive a liberty
   From heartiness, from bounty, fertile bosom,
   And well become the agent: 't may, I grant:
   But to be paddling palms, and pinching fingers,   115
   As now they are, and making practis'd smiles
   As in a looking-glass; and then to sigh, as 'twere
   The mort o'th'deer – O, that is entertainment

My bosom likes not, nor my brows. Mamillius,
  Art thou my boy?
Mam.   Ay, my good lord.
Leon.   I'fecks: 120
  Why that's my bawcock. What! Hast smutch'd thy nose?
  They say it is a copy out of mine. Come, captain,
  We must be neat; not neat, but cleanly, captain:
  And yet the steer, the heifer and the calf
  Are all call'd neat. – Still virginalling   125
  Upon his palm! – How now, you wanton calf!
  Art thou my calf?
Mam.   Yes, if you will, my lord.
Leon. Thou want'st a rough pash and the shoots that I have
  To be full like me: yet they say we are
  Almost as like as eggs; women say so,   130
  (That will say any thing): but were they false
  As o'er-dy'd blacks, as wind, as waters; false
  As dice are to be wish'd by one that fixes
  No bourn 'twixt his and mine, yet were it true
  To say this boy were like me. Come, sir page,   135
  Look on me with your welkin eye: sweet villain!
  Most dear'st, my collop! Can thy dam? – may't be? –
  Affection! thy intention stabs the centre:
  Thou dost make possible things not so held,
  Communicat'st with dreams; – how can this be? –   140
  With what's unreal thou coactive art,
  And fellow'st nothing: then 'tis very credent
  Thou may'st co-join with something; and thou dost,
  (And that beyond commission) and I find it,
  (And that to the infection of my brains   145
  And hard'ning of my brows).

(I.ii.108–46)

Shakespeare's blank verse here performs the function of a modern
zoom lens. Whereas, up to this point, the reader or spectator has
observed the public gestures of the dramatis personae, he or she is
now thrust into the mind of one of the speakers and confronted with
a highly disturbing gap between appearance and actuality. The
'aside' isolates the character from the rest of the group – like a
twentieth-century spotlight – while the movement of the blank

verse contrasts sharply with what has gone before. The stateliness of the opening exchange has given place to fragmentation and disorder. Insistent enjambement promoted by a variety of unstressed endings (cf. 111, 128, 133) send one line tumbling into the next, while strong internal pauses, occurring as the sense dictates, make it impossible to determine, when the passage is spoken rather than read, where the blank verse lines begin and end (cf. 111–14). Metrical irregularity too rips apart the poetic fabric to disclose the passion of the speaker. The disgust of line 125, for example, is signalled both by its brevity and the extreme irregularity of 'still virginalling', while the distrust and revulsion that now characterize his attitude towards women are evinced in the stresses of:

Álmŏst | ăs líke | ăs eǵgs; | wómĕn | sáy só.

(130)

The long, elegantly structured sentences of the opening exchange have given place to short questions and violent exclamations, while the elevated Latinate diction is now disturbingly juxtaposed against colloquialism (cf. 'smutch'd', (121) 'paddling palms' (115)) and innuendo (cf. 'virginalling' (125)). The effect is startling in two respects. In the first place, as noted above, the passage dramatically alters the relationship between the spectators and the dramatis personae. Whereas up to this point the members of the audience have watched the exchanges between the Bohemians and Sicilians with a species of wondering detachment, they are now abruptly drawn into the experience of mistrusting a wife and a friend through the emotion that Leontes' lines generate. At the same time, their assessment of the Sicilian court undergoes a swift revision. Induced to view Hermione and Polixenes through the distorted gaze of Leontes, the spectator is obliged to entertain, however briefly, the possibility that elegance and courtliness may be a facade for lust and bestiality, while simultaneously recognizing the corrosive passion underlying social harmony and grace.

The economy with which this shift of perspective is achieved is remarkable. The technique of speaking 'aside' and the broken rhythms of Leontes' utterance combine to produce the change of atmosphere which ominous music might indicate in a television drama, while the enactment, rather than statement, of emotion promotes that intimacy between protagonist and spectator which a close-up camera can effect today. No stage direction is necessary here in order to convey the speaker's state of mind. Though what he has to say is obviously important, it is the way in which he says it that determines how we relate to him, and which communicates most powerfully the threat which his attitudes constitute to the stability and harmony of the play world.

In the second half of scene ii the two contrasting styles are brought together. Leontes, obsessed by his jealousy, attempts to secure the assistance of Camillo in the murder of Polixenes. Suspicious that the courtier may be his queen's instrument, he begins by questioning his loyalty, eliciting an expression of concern that allows him to make his own diseased position clear:

Cam.	My gracious lord,	
I may be negligent, foolish, and fearful;		250
In every one of these no man is free,		
But that his negligence, his folly, fear,		
Among the infinite doings of the world,		
Sometime puts forth. In your affairs, my lord,		
If ever I were wilful-negligent,		255
It was my folly: if industriously		
I play'd the fool, it was my negligence,		
Not weighing well the end: if ever fearful		
To do a thing, where I the issue doubted,		
Whereof the execution did cry out		260
Against the non-performance, 'twas a fear		
Which oft infects the wisest: these, my lord,		
Are such allow'd infirmities that honesty		
Is never free of. But, beseech your Grace,		
Be plainer with me; let me know my trespass		265
By its own visage: if I then deny it,		
Tis none of mine.		
Leon.	Ha' you not seen, Camillo?	
(But that's past doubt: you have, or your eye-glass		
Is thicker than a cuckold's horn) or heard?		
(For to a vision so apparent rumour		270
Cannot be mute) or thought? (for cogitation		
Resides not in that man that does not think)		
My wife is slippery? If thou wilt confess,		
Or else be impudently negative,		

> To have nor eyes, nor ears, nor thought, then say   275
> My wife's a hobby-horse, deserves a name
> As rank as any flax-wench that puts to
> Before her troth-plight: say't and justify't!
> *Cam.* I would not be a stander-by, to hear
> My sovereign mistress clouded so, without   280
> My present vengeance taken: 'shrew my heart,
> You never spoke what did become you less
> Than this; which to reiterate were sin
> As deep as that, though true.
> *Leon.*   Is whispering nothing?
> Is leaning cheek to cheek? is meeting noses?   285
> Kissing with inside lip? stopping the career
> Of laughter with a sigh (a note infallible
> Of breaking honesty)? horsing foot on foot?
> Skulking in corners? wishing clocks more swift?
> Hours, minutes? noon, midnight? and all eyes   290
> Blind with the pin and web, but theirs; theirs only.
> That would unseen be wicked? is this nothing?
> Why then the world, and all that's in't, is nothing,
> The covering sky is nothing, Bohemia nothing,
> My wife is nothing, nor nothing have these nothings,   295
> If this be nothing.

(I.ii.249–96)

Superficially, the styles of the two speakers have much in common. Appropriately, when addressing the King, Camillo employs blank verse like his sovereign, rather than the informal prose of his earlier conversation with Archidamus. The verse of both men, moreover, conforms to the rhythms of natural speech, rather than strictly adhering to the conventions governing the poetic form. Enjambement, for example, occurs frequently in all four speeches (cf. 260–2, 275–8, 280–1, 286–8), while feminine (258), light (266) and weak (280) endings contribute throughout to the easy movement from one line to the next. The caesura falls in early (283) and late (269) positions, contributing to the breakdown of correspondence between syntactic and metrical units, while departures from the iambic pattern are frequent, and sometimes radical (cf. 250, 286, 291). Nevertheless, for all their superficial similarity, the styles of the two speakers are far from identical. Though both men are

governed by strong emotions, the disruptive nature of Leontes'
passion is emphatically contrasted with Camillo's legitimate
concern by the ragged movement of his lines. Whereas Camillo's
speeches largely conform to the iambic pattern, with minimal
variation for the purposes of emphasis, cf.

If ev|er Ĭ | were wil|ful-ne|gligent

(255)

Which oft | infects | the wi|sest: these, | my lord,

(262)

Ĭs ne|ver free | of. But, | beseech | your Grace,

(264)

Leontes' lines play against the rhythm of the verse, implying the
breakdown of the natural order:

Kissing | with in|side lip? | stopping | the career

(286)

Skulking | in cor|ners? wish|ing clocks | more swift?

(289)

Blind with | the pin | and web, | but theirs; | theirs on|ly.

(291)

At the same time, Leontes' emotional disorder is projected through
the staccato movement of his utterance. Whereas Camillo's
speeches consist of a series of long hypotactic sentences extending
over several lines, enacting the speaker's emotional and intellectual
control, Leontes' impassioned outbursts are much more loosely
constructed, degenerating, in the second of his two speeches, into a
torrent of increasingly elliptical questions that betray a racing mind
and fevered imagination. Once again, there is no need here of a
stage direction to indicate how the lines should be spoken, or of an

explicit statement defining the threat Leontes poses to his world. The rationality of one speaker and the emotional turmoil of the other are conveyed by the rhythm of their lines, while the collision between their styles enacts the irruption of a corrosive and potentially anarchic force into a stable and orderly world.

The effects discussed here depend, in large measure, upon the contrasts the dramatist engineers between kinds of discourse – prose and blank verse, formal and informal prose, regular and more flexible blank verse. Shakespeare's characters do not employ one single monolithic form of expression, nor is their mode of utterance arbitrarily selected. The vehicle they use is designed to communicate something about their status, mood, or proximity to the spectator, or to suggest the degree of homogeneity of their world. In many instances the members of the audience remain unconscious of the means by which their responses are manipulated, while on others a shift in style is drawn pointedly to their attention. The latter is frequently the case when Shakespeare abandons both blank verse and prose in favour of a more overtly structured form. As noted above, the songs interlarding a number of plays illustrate the use of a self-consciously poetic vehicle to indicate the intrusion of other-worldliness or romance into the day-to-day world, but departures from the dominant blank verse form may serve a variety of other purposes. The chorus speeches of *Pericles*, for example, are designed, not to suggest fancifulness, or spirituality, but to differentiate one level of artifice from another. All five acts of the play, and some scenes, are introduced to the spectators by the mediaeval poet, Gower, who claims to have returned from the dead in order to recount Pericles' life-history for their edification. The chorus to Act IV (a part of the play generally regarded as Shakespeare's) is typical of this character's style throughout:

Now to Marina bend your mind,   5
Whom our fast-growing scene must find
At Tharsus, and by Cleon train'd
In music's letters; who hath gain'd
Of education all the grace,
Which makes her both the heart and place   10
Of general wonder. But, alack,
That monster envy, oft the wrack

Of earned praise, Marina's life
Seeks to take off by treason's knife.

(IV Chorus 5–14)

Here, though the metre is iambic, cf.

Thăt món|stĕr én|vy̆, oft | thĕ wráck

(12)

there are only four feet in each line, while the passage is rhymed throughout. The four foot line, or *tetrameter*, is used to detach Gower from the play that he presents by means of the contrast that is set up between his dramatic idiom and that of Pericles, Marina and the rest who largely employ blank verse. Gower, as producer-commentator, belongs to a different order of reality from the 'motes and shadows' (IV.iv.21) that he presents, and his emphatically structured verse serves to isolate him from both the audience and the scenes which he interprets.

A much more famous passage, the opening scene of *Macbeth*, illustrates a very different use of the rhymed tetrameter:

> *Thunder and lightning. Enter three* WITCHES.
> *1 Witch.* When shall we three meet again?
>   In thunder, lightning, or in rain?
> *2 Witch.* When the hurlyburly's done,
>   When the battle's lost and won.
> *3 Witch.* That will be ere the set of sun.   5
> *1 Witch.* Where the place?
> *2 Witch.*   Upon the heath.
> *3 Witch.* There to meet with Macbeth.
> *1 Witch.* I come, Graymalkin!
> *2 Witch.* Paddock calls.
> *3 Witch.* Anon!   10
> *All.* Fair is foul, and foul is fair:
>   Hover through the fog and filthy air.

(I.i.1–12)

Here, the short, emphatically rhymed lines serve a number of purposes. The form is remote from natural speech, implying that the speakers do not belong to the everyday world, while the strong beat and insistent rhymes suggest the weaving of a spell, and have the hypnotic quality of a chant. What is most significant about the lines, however, is that they are not iambic. Whereas an iambic foot consists of an unstressed syllable followed by a stressed one, the metre the witches are assigned has the opposite pattern, cf.

Whén the | húrlў|búrly's | dóne,

(3)

Whére the | pláce?

Ŭ|pón the | heáth

(6)

Fáir ĭs | fóul, añd | fóul ĭs | fáir

(11)

The pattern of stresses employed here is conventionally described as *trochaic*. Each foot is made up of a stressed syllable followed by an unstressed one, while the last foot in each line frequently consists of one accented syllable only, to allow for an emphatic rhyme. The effect in this context is highly disturbing. The witches belong to a reversed world, in which 'Fair is foul, and foul is fair' (11), and the inversion of normality they embody is enforced by rhythmic, as well as lexical, means.

The divorce between the world of the weird sisters and that of beleaguered humanity (represented by Duncan's court) is indicated by the metrical shift that takes place following the Witches' departure. As the swirl of fog and filthy air dissipates, normality gradually reasserts itself in the form of Malcolm's blank verse:

This is the Sergeant,
Who, like a good and hardy soldier, fought
'Gainst my captivity. – Hail, brave friend!

Say to the King the knowledge of the broil,
As thou didst leave it.

(I.ii.3–7)

The economy with which meaning is communicated here constitutes a remarkable achievement. In fewer than twenty lines Shakespeare not only captures the attention of his audience by some highly spectacular effects (for the importance of this, see below p. 61), he also evokes the negative universe to which the witches belong, and initiates the conflict between opposing states of being upon which the subsequent action depends. Far from presenting a barrier to the modern reader, the poetic forms employed here actively promote understanding. The mesmeric power of 'Fair is foul, and foul is fair' (11) is experienced by the most unsophisticated spectator, as is the sense of release that occurs when the constriction of the rhymed tetrameter is loosened in Malcolm's blank verse.

The continuing hold that Shakespeare has exercised for nearly four hundred years over the imaginations of successive generations of play-goers arises, in part, from his inexhaustibility. The speeches that he assigns his characters cannot be readily paraphrased because their significance derives from an interaction between form and statement, and from the total context within which they are set. The way in which a statement is made is as important as the statement itself, and this aspect of Shakespeare's art is easily over-looked by the student, unfamiliar with Renaissance drama, closeted in a study with a printed text. Hence one route towards the discovery of Shakespeare's meaning lies through the forms of expression the dramatist employs – the study of which is far from the arid pursuit that is generally supposed. Shakespeare's power to invest the commonplace with meaning is experienced, if not conceptualized, by every theatre-goer, and a heightened awareness of the techniques that the playwright utilizes to govern the responses of his audience can be very helpful to the student or interested reader confronted with a text on a printed page. Cooking food over a fire, for example, and concepts of hardship or misfortune, are aspects of everyday life that might well be employed to evoke man's physicality, or the unchanging nature of the human lot. It is the rhymed trochaic tetrameter that transforms them into the ingredients of the world's most obscene rite:

Double, double toil and trouble:
Fire, burn; and, cauldron, bubble.

(*Macbeth*, IV.i.10–11)

2

Imagery and Spectacle

As the previous chapter has attempted to show, the blank verse line constituted one of the major poetic resources of the Renaissance dramatist. By metrical variation Shakespeare and his contemporaries were able to denote the emotional tempo of a specific scene, to engineer or frustrate dramatic involvement, and to distinguish one cast of mind or social group from another. Rhythm was not, however, the only poetic resource available to the dramatists of the period. The majority of Elizabethan–Jacobean playwrights were poets as well as dramatists, and they brought to their comedies and tragedies the same literary techniques that they employed in their non-dramatic works. Rhyme, alliteration,[1] and onomatopoeia[2] are all freely utilized, while poetic forms are sometimes transposed in their entirety, like the sonnet through which Romeo and Juliet first communicate (I.v.92–105), into the dramatic structure.

The use of imagery is an inevitable corollary of this easy interchange between dramatic and non-dramatic modes. Just as the epic poet looked to simile and metaphor to expand the arena of his action, or the song writer to analogy for ornament and illustration, so the playwright turned to imagery to suggest the atmosphere of a scene, to reveal the attitudes of his speakers, or define the nature of the universe in which his dramatis personae function. Where the rhythm of the blank verse line corresponds to the music which accompanies a modern television drama, the image structure of a Shakespearian play may be compared to the visual techniques (camera angle, set, costume, lighting) by means of which the twentieth-century film director can suggest a mental landscape or a universal condition.

The term *imagery* denotes the entire body of images that go to make up either a segment of a, or an entire, literary work. Such

1. The repetition of identical initial consonant or vowel sounds in a closely related group of words or syllables, e.g. 'You common cry of curs' (*Coriolanus*, III.iii.120).
2. The use of words which suggest their meaning through their sound, e.g. 'A drum! a drum! / Macbeth doth come' (*Macbeth*, I.iii.30–1).

images may be either *literal*, where a straightforward evocation of a specific object is involved, or *figurative*, where one object, or state, is defined in terms of another. Thus Oberon's speech –

> I know a bank where the wild thyme blows,
> Where oxslips and the nodding violet grows,   250
> Quite over-canopied with luscious woodbine,
> With sweet musk-roses, and with eglantine.
> There sleeps Titania sometime of the night,
> Lull'd in these flowers with dances and delight;
> And there the snake throws her enamell'd skin,   255
> Weed wide enough to wrap a fairy in –

> (*A Midsummer Night's Dream*, II.i.249–56)

may be described as a collection of literal images in that the lines conjure up a visual impression of a particular location, whereas Horatio's allusion to the coming of morning –

> But look, the morn in russet mantle clad
> Walks o'er the dew of yon high eastward hill –

> (*Hamlet*, I.i.171–2)

may be described as figurative in that it expresses the coming of day in terms of a human being, walking across a hill, wearing a red-brown cloak.

Figurative images fall into a number of categories – *personification* (the representation of an abstract concept or inanimate object in human terms, exemplified in Horatio's speech quoted above), *simile*, and *metaphor* being those most commonly discussed. A *simile* involves a comparison between one object and another, and is usually introduced by 'as' or 'like'. Falstaff and Prince Hal, for example, in *1 Henry IV*, define the former's melancholy state by comparing it to a series of animals and objects with gloomy associations:

> *Fal.*   'Sblood, I am as melancholy
>   as a gib cat, or a lugged bear.
> *Prince.* Or an old lion, or a lover's lute.
> *Fal.* Yea, or the drone of a Lincolnshire bagpipe.

Prince. What sayest thou to a hare, or the melancholy of 75
    Moor-ditch?
Fal. Thou hast the most unsavoury similes –   (I.ii.71–7)

while Viola, in *Twelfth Night*, describes her supposed sister's
response to unrequited·love in terms of the sublime resignation of a
statue on a tomb:

She sat like Patience on a monument,
Smiling at grief.

(II.iv.115–16)

Metaphor, by contrast, identifies, rather than compares, one object
with another, thus transferring the qualities of the second to the
first. When Lear, for example, exclaims:

When we are born, we cry that we are come
To this great stage of fools,

(IV.vi.184–5)

he assimilates the world to the platform on which the actor stands,
and thus reduces human life to play-acting; while Edgar, by
describing the blinded Gloucester's eye-sockets as:

      his bleeding rings,
Their precious stones new lost,

(*King Lear*, V.iii.189–90)

conveys the brilliance and value of the human eye by equating the
cavities in his father's face with the empty settings of pieces of
damaged jewellery.

    Two further categories, *emblem* and *symbol*, are also important in
Renaissance drama. The *emblem*, a very popular device in the
sixteenth and seventeenth centuries, is a picture (or combination of
picture and motto) that conveys an abstract idea. In *Pericles*, for
example, one of the suitors to the Princess Thaisa expresses the
extent of his devotion to her though an emblem painted on his
shield, consisting of:

a black Ethiop reaching at the sun;
The word [i.e. motto], *Lux tua vita mihi.*[3]

(II.ii.20–1)

An emblem is a species of symbol, but not all symbols are emblems.
A *symbol* evokes one object, or concept, while simultaneously
suggesting another, unrelated one. In *Pericles* again, the sea
journeys that the central figure undertakes represent his passage
through life, while the tempests that beset him are both literal
storms and the vicissitudes to which every human life is subject.

Shakespeare's dramatic language is highly figurative, and the
images that he employs serve a number of purposes. On the most
superficial level, they help to define the place and time of the
dramatic action, endowing the playwright's relatively bare stage
with colour, scenery, and changes of light. Horatio's lines quoted
above, for example, which form part of the concluding speech of the
night-time scene with which *Hamlet* opens, not only tell the
spectator how much time has elapsed since the play began, but
evoke the soft glow of coming morning, and help to dissipate the
darkness that the play's opening lines evoke. The concluding
speech of *Macbeth* III.ii, by contrast, serves the opposite purpose.
Macbeth is planning a second murder, and the darkness both of the
deed that he contemplates and the setting in which it is to be
accomplished are suggested by the literal and figurative imagery
with which he hails the coming of the night:

> Come, seeling Night,
> Scarf up the tender eye of pitiful Day,
> And, with thy bloody and invisible hand,
> Cancel, and tear to pieces, that great bond
> Which keeps me pale! – Light thickens; and the crow   50
> Makes wing to th'rooky wood;
> Good things of Day begin to droop and drowse,
> Whiles Night's black agents to their preys do rouse.

(III.ii.46–53)

A number of devices are used here to evoke the claustrophobic

3. 'Thy light is life to me.'

darkness which descends at this point upon the play world. Both night and day are personified, Night being seen as a cruel agent of evil, who blinds compassionate, yet vulnerable, Day. Light is described, metaphorically, as 'thickening' (50) as if it is being permeated by some alien element; while the literal image of the crow contributes to the idea of blackness, not only by the colour of the bird and implied gloom of the wood to which it flies, but through the association between roosting and night. It is not merely physical darkness, however, that these images suggest. The blinding of Day by Night (46–7), and the metaphorical 'tearing' of the order of nature (49), create an ominous sense of impending violence, while the perversity of the deed that Macbeth is contemplating is implied by the metaphor of wilting used in relation to the 'good things of Day' (52). The imagery here thus communicates a range of ideas to the spectator in a highly economical way. It informs him, or her, that it is now dusk, that the following scene takes place in darkness, that evil is now dominant over goodness, that violence and disorder have been loosed upon the world, and that fearful and perverse events are to be expected.

The use of imagery in Shakespeare's plays is not confined, however, to contexts in which an atmosphere or setting is evoked. Character is also defined, in part at least, by the figurative language that a speaker employs, or that is used by others in relation to him. The wicked daughters of King Lear, for example, are insistently equated with animals to suggest both their violence and their degeneracy. Albany describes them as 'Tigers, not daughters' (IV.ii.40), while Gloucester declares that he helped the King because he could not bear to see Goneril 'In his anointed flesh rash boarish fangs' (III.vii.57). In *Antony and Cleopatra*, by contrast, it is the superhuman quality of the central figures that the imagery implies. Cleopatra, speaking of the dead Antony, evokes a god-like figure by means of a series of similes and metaphors that define him in relation to the cosmos and the seasons of the year:

Cleo. I dreamt there was an Emperor Antony.
    O such another sleep, that I might see
    But such another man!
Dol[abella].   If it might please ye, –
Cleo. His face was as the heavens, and therein stuck
    A sun and moon, which kept their course, and lighted   80
    The little O, the earth.

Dol.   Most sovereign creature, –
Cleo. His legs bestrid the ocean, his rear'd arm
   Crested the world: his voice was propertied
   As all the tuned spheres, and that to friends:
   But when he meant to quail, and shake the orb,   85
   He was as rattling thunder. For his bounty,
   There was no winter in't: an autumn 'twas
   That grew the more by reaping: his delights
   Were dolphin-like, they show'd his back above
   The element they lived in: in his livery   90
   Walk'd crowns and crownets: realms and islands were
   As plates dropp'd from his pocket.

                    (V.ii.76–92)

Similarly, Enobarbus creates a vision of ultimate sensuousness and eroticism through the literal and figurative images he uses to describe Cleopatra:

   The barge she sat in, like a burnish'd throne
   Burn'd on the water: the poop was beaten gold;
   Purple the sails, and so perfumed that
   The winds were love-sick with them; the oars were silver,
   Which to the tune of flutes kept stroke, and made   195
   The water which they beat to follow faster,
   As amorous of their strokes. For her own person,
   It beggar'd all description: she did lie
   In her pavilion – cloth of gold, of tissue –
   O'er-picturing that Venus where we see   200
   The fancy outwork nature. On each side her,
   Stood pretty dimpled boys, like smiling Cupids,
   With divers-colour'd fans, whose wind did seem
   To glow the delicate cheeks which they did cool,
   And what they undid did.
Agr[ippa].   O, rare for Antony!   205
Eno. Her gentlewomen, like the Nereides,
   So many mermaids, tended her i'the eyes,
   And made their bends adornings. At the helm
   A seeming mermaid steers: the silken tackle
   Swell with the touches of those flower-soft hands,   210
   That yarely frame the office. From the barge

A strange invisible perfume hits the sense
Of the adjacent wharfs. The city cast
Her people out upon her; and Antony,
Enthron'd i'the market-place, did sit alone,   215
Whistling to the air; which, but for vacancy,
Had gone to gaze on Cleopatra too,
And made a gap in nature.

(II.ii.191–218)

In all these instances, the figurative language works upon the imagination of the spectator to enlarge the arena in which the action is set. The 'high eastward hill' of *Hamlet* (I.i.172), and the 'rooky wood' of *Macbeth* (III.ii.51), place the location in which the lines are spoken in a wider geographical context, sketching in a landscape with symbolic overtones. At the same time, the human beings who move about the stage become ciphers for something larger than themselves, participating in a conflict that has a wider significance than a clash between mundane individuals. Thus, Goneril, in terms of plot, is an ungrateful daughter who viciously abuses an aged father, but she becomes symptomatic, by virtue of the animal imagery linking her to the rest of the play's degenerate offspring, of the rapacity and bestiality that ensue when the bonds that bind the members of a society to one another are broken. Similarly, Antony, in terms of action, is Cleopatra's lover and Octavius Caesar's political rival, but he is also the embodiment of magnanimity, in opposition to policy, through the godlike generosity that differentiates him, through imagery, from his political opponents. Thus, while on one level the figurative language evokes an atmosphere or location, and defines the idiosyncratic nature of specific individuals, on another it contributes to the projection of theme, by aligning one character with another, or differentiating between groups.

Images that are drawn from a single area of experience, and which are used throughout a dramatic composition to widen the implications of the events that are enacted, are usually referred to as *iterative*, and they form one of the principal routes by which the meaning of a specific play may be explored. In *Hamlet*, for example, images of disease pervade the dramatic language, suggesting not merely the corruption of one individual but the degeneration of an entire society. In the first scene of the play, before fifty words have been spoken, Francisco, one of two sentries, declares that he is not merely cold, but 'sick at heart' (9). Less than forty lines later, Barnardo, another sentry, remarks that Horatio, a scholar, 'tremble[s] and look[s] pale' (56), while Horatio extends the unhealthiness of individuals to the natural world by describing the moon as 'sick almost to doomsday with eclipse' (123) on an occasion similar to that which has brought the men together. In the following scene, Hamlet himself takes up the image, bringing together human and natural corruption. To him the whole of Denmark is 'an unweeded garden / That grows to seed; things rank and gross in nature / Possess it merely' (135–7), while Laertes, a scene later, uses the diseases to which the natural world is subject to illustrate the vulnerability of virtue in the play world:

> The canker galls the infants of the spring
> Too oft before their buttons be disclos'd,   40
> And in the morn and liquid dew of youth
> Contagious blastments are most imminent.

(I.iii.39–42)

What is significant here is the range of speakers involved. The recurrence of the strand of imagery implies that it is not one individual who is diseased in himself, or sees his world with a jaundiced eye, but an entire society that is somehow contaminated, though the causes of that contamination are, as yet, undefined. In I.v. the source of the corruption to which the dramatis personae unconsciously attest becomes clear, when the former King reveals the manner of his death:

> Sleeping within my orchard,
> My custom always of the afternoon,   60
> Upon my secure hour thy [Hamlet's] uncle stole
> With juice of cursed hebenon in a vial,
> And in the porches of my ears did pour
> The leperous distilment, whose effect
> Holds such an enmity with blood of man   65
> That swift as quicksilver it courses through
> The natural gates and alleys of the body,
> And with a sudden vigour it doth posset
> And curd, like eager droppings into milk,

The thin and wholesome blood. So did it mine,   70
And a most instant tetter bark'd about,
Most lazar-like, with vile and loathsome crust
All my smooth body.

(I.v.59–73)

The poisoning of the king, the head of the body politic, emerges here as the fount of the sickness that pervades the play world. The poison poured by Claudius into Old Hamlet's ear has corroded the fabric not merely of an individual but of an entire society, and it is the progress of the members of a diseased state that the play is concerned to trace.

The imagery of inversion that pervades *Macbeth* serves a similar function in defining the world in which the action of the drama is set. At the outset of the play, the Witches establish that in the perverse universe in which they function 'Fair is foul, and foul is fair' (I.i.11), and it is with this inverted world that Macbeth identifies himself by murdering a man who is at once his king, his kinsman, and his guest. From the moment that Macbeth, and subsequently Lady Macbeth, begin to contemplate the unnatural deed, literal and figurative images expressive of the overthrow, not merely of the social, but the natural, order accumulate. On first hearing that two of the Witches' statements in relation to him are confirmed, Macbeth feels his

seated heart knock at [his] ribs,
Against the use of nature,

(I.iii.136–7)

and finds himself drawn into a confused state of being in which

function is smother'd in surmise,
And nothing is, but what is not.

(141–2)

Lady Macbeth summons darkness to engulf the world –

> Come, thick Night,   50
> And pall thee in the dunnest smoke of Hell,
> That my keen knife see not the wound it makes,
> Nor Heaven peep through the blanket of the dark,
> To cry, "Hold, hold!" –

                                        (I.v.50–4)

and declares that had she sworn to perform the murder of Duncan,
as Macbeth has done, she would have plucked the nipple from the
boneless gums of the baby at her breast, and dashed the child's
brains out (I.vii.56–8) rather than broken her oath. Once the murder
has been performed, and the natural order subverted, the imagery
becomes yet more insistent. Macbeth thinks that a voice cries out
'Macbeth does murther Sleep' (II.ii.35), Lennox, one of the Scottish
lords, describes the extraordinary occurrences of the night –

> where we lay,   55
> Our chimneys were blown down; and, as they say,
> Lamentings heard i'th'air; strange screams of death,
> And, prophesying with accents terrible
> Of dire combustion, and confus'd events,
> New hatch'd to th'woeful time, the obscure bird   60
> Clamour'd the livelong night: some say, the earth
> Was feverous, and did shake –

                                        (II.iii.55–62)

while another lord, Rosse, and an Old Man express the
unnaturalness that has entered the play world in even more extreme
terms:

> *Old M.* Threescore and ten I can remember well;
>   Within the volume of which time I have seen
>   Hours dreadful, and things strange, but this sore night
>   Hath trifled former knowings.
> *Rosse.*   Ha, good Father,
>   Thou seest the heavens, as troubled with man's act,   5
>   Threatens his bloody stage: by th'clock 'tis day,
>   And yet dark night strangles the travelling lamp.
>   Is't night's predominance, or the day's shame,

That darkness does the face of earth entomb,
When living light should kiss it?
Old M.   'Tis unnatural,   10
Even like the deed that's done. On Tuesday last,
A falcon, towering in her pride of place,
Was by a mousing owl hawk'd at, and kill'd.
Rosse. And Duncan's horses (a thing most strange and certain)
Beauteous and swift, the minions of their race,   15
Turn'd wild in nature, broke their stalls, flung out,
Contending 'gainst obedience, as they would make
War with mankind.
Old M.   'Tis said, they eat each other.
Rosse. They did so.

(II.iv.1–19)

From this point the grotesque becomes the familiar – ghosts walk, innocent children are slain, woods move – with the figurative language of the play endowing these events with a significance that extends far beyond the physical arena in which the action is played out. What, in terms of plot, is merely the story of the murder of a good king by an ambitious subject, becomes a record, through the iterative imagery, of the cosmic upheaval consequent upon the fracturing of natural bonds, and a horrifying vision of a mental landscape born of the individual's violation of his own moral nature.

The poetic fabric of a drama lends itself to private study. Once alerted to the importance of imagery in evoking an atmosphere, defining a location, delineating character, or contributing to the projection of theme, the student of Shakespearian drama has merely to apply himself to the text in order to appreciate the rewards that are to be reaped from close consideration of the language of the plays. Moreover, since the 1930s when the study of imagery first emerged as a major critical preoccupation, a number of books and articles have appeared on the figurative language of specific plays,[4] so that, once again, the interested reader has merely to transfer the course charted by the literary critic to his or her own study of the printed page in order to appreciate the expanding circle of significance that the imagery of a play generates. What is much

4. Classic examples are Robert B. Heilman's *This Great Stage* (Baton Rouge, La., 1948) and *Magic in the Web* (Lexington, Ky., 1956) which explore the imagery of *King Lear* and *Othello* respectively.

harder for the reader, as opposed to the theatre-goer, to perceive is the close relationship that exists in Shakespearian drama between stage spectacle and figurative language. Whereas the reader is at liberty to devote time and attention to the word-by-word exploration of a specific passage while the play-goer is denied the facility of an 'action-replay' that might alert him to the nuances of a word or phrase, the reader is deprived of the visual effects that transform the poetic expression of a concept into the dramatic realization of it. The reader's loss, perhaps surprisingly in view of the richness of the linguistic fabric, is the greater of the two. Shakespeare's poetry is designed to work upon the imagination of the spectator as the drama evolves. Its effects may not be conceptualized while the play is in progress, but they are, nevertheless, experienced, whereas the disposition of a scene is entirely lost to the reader whose attention is focused upon words alone. For this reason it is essential for the student of Shakespearian drama to attempt to realize, in the theatre of the imagination if nowhere else, the visual effects which the dramatist engineers, and to consider the relationship between those effects and the mental images that are evoked.

Richard II affords a straightforward example of figurative language and stage spectacle complementing one another. Bolingbroke, having been banished by King Richard, returns to England in arms – ostensibly to reclaim lands distrained by the King – and thus initiates a challenge to the throne that is to end in Richard's deposition and death. Act III constitutes the pivotal point in the see-saw opposition between the two men, and their changing relationship is conveyed to the audience by a combination of action, imagery and spectacle. The Elizabethan stage did not consist of a single flat platform. It had a trap-door from which devils, etc. could enter from below, and it had a gallery at the back which could represent a balcony, upper room, etc. In III.iii a company of rebels, including Bolingbroke and Northumberland, approach Flint castle where Richard has taken refuge. At this point in the action, Richard is still King, and Bolingbroke still maintaining that he has returned to England only to reclaim his own lands. The imagery that Bolingbroke employs denotes his deferential relationship to his sovereign, and emphasizes the discrepancy between their social stations:

Henry Bolingbroke   35
On both his knees doth kiss King Richard's hand,
And sends allegiance and true faith of heart
To his most royal person; hither come
Even at his feet to lay my arms and power,
Provided that my banishment repeal'd   40
And lands restor'd again be freely granted;
If not, I'll use the advantage of my power
And lay the summer's dust with showers of blood
Rain'd from the wounds of slaughtered Englishmen –
The which, how far off from the mind of Bolingbroke   45
It is such crimson tempest should bedrench
The fresh green lap of fair King Richard's land,
My stooping duty tenderly shall show.

(35–48)

The stability of the hierarchical relationship implied in the first five lines of the utterance is undermined, however, by the conditional nature of what follows. The deferential attitude the speaker posits is dependent upon the king submitting to the subject's will, and the diminished majesty that this implies is caught up in the following lines, in which the physical setting in which the action takes place is emphasized. Bolingbroke continues:

Let's march without the noise of threat'ning drum,
That from this castle's tottered battlements
Our fair appointments may be well perus'd.

(51–3)

The word 'tottered' (52) is important here. While being a literal description of the castle in that it is ragged at the top (i.e. crenellated), it also implies that it is 'tattered' in the sense of ruined, and 'tottering' as if about to fall. The description of the castle clearly has reference to its occupant, the imagery serving to suggest the insecurity, not merely of Richard's physical sanctuary, but of his social position. At this point, the King himself appears on the upper stage – now representing the castle walls. His physical elevation above Northumberland, Bolingbroke's messenger, is an emblematic representation of his superior social status, and the 'height' of his majesty is given further significance by the figurative language through which he is then described:

> See, see, King Richard doth himself appear,
> As doth the blushing discontented sun
> From out the fiery portal of the East,
> When he perceives the envious clouds are bent   65
> To dim his glory and to stain the track
> Of his bright passage to the occident.

            (62–7)

The King is the sun, in that it is he who brings glory, hope and prosperity to his people, and this aspect of his role within the state is realized in visual terms by Richard's appearance, richly clad, upon the upper stage. At the same time, the elaboration of the simile anticipates the movement of the remainder of the scene. Just as the sun can be obscured by clouds, so the King's glory may be dimmed by envious nobles, while the closing reference to the occident looks forward to the physical descent with which the scene is to conclude. It is not only the sun to which Richard is compared, however. York exclaims:

> Yet looks he like a king. Behold, his eye,
> As bright as is the eagle's, lightens forth
> Controlling majesty.   70

            (68–70)

Once again, the physical height of Richard above the nobles on the stage below him lends force to the simile. The eagle is the king of birds, as Richard is a king among men. The eagle soars high above the earth, scanning the world below him with an acute gaze, as Richard, in his majesty, over-sees the activities of his subjects. The King's appearance on the upper stage fuses these concepts. He looks down, literally, upon those beneath him, surveying them, clear-sightedly, from his position of pre-eminence.

Northumberland's response to the King's appearance on the

castle wall, implicit in Richard's opening address to him, is highly significant:

> *Rich.* [*To North.*] We are amaz'd, and thus long have we stood
>   To watch the fearful bending of thy knee,
>   Because we thought ourself thy lawful king;
>   And if we be, how dare thy joints forget   75
>   To pay their awful duty to our presence?

> (72–6)

Here, it is an omission, rather than an action, that communicates the declining power of the sovereign and the diminishing distance between king and subject. By failing to kneel to the monarch, Northumberland not only withholds a gesture of respect, but enforces, in visual terms, his own stature in relation to the man standing upon the walls above him. Unable to impose his authority, Richard is obliged to acquiesce to Bolingbroke's demands, his capitulation again being seen in terms of a lowering of status:

> *Rich.* We do debase ourselves, cousin, do we not,
>   To look so poorly, and to speak so fair?

> (127–8)

The word 'debase' is the significant one here. When Northumberland, having communicated Richard's response to Bolingbroke, returns to confront the King for the second time, the second element of the word is caught up in a series of puns that draw together the stage spectacle and the worldly fortunes of the King. The ironic terms in which Richard now salutes Bolingbroke's messenger indicate the reversal of roles that is inexorably taking place:

> Most mighty prince, my Lord Northumberland,
> What says King Bolingbroke? Will his Majesty
> Give Richard leave to live till Richard die?
> You make a leg, and Bolingbroke says "ay".   175
>   *North.* My lord, in the base court he doth attend
> To speak with you; may it please you to come down?

Rich. Down, down I come, like glist'ring Phaeton,
　　Wanting the manage of unruly jades.
　　In the base court? Base court, where kings grow base   180
　　To come at traitors' calls, and do them grace!
　　In the base court? Come down? Down, court! down, king!
　　For night-owls shriek where mounting larks should sing.

(172–83)

At this point in the action Richard descends from the castle walls to
the base court (i.e. to the castle courtyard) – or from the upper to the
lower stage. The movement denotes his submission to superior
force, but it also enacts a descent from kingship to 'baseness', from
supremacy over others to the common human condition. At the
same time, the significance of the stage spectacle is enriched by the
figurative language that accompanies it. Richard does not merely
quibble upon the word 'base', he also plays upon the sun image
conventionally used in relation to the sovereign. His comparison
between himself and Phaeton (78–9) constitutes a significant
departure, however, from the traditional sun/king analogy.
Phaeton was the son of Apollo (god of the sun), who attempted to
drive his father's chariot across the sky, failed to control the horses
which drew it, and was killed by Jove with a thunderbolt in order to
save the world from destruction. The image transforms Richard from
the true, sun-like monarch, to an aspirant to that role, with his
descent from the upper stage enacting his waning authority, and
foreshadowing his destruction.

The visual and verbal imagery of ascent and descent is continued
when Richard is on the same physical level as Bolingbroke and his
followers. Though the nobility are now grouped together in the
'base court', Bolingbroke kneels in recognition of Richard's status, a
gesture which the King brushes aside as empty of meaning:

Bol. Stand all apart,
　　And show fair duty to his Majesty.
　　　　　　　　　　　　　　[He kneels down.]
　　My gracious lord.
Rich. Fair cousin, you debase your princely knee   190
　　To make the base earth proud with kissing it.
　　Me rather had my heart might feel your love,
　　Than my unpleased eye see your courtesy.

Up, cousin, up; your heart is up, I know,
Thus high at least, although your knee be low.   195

(187–95)

Not only does Richard raise Bolingbroke to the same level as himself, with his 'Up, cousin, up' (194) paralleling his earlier 'Down, court! Down, king!' (182), but his gesture towards the crown in 'your heart is up, I know, / Thus high at least' (194–5) points towards the ultimate nature of the predominance that Bolingbroke is to gain. From this point onwards it is Bolingbroke who is in the ascendancy and Richard who is doomed to decline. The aspirants to the crown of England, as the deposed King comments in the following act, are like two buckets in a well, the elevation of one inevitably entailing the decline of the other:

Now is this golden crown like a deep well
That owes two buckets, filling one another,   185
The emptier ever dancing in the air,
The other down, unseen, and full of water,
That bucket down and full of tears am I,
Drinking my griefs, whilst you mount up on high.

(IV.i.184–9)

It is this alternation of fortunes that the stage spectacle and the figurative language combine, in III.iii, to illuminate.

The figurative language of *Othello* also turns upon a contrast which is realized in terms of stage spectacle, but in this instance it is built upon colour rather than height. From the very outset of the play images evocative of darkness and light are in opposition to one another – speaker after speaker reiterating the motif with its traditional metaphysical connotations. In the first scene, for example, Iago calls out to Brabantio, not that his daughter has eloped with a moor, but that

an old black ram
Is tupping your white ewe;

(I.i.88–9)

while Roderigo confirms that the 'fair' Desdemona has been carried off in the 'dull watch o'the night' (122–3). In scene ii Brabantio himself refers to his daughter as 'fair', and her husband, Othello, as 'sooty' (66 and 70), while in scene iii he alleges that the Moor has employed 'practices of cunning hell' (102) to win his 'jewel' (195). At the close of the act, the emphasis upon the encroachment of the darkness of hell upon the play world is yet more pronounced. Iago, having conceived his plot to destroy Othello, exclaims:

> I ha't, it is engender'd; Hell and night
> Must bring this monstrous birth to the world's light.

> (I.iii.401–2)

Throughout this act, the figurative language is reinforced by the spectacle with which the theatre audience is presented. As the action evolves, the spectator gathers, even in an unlit, Shakespearian-style theatre, that the scenes he is witnessing take place at night. During the first sixty-five lines of dialogue the time of day remains uncertain, with two gentlemen simply conversing in a street, but from this point onwards the literal darkness in which the action is set becomes evident. By line 67 Iago and Roderigo are standing beneath the window of Brabantio's house, and the following exchange takes place:

> *Rod.* Here is her father's house, I'll call aloud.
> *Iago.* Do, with like timorous accent, and dire yell,   75
>   As when, by night and negligence, the fire
>   Is spied in populous cities.
> *Rod.* What ho! Brabantio, Signior Brabantio, ho!
> *Iago.* Awake! what ho, Brabantio! thieves, thieves, thieves!
>   Look to your house, your daughter, and your bags.   80
>   Thieves, thieves!

> BRABANTIO *at a window.*
> *Bra.* What is the reason of this terrible summons?
>   What is the matter there?
> *Rod.* Signior, is all your family within?
> *Iago.* Are all doors lock'd?
> *Bra.*   Why, wherefore ask you this?   85

Iago. Zounds, sir, you are robb'd, for shame put on your gown,
   Your heart is burst, you have lost half your soul;
   Even now, very now, an old black ram
   Is tupping your white ewe; arise, arise,
   Awake the snorting citizens with the bell,   90
   Or else the devil will make a grandsire of you,
   Arise I say.
Bra.   What, have you lost your wits?
Rod. Most reverend signior, do you know my voice?
Bra. Not I, what are you?
Rod. My name is Roderigo.   95

                                          (I.i.74–95)

A host of devices are used here to communicate the night-time setting to the audience. Iago's simile beginning 'with like timorous accent' (75–7) encourages the spectator to associate the present action with the tumult of a night lit by the flames of a fire; the injunction 'awake!', and repeated cry of 'thieves' (79 and 81) before Brabantio appears, suggest that the occupants of the house are not going about their daily tasks but have to be roused; while Brabantio's appearance at a window (on the upper stage), rather than at his door, invites the supposition that he is in his bedchamber. The urgent questions that are addressed to him – 'is all your family within / Are all doors lock'd?' (84–5) could have relevance, in a peaceful city, only at night, while Iago's injunction to him to put on his gown (86) is a clear indication that the old man is dressed only in his nightshirt. The reference to the consummation of the marriage between Othello and Desdemona (88–9) also suggests the lateness of the hour, while the explicit 'Awake the snorting citizens with the bell' (90) confirms that the whole town is asleep. It is clear too, by the close of the exchange, that Brabantio can see neither of his interlocutors. Though Roderigo, who has been a suitor to his daughter, is well known to him, he is obliged to ask who he is, and he directs the same question, a few lines later, to Iago (114).

   Up to this point, the darkness of the play world has been implied by the nature of the characters' exchanges, by the imagery, and the disposition of the actors on the upper and lower stage. From line 140 it is conveyed by invoking its opposite. Brabantio, stirred into action by the cries of the men below him, begins to call for light, thus confirming the blackness in which the action has hitherto taken place:

> Bra.   Strike on the tinder, ho!   140
> Give me a taper, call up all my people:
> This accident is not unlike my dream,
> Belief of it oppresses me already:
> Light I say, light!   [*Exit above.*]
>
>   (140–4)

When he reappears on the lower stage, the night-time setting is reaffirmed by his costume, and the torches carried by his attendants,[5] while he again calls, distractedly, for more lights:

> Enter BRABANTIO *in his night-gown, and Servants with*
>   *torches.*
> Bra. It is too true an evil, gone she is,   160
>   And what's to come, of my despised time,
>   Is nought but bitterness. Now Roderigo,
>   Where didst thou see her? (O unhappy girl!)
>   With the Moor, say'st thou? (Who would be a father?)
>   How didst thou know 'twas she? (O thou deceivest me   165
>   Past thought!) What said she to you? Get more tapers.
>
>   (160–6)

Finally convinced of his daughter's flight, he sends his attendants 'Some one way, some another' (177), and finally exits to 'raise some special officers of night' (183).

It is at this point in the action that Othello enters in one of Shakespeare's most striking stage spectacles. The continuing darkness is immediately established by the stage direction – *Enter OTHELLO, IAGO, and attendants with torches* – but the blackness is now embodied in the person of the Moor as he and the white Iago emerge from the night together. Though the Moor is physically

---

5. It should be pointed out that the stage directions discussed here derive from early editions of the play, and have not simply been supplied by modern scholars. Given the textual history of *Othello* it may be assumed that they originate either from Shakespeare's own manuscript or from the prompt book of the company for which he wrote.

associated with the surrounding darkness, however, the figurative language that he employs carries positive, rather than negative, connotations, contributing to the confusion and uncertainty that the shadowy location evokes. Moreover, within a few lines the omnipresent blackness is again enforced both by visual means, by the use of torches, and by the difficulty that the characters experience in identifying one another. When Othello comments 'But look what lights come yonder' (I.i.28), Iago mistakenly responds that the newcomers must be Brabantio and his followers, but it is Cassio, not Brabantio, who then enters '*with Officers, and torches*' (s.d.), and his brief colloquy with Othello again suggests darkness and uncertainty:

Oth. The goodness of the night upon you, friends!   35
    What is the news?
Cas.   The duke does greet you, general,
    And he requires your haste post-haste appearance,
    Even on the instant.
Oth.   What's the matter, think you?
Cas. Something from Cyprus, as I may divine;
    It is a business of some heat, the galleys   40
    Have sent a dozen sequent messengers
    This very night, at one another's heels:
    And many of the consuls, rais'd and met,
    Are at the duke's already; you have been hotly call'd for,
    When, being not at your lodging to be found,   45
    The senate sent about three several quests
    To search you out.

                                        (I.ii.35–47)

As Othello prepares to comply with the Duke's summons, Brabantio and his attendants enter with '*lights*' and '*weapons*' (s.d.) and confusion mounts. Shouts are exchanged, swords drawn, and the incipient riot in the flickering torch light is quelled only by the intervention of the Moor, who stills the rising tumult with an image redolent of brilliance rather than opacity:

Keep up your bright swords, for the dew will rust 'em.

                                        (I.ii.59)

The combined significance of spectacle and imagery in these scenes would have been much more evident to the Elizabethan play-goer than to the twentieth-century reader. Not only is it more difficult to respond to visual effects in the study than in the play-house, but the images familiar to Renaissance society are no longer readily understood today. Whereas it is relatively easy to establish, by a line-by-line analysis of the text, that animality and darkness are in opposition to beauty and light, it is less easy for the reader to create, in the theatre of the imagination, the on-stage confusion, violence and leaping flames that translate the hell evoked by the figurative language into literal terms. Even more difficult for the modern reader to appreciate is the significance of Othello's colour in this context. Not only is black conventionally associated with evil, but the devil was frequently depicted, from the mediaeval period onwards, as a grotesque black man, surrounded by leaping flames, and prone to carry off souls (depicted as female), as Othello has apparently carried off Desdemona. By scene ii, when the Moor and Iago emerge from the darkness, side-by-side, the iterative imagery has predisposed the members of the theatre audience to think of the action in terms of a metaphysical conflict, and Othello's appearance appears to confirm that he is the diabolical force from which the hellish nature of the play world proceeds. In short, from the opening lines of the play in which two gentlemen converse about a third, the verbal and visual imagery combine to carry the spectator forward into a species of hell – a hell in which darkness is omnipresent, animal appetites are satisfied, physical violence is threatened, confusion reigns, and the devil walks.

The visual impact of these opening scenes is crucial to the meaning of the play as a whole. The plot turns upon the destruction of Othello by Iago, that destruction being brought about through sexual jealousy. The success of Iago's diabolical stratagem depends upon his pose of unswerving honesty – a pose which none of the other characters, not even his wife, is able to penetrate. The literal and figurative imagery of Act I contributes to the audience's comprehension of these events in a number of ways. The dramatic language and stage spectacle combine to involve those outside the play world in that process of mistaking appearance for reality which is to be the downfall of the central figure, in that they invite the audience to associate evil with black and virtue with white, when the reverse is, in fact, the case. At the same time, they place a tawdry story of sexual jealousy in a much larger context, widening the arena of the action from the domestic to the universal. It is not a marriage that is at stake, but a human soul, and the spectator is aware of this larger issue, through the imagery, from very early in the play. Above all, these opening scenes ensure a very high level of audience attention from the outset. Not only are they full of action and movement, but they are deeply unsettling, in that they evoke stereotype responses only to undermine them. Presented with a visual image of hell, several upholders of virtue and a seeming embodiment of the devil, the members of the theatre audience find the language of those they expect to admire deeply repellent, while that of the figure they ought to reject is moving and powerful. While Iago talks in terms of hatred and animality, of 'an old black ram/. . . tupping your white ewe' (I.i.88–9), Othello asserts his 'love' for the 'gentle Desdemona' (I.ii.25), and seeks to allay the violence and tumult that Iago has instigated. The spectator is thus obliged to move from the stereotype response evoked by the stage picture, through confusion, to the recognition that it is not the black Othello who is the instigator of evil, but the 'honest' Iago, and it is from this recognition that much of the intellectual excitement of the play springs. 'Hell and night' certainly conspire in this play to bring a 'monstrous birth' to 'the world's light' (I.iii.401–2), but the paradox on which the play is constructed is that it is the white man, not the black, who is the agent of destruction. Unless the reader is able to visualize, and appreciate the significance of, the stage pictures of Act I and to recognize their relationship to the figurative language of the play, much of the startling originality both of Shakespeare's conception, and the audience alignment that he engineers, is lost.

King Lear illustrates a different kind of interaction between spectacle and figurative language. Where the iterative imagery and stage pictures combine in *Richard II* to illustrate a process, and the dramatic language of *Othello* enforces a polarized opposition between darkness and light that runs counter, initially at least, to their human embodiments, stage spectacle in *King Lear* serves to actualize the concepts upon which the imagery of the play turns. *King Lear* traces the disintegration of order in a realm, consequent upon the blindness of a sovereign in relation to the relative worth of his off-spring and the implications of his own actions. At the outset of the play Lear declares his intention to divide his kingdom between his daughters in proportion to the love that they bear him, conferring the realm on his two elder daughters and their husbands when his youngest child fails to express her affection in sufficiently eloquent terms. The implications of his decision are communicated to the audience by a piece of stage business that is easily overlooked on the printed page:

Lear.   Cornwall and Albany,

. . . .
> I do invest you jointly with my power,   130
> Pre-eminence, and all the large effects
> That troop with majesty. Ourself, by monthly course,
> With reservation of an hundred knights
> By you to be sustain'd, shall our abode
> Make with you by due turn. Only we shall retain   135
> The name and all th'addition to a king; the sway,
> Revenue, execution of the rest,
> Beloved sons, be yours: which to confirm,
> This coronet part between you.

(I.i.127–39)

The division of the kingdom between the Dukes that the King propounds here may well arouse concern in the mind of the spectator, and these concerns are expressed visually by the action which is implied in Lear's closing lines. The King takes his regal coronet, symbolic here both of his dignity and the realm, and hands it to his sons-in-law with the injunction to part it between them. The significance of the action lies in the manifest impossibility of dividing a crown. Whereas it is possible, in theory, to envisage the division of a kingdom, the division of a coronet is inconceivable, and the problems involved in sharing the one are transferred by the audience to the other. Half a crown is patently worthless, and the spectacle of Cornwall and Albany, each with one hand on the coronet, or stepping forward, simultaneously, to accept it, is a highly ominous one, suggesting the possibility of future competition between the two men for meaningful sovereignty. At the same time, the King's injunction to divide the crown involves the fragmentation or destruction of an indivisible entity. Just as the crown cannot be broken apart without destroying its value and integrity, so the state cannot be parcelled out at the whim of the monarch in that it constitutes an organic whole. The stage spectacle here thus communicates a range of ideas to the audience of which the three actors in the scene are unaware. It encourages those outside the play world to pass an adverse judgement upon Lear's action; it creates a sense of foreboding; and suggests that a process of unnatural division has been set in motion.

The process of division is emphasized from the very beginning of the play. The partition of the kingdom is the subject of the opening exchange and the principal business of the first scene, and it is the implications of this partition in political terms that the stage spectacle discussed above primarily enacts. At the same time, however, the process of fragmentation that Lear has set in motion does not merely involve the body politic. The two men who stand on either side of the crown are members of the same family, while the crown itself, as noted above, represents not merely the state, but the abstract notion of kingship, the division of this symbol of authority suggesting a division of loyalties, and the overthrow of the hierarchical order. It is these concepts, implicit in the visual image with which the audience is presented, that the figurative language takes up, progressively widening Lear's misguided action into a cataclysmic event. In I.iv, for example, Lear has the following exchange with his Fool:

> *Fool.* Nuncle, give me an egg, and I'll give thee two
> crowns.
> *Lear.* What two crowns shall they be?
> *Fool.* Why, after I have cut the egg i'th'middle and   165
> eat up the meat, the two crowns of the egg.
> When thou clovest thy crown i'th'middle, and
> gav'st away both parts, thou bor'st thine ass on
> thy back o'er the dirt: thou hadst little wit in thy
> bald crown when thou gav'st thy golden one   170
> away.   (I.iv.162–71)

Here, the Fool uses an egg that has been cut in half as an image of Lear's conduct in relation to the crown, but his elaboration of the comparison expands the significance of what has taken place in the preceding scene, rather than merely reiterating it. Whereas the King spoke of *dividing* his coronet, the Fool refers to Lear as having *cloven* his crown in two (167), a much more violent and disturbing image that confirms the ominous implications of the earlier scene. At the same time, the subversion of the social hierarchy implicit in the abdication of authority and the division of the kingdom, is now seen in terms of the inversion of the natural order. Where Lear envisaged

yielding his power to his 'beloved sons' (I.i.138), the Fool sees him
as bearing 'thine ass on thy back o'er the dirt' (168–9), evoking an
anarchic universe in which the bestial dominates over the humane,
rather than a world of familial bonds. Above all, the insistent
punning upon the word 'crown' (symbol of kingly authority/
halved egg/head) serves to link the process of cleaving with Lear
himself. The crown is the crown of Lear's own head, and the
cleaving of it the rending of his own being as individual, father, and
king.

In Act III, stage spectacle and figurative language combine to
enlarge the arena of the action still further. Lear, now mad, enters
on a 'heath' representative of a de-localized, universal arena, and
confronts a storm symbolic of universal chaos:

> *Lear.* Blow, winds, and crack your cheeks! rage! blow!
>   You cataracts and hurricanoes, spout
>   Till you have drench'd our steeples, drown'd the cocks!
>   You sulph'rous and thought-executing fires,
>   Vaunt-couriers of oak-cleaving thunderbolts,   5
>   Singe my white head! And thou, all-shaking thunder,
>   Strike flat the thick rotundity o'th'world!
>   Crack Nature's moulds, all germens spill at once
>   That makes ingrateful man!
>
>   (III.ii.1–9)

Image after image here evokes the process of splitting asunder. Lear
personifies the wind, calling upon him to 'crack' (1) his cheeks with
the violent eruption of his breath, evoking the destruction, through
severance, of the elements themselves. He refers to 'oak-cleaving
thunderbolts' (5), fusing the division of the sky by a plunging
meteor with the splitting apart of both the physical world and his
own being, through the oak's traditional associations with kingship,
stability, and strength. The word 'cleaving' itself looks back to the
Fool's 'clovest' (I.iv.167), while the blow it implies is caught up in
'strike' (7), and in the final, and most terrible, 'crack' of line 8 which
is to fracture the 'moulds' of nature and scatter the seeds of
regeneration.

It will be apparent from the above that the stage spectacle of Act I
constitutes a visual representation of an abstract idea. Lear's action
in handing his coronet to Albany and Cornwall is emblematic of the

concept of unnatural sundering, and it is this concept that the figurative language extends and explores. The realization of metaphor in literal terms is characteristic of *Lear*, which has long enjoyed the reputation of being among the most 'poetic', and thus least actable, of Shakespeare's plays while in fact being among those in which the dramatist conveys his meaning most forcefully through visual effects. Lear's decline in power, for example, is carefully charted through the diminishing number of his followers; his equation between man and beast is registered by his attempt to fling off his clothes (III.iv.105–12); while the humility that he learns in the course of the play is signalled by a movement to kneel to his own daughter (IV.vii.59). It is the blinding of Gloucester, however, the most startling and horrific scene in the whole of Renaissance drama, which demonstrates most vividly the close relationship between stage spectacle and figurative language in this play. As noted above, Lear's decision to divide his kingdom between his elder daughters and their husbands is a product of a metaphorical blindness. He is unable to discern either the relative worth of his daughters, or the nature of his own responsibilities as king, and this fact is drawn to the attention of the audience by an accumulation of imagery relating to sight. Goneril, Lear's eldest daughter, for example, claims that she loves her father 'Dearer than eye-sight' (I.i.56), while Kent, appalled by Lear's conduct and threatened with banishment himself, urges:

> See better, Lear; and let me still remain
> The true blank of thine eye.

(I.i.158–9)

Lear's situation is closely paralleled by that of the Duke of Gloucester,[6] who is similarly blind to the relative worth of his offspring, and it is through Gloucester that this aspect of Lear's position is expressed. Betrayed by the son he had trusted, Gloucester is physically blinded, on stage, in a scene woven around references to sight:

> *Re-enter Servants, with* GLOUCESTER *prisoner.*
> *Reg[an].* Ingrateful fox! 'tis he.

6. For a fuller discussion of the relationship between the two plots, see below pp. 114–15.

Corn[*wall*]. Bind fast his corky arms.

. . . .

Corn. Where hast thou sent the King?
Glou[*cester*].   To Dover.   50
Reg. Wherefore to Dover? Wast thou not charg'd at peril –
Corn. Wherefore to Dover? Let him answer that.
Glou. I am tied to th'stake, and I must stand the course.
Reg. Wherefore to Dover?
Glou. Because I would not see thy cruel nails   55
   Pluck out his poor old eyes; nor thy fierce sister
   In his anointed flesh rash boarish fangs.
   The sea, with such a storm as his bare head
   In hell-black night endur'd, would have buoy'd up,
   And quench'd the stelled fires;   60
   Yet, poor old heart, he holp the heavens to rain.
   If wolves had at thy gate howl'd that dearn time,
   Thou should'st have said "Good porter, turn the key."
   All cruels else subscribe: but I shall see
   The winged vengeance overtake such children.   65
Corn. See't shalt thou never. Fellows, hold the chair.
   Upon these eyes of thine I'll set my foot.
Glou. He that will think to live till he be old,
   Give me some help! O cruel! O you Gods!
Reg. One side will mock another; th'other too.   70
Corn. If you see vengeance, –
First Serv[*ant*].   Hold your hand, my Lord.
   I have serv'd you ever since I was a child,
   But better service have I never done you
   Than now to bid you hold.
Reg.   How now, you dog!
First Serv. If you did wear a beard upon your chin   75
   I'd shake it on this quarrel.
Reg.   What do you mean?
Corn. My villain!   [*They draw and fight.*]
First Serv. Nay then, come on, and take the chance of anger.
Reg. Give me thy sword. A peasant stand up thus!
       [*Takes a sword and runs at him behind.*]
First Serv. O! I am slain. My Lord, you have one eye left   80
   To see some mischief on him. Oh!   [*Dies.*]
Corn. Lest it see more, prevent it. Out, vile jelly!
   Where is thy lustre now?

Glou. All dark and comfortless. Where's my son Edmund?
   Edmund, enkindle all the sparks of nature   85
   To quit this horrid act.
Reg.   Out, treacherous villain!
   Thou call'st on him that hates thee; it was he
   That made the overture of thy treasons to us,
   Who is too good to pity thee.
Glou. O my follies!   90

(III.vii.28–90)

This scene serves a number of purposes. It advances the 'story' of
Gloucester himself, and reveals the extent of his betrayal by the son
he had trusted; it exposes the viciousness of Cornwall, and the
unnatural cruelty of Regan; and it enforces, through its insistent
references to animals, the degeneracy of the play world. Over and
above these functions, however, the stage spectacle locates
Gloucester's experience in a wider process that endows his 'story'
with universal relevance. The putting out of his eyes transforms a
metaphor into an event, and in doing so allows the audience to
understand the significance of the careers of Lear and Gloucester
more fully. Before he was physically blinded Gloucester was
metaphorically 'dark and comfortless' (84) in that he had no true
understanding of his situation and placed his trust in those who
hated him. Once physically blind, he comes to 'see' in a
metaphorical sense more clearly. He perceives the truth about
Edmund, and comes to recognize his own folly. The iterative
imagery serves to link this development with that of Lear. He too is
'blind' to the realities of his own situation and comes to 'see' through
suffering. The stage spectacle thus communicates a central paradox
that has acquired universal status through a process of repetition.
Emerging, with terrible inevitability, from the reiterated images –
'dearer than eye-sight' (I.i.56), 'the true blank of thine eye' (I.i.159) –
the scene burns the significance of the progress of the play's fathers
into the consciousness of the audience, heightening their sensitivity
to the emphatic references to 'seeing' that are to follow.
    Iterative imagery is one of the principal means by which the
Renaissance dramatist transmutes a bare stage into a changing
landscape, and trivial or familiar incidents into universally relevant
events. It fills the imagination of the spectator with sound and
colour, defines the world in which a given action is set, and ushers

the members of a theatre audience into the inner recesses of a speaker's consciousness. The figurative language of the plays is thus one of the most rewarding avenues by which to approach Shakespeare's meaning, and one which is as accessible to those unable to witness the plays in performance, as to those lucky enough to be able to do so. It is essential to bear in mind, however, that Shakespeare was a working dramatist – a man of the theatre – rather than a poet like Spenser or Donne. He was a member of a theatrical company, part-owner of London's principal playhouse, and an actor in his own right. Not only did he write his plays with a particular group of performers and a particular stage in mind, but he probably shared in their direction and took minor parts in them himself. As the insistent theatrical imagery throughout his work testifies, he thought in terms of the stage, and it is through the combination of words and spectacle, not through words alone, that the meaning of the play is generated. When studying the text of a Shakespearian play, the student or interested reader should explore, not merely the verbal imagery, but the stage directions, stated or implied, through which the disposition of a scene, or significant actions, are communicated. Only by living out the drama, either in the playhouse itself, or in the theatre of the mind, can the relationship between verbal and visual image be appreciated – and it is in this relationship that the fullest meaning of Shakespeare's imagery resides.

3

Shakespeare's Expositions

The opening scenes of a drama are crucial in determining the responses of a theatre audience to the events that are to be enacted. They must catch the attention of the spectators – a much more difficult task in a Renaissance playhouse than a modern one, where no dipping of the lights helped to create an expectant hush prior to the entrance of the characters – and they must acquaint the members of the audience with any information necessary for an understanding of what is to follow. Over and above these more obvious functions, however, the exposition also determines the *mode* of the ensuing action, and it is this aspect of the opening scene that is most readily overlooked by the reader or spectator when caught up in the onward flow of events.

The relationship between a play and its audience is an infinitely variable one. At one extreme, as in a mediaeval morality play, the members of the cast may mingle with the spectators, dissolving the boundary between the fictional world and the real one by directly addressing those present and inviting their participation in events, while at the other extreme, as in oriental drama, the actor may remain remote from the onlooker, enforcing the distance betweeen art and life by a highly formal mode of expression that transmutes experience into ritual. In the course of his theatrical career Shakespeare experimented with a variety of means of initiating events and communicating preliminary information to his audience, and he exploited, in the process, a whole range of relationships between play and spectators. *Richard III*, for example, opens with a soliloquy which serves to place those outside the play world on intimate terms with the central figure, while *Pericles*, by contrast, is presented by a narrator, who stands between the dramatis personae and the audience, and thus distances the one from the other. *The Tempest* generates a sense of excitement and wonder by its opening spectacle, while *Henry V* enforces the theatricality of the representation through the use of a Chorus, who laments the incapacity of the playhouse to do justice to the theme. The choice of opening scene in each of these instances is clearly not

61

random. The exposition is geared to the nature of the play that is to follow, and determines the stance of the audience towards the action that ensues. It is for this reason that the study of the way in which Shakespeare sets his dramas in motion may be seen as one of the most useful ways of approaching the plays, in that it affords an insight, not only into the meaning of specific works, but into the complex ways in which the corpus as a whole functions.

The Comedy of Errors and *Hamlet* illustrate two very different methods of capturing the attention of the spectator and placing him in possession of essential information. *The Comedy of Errors* opens with a spectacle. The Duke of Ephesus, accompanied by his attendants, enters with a jailor and a captive merchant, Egeon, whose opening words instantly command attention:

Proceed, Solinus, to procure my fall,
And by the doom of death end woes and all.

(I.i.1–2)

Here, the members of the audience are stilled by suddenly finding themselves plunged into the midst of a trial involving life and death issues. The speaker is apparently on the point of execution, and the danger he is in is confirmed in the following speech in which the Duke makes clear that any Syracusan found in Ephesus is customarily put to death. Once the attention of the spectators is gained, however, the forward motion of the scene is arrested, and its naturalism violated. The Duke enquires, quite gratuitously since it seems that the information can in no way influence his judgement, why Egeon has placed himself in the jeopardy in which he stands, and there then follows a speech of over one hundred lines, broken by only two brief interjections by the Duke, in which the prisoner painstakingly relates what has happened to him, and in doing so explains the pre-history upon which the subsequent action depends. His story is a complicated one, involving the birth of two sets of identical twins and their separation in infancy, and the fates of all four children, as far as they are known to the speaker, are carefully unfolded before the merchant is led away to try to raise the ransom required to save his life. Egeon's long speech here is plainly designed to convey information, not to the Duke – to whom it has no relevance – but to the audience, and it serves to place those watching the play in a position of awareness superior to that of any of the characters subsequently introduced. Armed with the information Egeon has furnished, the reader or spectator is able to deduce the relationship between the doomed Syracusan and a prominent member of Ephesian society, and thus to anticipate the former's release, while he or she is aware that each of the four principal characters has a physical counterpart, a fact of which those within the play world have no suspicion and upon which the ensuing misunderstandings depend. The exposition thus ensures that while the dramatis personae plunge into ever greater alarm and confusion, the members of the audience are free to laugh at their misapprehensions, secure in the knowledge that an answer to their problems is available to them, and that time will bring it to light.

The exposition of *Hamlet* is much more complex, and it places the audience in an entirely different relationship to the central action. The play opens with two men challenging one another, and their initial interchange suggests uncertainty and fearfulness. The first speaker – as yet unidentified – calls 'Who's there?' (I.i.1), while the second, rather than responding directly, questions in return – 'Nay, answer me. Stand and unfold yourself' (I.i.2). A password is given, one man recognizes the other, and the two, now revealed (perhaps ominously) to be sentries, are about to exchange places when others are heard approaching, and the tense questioning – again suggesting confusion and an all-enfolding darkness – begins afresh: 'Who is there?' (15), 'who hath reliev'd you?' (18), 'is Horatio there?' (21).

Up to this point in the action the attention of the audience has been gained, not by silencing its members with a spectacle or telling them a story, but by generating a sense of alarm and obliging them to deduce what is happening. The origins of the situation are with-held, rather than stated; the characters are not immediately identified; and it is an atmosphere that is communicated to the spectator not factual information. Once the audience is stilled, however, the dramatist again engineers an opportunity for the pre-history of the play to be related. Barnardo invites Horatio to listen to an account of what has occurred:

> Sit down awhile,
> And let us once again assail your ears,
> That are so fortified against our story,   35
> What we have two nights seen –
>
>   (33–6)

and Horatio concurs:

> Well, sit we down.
> And let us hear Barnardo speak of this.

(36–7)

Superficially, the dramatist seems on the point here of employing a similar technique to that used in *The Comedy of Errors*. One character invites another to recount what has happened, and the audience prepares to be informed of the events from which the situation has sprung. But in *Hamlet*, unlike the earlier play, the management of the scene maintains rather than violates the naturalism of the opening, and thus places the audience in a very different relationship to the events which follow. Barnardo's suggestion that he should relate what he has seen springs naturally from the situation in which he is placed, and it has been prepared for in previous speeches. Marcellus' lines –

> Horatio says 'tis but our fantasy,
> And will not let belief take hold of him,
> Touching this dreaded sight twice seen of us.
> Therefore I have entreated him along
> With us to watch the minutes of this night,   30
> That if again this apparition come,
> He may approve our eyes and speak to it –

(I.i.26–32)

establish that Horatio is present in order to witness a recurrence of the incidents that are to be related, and he has already enquired, 'has this thing appear'd again tonight?' (24). The illusion that the characters are talking to one another, rather than overtly addressing the audience, is also maintained. The four men are in possession of shared knowledge, that allows them to allude to events of which those outside the play world are in ignorance, obliging the spectator to piece together the situation from those items of information that emerge as the conversation proceeds. The speakers mention, for example, that a 'thing' has 'appear'd' (24) on two previous occasions (28), that the reality of what they have seen is in doubt (26–8), and that those who have witnessed the occurrence were filled with fear by it (28). By line 31 the 'thing' has become an 'apparition', a term that enables those watching the play to conclude that the sentries have seen some kind of ghost *before* Barnardo embarks on his narrative. Moreover, though Barnardo begins his account with all the circumstantial detail that would lead the spectator to expect a formal exposition –

> Last night of all,
> When yond same star that's westward from the pole,
> Had made his course t'illume that part of heaven   40
> Where now it burns, Marcellus and myself,
> The bell then beating one –

> (38–42)

he is interrupted by the entrance of the Ghost before he has done more than set the scene, further explanation becoming superfluous as those on stage and off are plunged into the experience that has generated the situation, rather than being told, by others, about it.

Even at this point, however, the knowledge of those within the play world remains superior to that of the spectators, who continue to compile an understanding of events from the scraps of information that emerge through the whirlwind exclamations and awed comments that follow. The audience gleans, for example, that the head of state has died recently, since the spectre resembles 'the King that's dead' (44), and gathers that the Danish monarch was distinguished by his valour since he 'th'ambitious Norway combated' (64), and 'smote the sledded Polacks on the ice' (66). From this information, together with the evident nervousness of the sentries, the spectator may well deduce that the loss of a redoubtable leader has placed the Danish state at the mercy of external aggression, and this deduction would appear to be confirmed by the exchanges immediately preceding the second entrance of the Ghost in which Marcellus enquires why the kingdom is preparing for war, and Horatio, in a second expository speech, explains the hostile intentions of young Fortinbras towards Denmark (73–110). What is significant here is that the members of the audience have been led, like the dramatis personae, to try to account for the appearance of the Ghost, and have come to a false conclusion. Far from sitting back in a position of amused superiority, like the spectators of *The Comedy of Errors*, the reader or listener has been obliged to grapple with darkness, half-truth, and innuendo, and has thus been drawn, inexorably, into the chiaroscuro world in which Hamlet himself has to function. By the close of the scene, those outside the play world, like those within it, are unsure of the meaning of what they have witnessed, while, as the closing references to a 'young Hamlet' (175) indicate, they still possess less information about the play universe than those who leave the stage.

It will be clear from the above that the expositions of *The Comedy of Errors* and *Hamlet* are directed towards very different ends. While the opening scene of the former is structured with a view to communicating information and imposing dramatic distance, the preliminary exchanges of the latter are designed to evoke an atmosphere, to suggest the difficulty of assessing sensory data, and to implicate the audience in that process of probing that is to span the entire play. The amount of factual information each conveys is radically different – and the stance of the audience towards the ensuing action is determined, to some extent at least, by the degree to which the awareness of those watching the play is superior or inferior to that of the dramatis personae. The distance between a drama and its audience does not always depend, however, upon the amount of knowledge possessed by the spectator. The expositions of *King Lear* and *Cymbeline*, for example, have much in common both in terms of the amount of factual information they convey and the means by which they convey it, yet they differ sharply in dramatic effect. Both plays open with a conversation between two gentlemen (a type of exposition Shakespeare employs on a number of occasions) and their plots are superficially similar. Each turns upon the estrangement between a monarch and the members of his family, and draws heavily upon folk-tale. In *King Lear*, the King proposes to divide his realm among his three daughters in proportion to the love each bears him, disowning his most devoted daughter, Cordelia, when she is unable to put her affection into words, and consigning himself and his kingdom to his more obsequious offspring, who subsequently abuse both. Similarly, in *Cymbeline*, the King, whose sons have been stolen in infancy, turns upon his loving daughter, Imogen, when she marries a social inferior, thus rendering himself vulnerable to the schemes of his vicious Queen on behalf of her ignoble son, Cloten. In both cases, the misguided conduct of the monarch jeopardizes the safety of individuals and the realm, one play moving towards a tragic denouement, and the other towards a comic one, as the banished daughter of Lear and the lost sons of Cymbeline attempt to succour the kingdom and their respective parents.

The conversations that open the two dramas are strikingly similar in substance. Both introduce the two interlocking actions with which each play is to be concerned, while supplying the pre-history of a nobly derived individual who is to be responsible for a vicious and unnatural act. Thus the opening words of *Lear* refer directly to the division of the kingdom, while the conversation moves swiftly to the conception of Edmund, who is to be instrumental in the blinding of his own father, and who is the sub-plot equivalent of Lear's unnatural daughters (see below pp. 114ff.). Similarly, in *Cymbeline* the conversation opens with an allusion to the banishment of the King's daughter, moves quickly to an account of the ancestry and upbringing of Posthumus, the banished husband of Imogen, who is later to order his wife's death, and concludes with the disappearance of the sons of Cymbeline with whose recovery the sub-plot is to deal.

The similar content of these opening scenes is offset, however, by the contrasting modes in which they function. In *King Lear* every aspect of the scene is designed to root the extraordinary actions of the King, and the horrifying events that flow from them, in a credible dramatic universe, while in *Cymbeline* the folk-tale nature of the plot material is stressed from the very outset. The conversing gentlemen of *King Lear* are named individuals, who play a prominent part in the subsequent action, and have shared knowledge of the situation they are instrumental in presenting. Their questions and responses are directed towards one another, and arise naturally from their circumstances, placing the spectator in the position of an uninformed third party, eavesdropping upon a conversation between individuals with a past, and a clearly defined place in a coherently structured society. In *Cymbeline*, by contrast, the reverse is the case. The gentlemen are unnamed; they play no part in the subsequent action; and they function as speaker and interlocutor, informing the audience, rather than one another, about events they regard as extraordinary and a social structure from which they are almost wholly detached.

One of the principal devices by which the naturalism of *King Lear* is promoted is the presence on stage of the virtually silent figure of Edmund, about whom questions can legitimately be asked. The scene opens with an exchange that is remarkable for its economy:

Kent. I thought the King had more affected the Duke
of Albany than Cornwall.

Glou[cester]. It did always seem so to us; but now, in the
division of the kingdom, it appears not which of
the Dukes he values most; for equalities are so   5
weigh'd that curiosity in neither can make choice
of either's moiety.

(I.i.1–7)

On the simplest level these lines clearly prepare the audience for
Lear's division of the kingdom in the second half of the scene. They
inform those watching or reading the play that the King has been
engaged in sharing his lands between the Dukes of Cornwall and
Albany (and possibly others), and that he has been impartial in the
division of the realm for all his known preference for one of the two
Dukes. At the same time, the exchange reveals something about the
speakers. Their familiarity with affairs of state suggests a high rank
(confirmed in the following line in which the first speaker addresses
the second as 'my Lord'), while a contrast is suggested between the
characters of the two through the straightforward, uncomplicated
style of the first speaker and the more prolix response of the second.
The mode by which the information is conveyed is also important.
The two men are clearly talking to one another rather than to the
audience. They enter in the midst of a conversation – a conversation
that endows both them, and their society, with a past – and they are
able to allude to matters the reader or spectator does not yet fully
understand. Though they belong to the higher echelons of society,
they employ prose rather than blank verse, the less elevated style
suggesting informality, or intimacy, and enforcing the sense of an
established relationship. Above all, the way in which they frame
their observations alerts the audience to a possible discrepancy
between what seems to be and what is. The first speaker '*thought* the
King had more affected the Duke of Albany than Cornwall' (1–2),
implying that his judgement may have been at fault, while the
second agrees that 'It did always *seem* so to us' (3), suggesting that
events appear to have proved him (and others) wrong.

Significantly, it is at this juncture that the third person on stage is
introduced. The first speaker enquires:

Is not this your son, my Lord?

(8)

– a question plainly designed to allow the hitherto silent member of the group to be identified. This process of identification, however, in no way violates the naturalism of the opening exchange. The second gentleman is accompanied by a much younger man, who may resemble him, and who is obviously not a servant, and it would be highly unnatural for the first gentleman not to enquire who he is. The second speaker's response to the query, for all its circumlocutory, jocular style, is again highly economical in the amount of information that it conveys:

> *Glou.* His breeding, Sir, hath been at my charge: I
>   have so often blush'd to acknowledge him, that   10
>   now I am braz'd to't.
> *Kent.* I cannot conceive you.
> *Glou.* Sir, this young fellow's mother could; where-
>   upon she grew round-womb'd, and had, indeed,
>   Sir, a son for her cradle ere she had a husband   15
>   for her bed. Do you smell a fault?
> *Kent.* I cannot wish the fault undone, the issue of it
>   being so proper.
> *Glou.* But I have a son, Sir, by order of law, some
>   year elder than this, who yet is no dearer in my   20
>   account: though this knave came something
>   saucily to the world before he was sent for, yet
>   was his mother fair; there was good sport at his
>   making, and the whoreson must be acknowledged.
>   Do you know this noble gentleman, Edmund?   25
> *Edm.* No, my Lord.
> *Glou.* My Lord of Kent: remember him hereafter as
>   my honourable friend.
> *Edm.* My services to your Lordship.
> *Kent.* I must love you, and sue to know you better.   30
> *Edm.* Sir, I shall study deserving.
> *Glou.* He hath been out nine years, and away he shall
>   again.
>   (I.i.9–33)

A number of items of information are disclosed here through the introductions that the first speaker's question quite naturally invites. The reader or spectator learns that the enquirer is the Earl of Kent, and that the much younger man is the bastard son of the, as yet unidentified, second speaker. The familial circumstances of father and son are also filled out. The members of the audience learn that the second speaker has another, legitimate, son; that Edmund is the younger of his two children; and that the two are equal in their father's affections, though the younger has spent much of his life abroad. Something of Edmund's physical appearance (which is to be of significance in subsequent scenes) is also indicated. Asked whether he disapproves of the moral laxity that led to the young man's conception, Kent replies:

> I cannot wish the fault undone, the issue of it
> being so proper [i.e. well-made].

> (17–18)

Once again, however, it is not simply hard facts that these lines communicate. The tone of the second speaker is as important as that which he has to say, and it is this tone which determines, for the audience, the significance of the situation. Though it appears that he was once ashamed to acknowledge his illegitimate offspring, the jocular, man-of-the-world tone with which he now describes his conception suggests that his sense of moral responsibility is no longer as acute as it once was, while his references to his son's 'saucy' entrance into the world (22) and the 'sport' (23) involved in his 'making' (24) imply considerable insensitivity on his part towards the feelings of the youth in whose presence these remarks are made. His salacious play on the word 'conceive' (13), his casual reference to the product of an adulterous relationship as 'the whoreson' (24), and apparent indifference to the ultimate welfare of Edmund's mother, all suggest a disturbing degree of levity in a man of his age, which, together with his garrulousness, points to an imbalance between his years and his wisdom. The formality of Edmund's responses is also suggestive. He is introduced immediately after the audience has been alerted to the possibility that a dichotomy may exist in the play world between appearance and reality, and the contrast between his reserve and his father's loquacity, together with the older man's lack of sensitivity towards him, might well lead the spectator to question the sincerity of the dutifulness which he displays.

The conversation between the two gentlemen is brought to a close by a 'sennet' (s.d.) heralding the arrival of the King – Lear's opening words, 'Attend the Lords of France and Burgundy, Gloucester' (I.i.34) at once identifying the second speaker and drawing him into the action with which the remainder of the scene is to deal. The nature of that action is extraordinary to say the least. The King invites his three daughters to tell him how much they love him, proposing to divide his kingdom among them in proportion to the filial piety each displays. Without the exchange between Kent and Gloucester which precedes these events, the audience might well be inclined to dismiss them as ludicrous, or to sit back and enjoy them as the fairy-tale happenings of a never-never-land kingdom. The brief introductory scene ensures a very different response. On a factual level the opening exchange has already prepared those watching for the division of the kingdom, and has stressed the King's impartiality, thus alerting the audience to the fact that the public apportioning of the realm is no more than a device, engineered to ratify, by a process most gratifying to the King's vanity, a political decision that has already been reached. At the same time, the first thirty-three lines of the play have disposed the spectators to accept that they are watching credible human beings functioning in a self-contained dramatic universe not unlike their own. The opening speeches have encouraged them to speculate about the characters of the dramatis personae, to make deductions about their motives, and to view their world as a complex one in which appearance and reality do not always coincide. The speakers have not leaped onto the stage through a trap-door opening upon a vacuum; they emerge from a past about which they can chat together and are composed of a realistic mixture of good and bad qualities. Kent disapproves of Gloucester's adultery, but cannot condemn its outcome, Gloucester has committed an immoral act but appears to be a kindly, well-meaning individual. The merging of these complex figures into Lear's court serves to locate the rash actions of the King, when his purposes are frustrated, in the context of a recognizable human society, increasing the horror of the deviation from rational conduct which the banishment of Cordelia represents.

One function of the expository speeches of Lear is thus to make the incredible credible, and in doing so to diminish the distance between the play world and actuality. But the conversation between Kent and Gloucester has a larger purpose in relation to the economy of the drama as a whole. Not only does it convey information to the audience, and root Lear's irrationality in a plausible dramatic universe, it also places the reader or spectator, by the mode in which it communicates, in a particular relationship to the events that are to be enacted. The naturalistic conversation between acquaintances who share knowledge about their society and have a personal history that antedates the opening of the play obliges the members of the audience, as in *Hamlet*, to deduce the significance* of the situation from that which they overhear, and to speculate about character and motive, rather than being informed of them directly. As a result, those outside the play become intellectually implicated in the dramatic experience; they become participators in, rather than observers of, the events that take place, feeling their own way, through the gaps in the dialogue, to the inner reality of the play world. In this way, the process is initiated whereby the experience of the dramatis personae becomes the spectator's experience, the suffering of Lear the suffering of every man or woman, drawn by a series of interrelated devices – of which the nature of the exposition is only one – to endure with him upon the heath. A more overtly contrived opening scene, which announced the speakers' names, roles and personalities directly to the audience would have created a much more formal framework for Lear's sudden outburst of rage and the cataclysm of Cordelia's banishment, placing those outside the play world in a very different relationship to the events which spring from them.

It is this kind of formal framework which the exposition of *Cymbeline* supplies. As noted above, the vehicle by which the pre-history of the action is disclosed is once again a conversation between two gentlemen, one at least of whom appears to be a courtier. In all other respects the contrast between the management of the two scenes could hardly be more striking. The speakers in *Cymbeline* have no names, nothing whatsoever emerges about their personalities or their motives, and no place is assigned them in the society upon which they comment. Their dialogue is worth quoting in full:

> *First Gent.* You do not meet a man but frowns: our bloods
> No more obey the heavens than our courtiers
> Still seem as does the king's.
> *Sec. Gent.*   But what's the matter?
> *First Gent.* His daughter, and the heir of's kingdom (whom
> He purpos'd to his wife's sole son – a widow   5
> That late he married) hath referr'd herself

Unto a poor but worthy gentleman. She's wedded,
Her husband banish'd; she imprison'd, all
Is outward sorrow, though I think the king
Be touch'd at very heart.
Sec. Gent.   None but the king?   10
First Gent. He that hath lost her too: so is the queen,
That most desir'd the match. But not a courtier,
Although they wear their faces to the bent
Of the king's looks, hath a heart that is not
Glad at the thing they scowl at.
Sec. Gent.   And why so?   15
First Gent. He that miss'd the princess is a thing
Too bad for bad report: and he that hath her
(I mean, that married her, alack good man,
And therefore banish'd) is a creature such
As, to seek through the regions of the earth   20
For one his like; there would be something failing
In him that should compare. I do not think
So fair an outward, and such stuff within
Endows a man, but he.
Sec. Gent.   You speak him far.
First Gent. I do extend him, sir, within himself,   25
Crush him together, rather than unfold
His measure duly.
Sec. Gent.   What's his name and birth?
First Gent. I cannot delve him to the root: his father
Was call'd Sicilius, who did join his honour
Against the Romans with Cassibelan,   30
But had his titles by Tenantius, whom
He served with glory and admired success:
So gain'd the sur-addition Leonatus:
And had (besides this gentleman in question)
Two other sons, who in the wars o'th'time   35
Died with their swords in hand. For which their father,
Then old, and fond of issue, took such sorrow
That he quit being; and his gentle lady,
Big of this gentleman (our theme) deceas'd
As he was born. The king he takes the babe   40
To his protection, calls him Posthumus Leonatus,
Breeds him, and makes him of his bed-chamber,
Puts to him all the learnings that his time

Could make him the receiver of, which he took,
As we do air, fast as 'twas minister'd,   45
And in's spring became a harvest: liv'd in court
(Which rare it is to do) most prais'd, most lov'd;
A sample to the youngest, to th'more mature
A glass that feated them, and to the graver
A child that guided dotards. To his mistress,   50
(For whom he now is banish'd) her own price
Proclaims how she esteem'd him; and his virtue
By her election may be truly read
What kind of man he is.
Sec. Gent.   I honour him,
Even out of your report. But pray you tell me,   55
Is she sole child to th'king?
First Gent.   His only child.
He had two sons (if this be worth your hearing,
Mark it) the eldest of them at three years old,
I'th'swathing-clothes the other, from their nursery
Were stol'n; and to this hour no guess in knowledge   60
Which way they went.
Sec. Gent.   How long is this ago?
First Gent. Some twenty years.
Sec. Gent. That a king's children should be so convey'd,
So slackly guarded, and the search so slow
That could not trace them!
First Gent.   Howsoe'er 'tis strange,   65
Or that the negligence may well be laugh'd at,
Yet is it true, sir.
Sec. Gent.   I do well believe you.

                                                    (I.i.1–67)

A number of points are notable about this exchange. As in *King
Lear*, information is conveyed here by means of question and answer
but the questions that are asked do not, in this instance, spring from
either the personalities or the situations of the speakers. Kent's
query, 'Is not this your son, my Lord?' (8) is a perfectly natural one,
given the presence of Edmund on stage. Gloucester's 'Do you know
this noble gentleman, Edmund?' (25) is the conventional social
response that the situation requires. By contrast, the questions that
the Second Gentleman asks are extraordinary. His opening query,

'But what's the matter?' (3) could be accounted for naturalistically by some difference in social rank between the two speakers that allows one a greater degree of intimacy with persons of state than the other, but his subsequent enquiries reveal an abyss of ignorance about the play world that defies explanation. He asks if the King is the only person grieved at the marriage of Imogen (10), why the courtiers are glad that she married Posthumus rather than the Queen's son (15), what the name and ancestry of the Princess's husband are (27), how many children the King has (56), and when the King's sons were lost (61). Moreover, the circumstantial replies of the First Gentleman, in which he carefully expounds the immediate history and personal relationships of all the members of the royal family and indicates the esteem in which they are held, suggest an even greater degree of ignorance on the part of his companion than his questions denote. No explanation is offered by either speaker for the Second Gentleman's extraordinary ignorance, and it is very hard to supply one. A country gentleman, for example, newly come to court, would be unlikely to have no knowledge of his own king's lack of a male heir, while a stranger from overseas would be very unwise not to have armed himself in advance with some minimal information about the court he proposed to visit. This gentleman appears to have issued from another planet. He knows nothing about the world in which he functions, no information is given about him, and he disappears from the stage into the vacuum from which he emerged once he has asked the questions he exists to propound.

The first speaker is almost equally devoid of personality. His knowledge of state affairs and the attitudes of those surrounding the King suggest that he is a member of the court, but no explicit reference is made to his role in the society he describes. Though he is as garrulous as Gloucester, his long, parenthetic speeches convey facts about a situation, rather than affording an insight into his character, and he offers no idiosyncratic view or opinion upon the events he relates. His relationship with the Second Gentleman, too, remains obscure. No context is supplied for their conversation, and the first speaker, like the second, disappears into a void once his role as informant is at an end.

The medium in which the exposition is conducted is also significant. The two gentlemen employ blank verse, rather than prose, while their syntax and diction contribute to an elevated style remote from natural speech. The First Gentleman's sentences are much longer than those of his *King Lear* counterpart, Gloucester, and they evolve through a series of dependent clauses and parentheses extending over a considerable number of lines (cf. 28–36). The violation of conventional word order (cf. 'from their nursery / Were stol'n' (59–60)), and the elliptical structure of several passages (cf. 'As we do air, fast as 'twas minister'd' (45)) contribute to the convoluted nature of the style, making the account, for all its circumstantial detail, surprisingly hard to follow. The vocabulary, too, is at a considerable remove from day-to-day usage. In place of Gloucester's colloquial 'young fellow's' (13), 'round-womb'd' (14), 'knave' (21), 'saucily' (22), 'whoreson' (24), the First Gentleman employs the more formal 'sur-addition' (33), 'deceas'd' (39), 'learnings' (43), 'minister'd' (45), 'election' (53). The use of *functional shift* (i.e. the conversion of one part of speech into another) as in 'outward' (23), and of coinages, as in 'feated' (49) also add to the sense of unfamiliarity which the language as a whole promotes. In short, where the informal, personal style of *King Lear* creates the illusion of real people talking to one another in a universe not unlike the spectator's own, the opening exchanges of *Cymbeline* do not seek to convince the audience of the credibility of the dramatic fiction and are designed to distance the play world from the audience.

The sense of remoteness generated by the opening scene of *Cymbeline* is not solely a product, however, of the non-naturalistic nature of the dialogue. The kind of information that is conveyed also contributes to the creation of distance. Whereas the opening speeches of *Lear* help to establish the credibility of the events which follow by locating them in a world of fallible human beings capable of being misled by false appearance, the initial exchanges of *Cymbeline* stress the fairy-tale nature of the play's concerns by the black-and-white terms in which the characters are presented. Thus the Queen's son is not simply unlikeable, he is 'Too bad for bad report' (17), while Posthumus is not merely well-disposed, he is 'a creature such / As, to seek through the regions of the earth / For one his like; there would be something failing / In him that should compare' (19–22). Cymbeline's courtiers like and dislike with unrealistic unanimity, while the First Gentleman has no difficulty in penetrating the facades of his fellow courtiers, and is untroubled by any doubt that motives may be too complex to comprehend. Folk-tale motifs, too, are emphasized, rather than being assimilated into a naturalistic framework. Whereas in *King Lear* the traditional elements of the main and sub plots (the love test, and the innate malevolence of those born outside wedlock) are brought into contact with the everyday world, in that the professions of love are designed to ratify a more conventional agreement, while Edmund's degeneracy may be a product of his experience, in *Cymbeline* the archetypal elements of the situation are highlighted by the First Gentleman's insistence upon the exceptional virtue of the posthumous child, and by both gentlemen's emphasis upon the extraordinary nature of the abduction of the King's sons.

The stance of the two gentlemen towards the events they discuss also differs from that of Kent and Gloucester. Where the two courtiers of *King Lear* express some surprise that their expectations in relation to a specific situation have been overthrown, the First and Second Gentlemen note the improbability of the events the former retails, and comment upon their ludicrousness. Thus the Second Gentleman exclaims:

> That a king's children should be so convey'd,
> So slackly guarded, and the search so slow
> That could not trace them!

> (63–5)

to which the First Gentleman responds:

> Howsoe'er 'tis strange,
> Or that the negligence may well be laugh'd at,
> Yet is it true, sir.

> (65–7)

Once again this is an interchange that is designed to draw attention to the non-naturalistic nature of events rather than to convince the audience that what is being presented is 'real life'. It establishes that the dramatist is fully aware of the improbability of his fiction, and it invites the spectator to accept a situation that is patently unlikely as a starting point for an exploration that will have its own kind of truth. This kind of exchange, which generates an awareness of artifice (see Chapter 8 below), places the audience in a highly objective relationship to that which is being enacted. The reader or spectator is induced to think of the play as a work of art, rather than being drawn into the dramatic experience, and is thus encouraged to view that which is to ensue with a far greater degree of detachment than the opening speeches of *Lear* permit.

The role of the audience as spectators, rather than participants, is also ensured by the highly explicit nature of the exposition. Everything that those outside the play world need to know is carefully spelt out. The motives of the King, the Queen and their offspring are clearly stated, and the ancestry of Posthumus is expounded in what appears, at this stage in the play, to be superfluous detail. Nothing whatsoever here is left to the imagination. Where *King Lear* encourages the reader or listener to ponder the possible implications of the situation and to speculate upon character and motive, *Cymbeline* frustrates audience involvement by the absolute terms which it employs and the fullness of its account. Significant items of information are drawn, pointedly, to the spectator's attention. For example, the First Gentleman introduces the loss of the King's sons with:

He had two sons (if this be worth your hearing,
Mark it)

(57–8)

– the parenthesis very obviously being designed to alert those outside the play world to the importance of what is to follow, rather than being dictated by the dramatic situation. No concession is made here either to naturalism on the one hand or emotional involvement on the other. It is an alert mind and an appreciation of bold outline that the artefact demands.

To a twentieth-century reader the contrast between the expositions of *King Lear* and *Cymbeline* may appear, at first glance, to be a matter, not of divergent dramatic techniques, but of success and failure, good art and bad. A present-day audience, accustomed to the conventions of the modern novel and the realism of television drama, is conditioned to measure the achievement of a work of art in proportion to the degree to which it conveys the illusion that it is presenting real life, and thus to respond adversely to the overtly artifical. In fact, all art, however superficially realistic, depends upon a process of selection. The artist does not (and could not) reflect life in all its confusion and complexity; he shapes it in accordance with a preconceived purpose, even when that purpose is to document a real event. Though the exploration of human character is one legitimate province of the dramatist, it is not the only province, nor is a high degree of proximity between actors and audience an essential element of a major dramatic work. As noted at the outset of this chapter, the relationship between play and spectators varies from drama to drama and from society to society, and no histrionic mode is, by nature, superior to the rest. The success or failure of a specific work depends, not upon the degree of its 'realism' but upon its internal coherence and the truth of its vision, and this kind of truthfulness is not dependent upon a simple adherence to the minutiae of everyday life. *King Lear* and *Cymbeline*, for all their joint dependence upon folk-tale, represent contrasting dramatic modes, and it is the kind of play each is to be that their opening lines seek to establish. *King Lear* foregrounds individuals, to whom the members of the audience are encouraged to relate, and through whose experience they come to perceive the workings of a larger, universal process. Gloucester, for example, is a person, not a type. He is well-meaning, insensitive, kindly, weak, superstitious, capable of learning from his experience, and so on. At the same time, however, he has a larger, generic role which he shares with Lear. He is a suffering father, abused by the offspring in whom he placed his trust, an archetypal victim of filial ingratitude. The opening scene of the play initiates this dual role and dictates the primacy of the first of its elements. It establishes Gloucester's character, and the situation for which he is responsible, while paying just sufficient attention to the universal to initiate the process whereby the larger significance of the individual's personal experience is unfolded. *Cymbeline*, by contrast, evolves in the opposite direction. It is pattern, here, rather than individuality which is to the fore. The play is concerned with a cyclical process of loss and recovery, of which the experience of the dramatis personae is merely symptomatic, and it is therefore the traditional roles to which the characters conform, rather than their personal idiosyncracies that are stressed. Imogen, for example, is the embodiment of wifely devotion and fertility. Her imprisonment and subsequent rejection by her husband represent the frustration of the natural processes of growth and renewal, both in personal and national terms. Hence it is as princess and wife that she is first presented. No name is assigned to her in the opening exchange, and it is upon her archetypal role as king's daughter, and victim of a stepmother's ambitions, that attention is initially focused.

The degree of distance between the play world and its audience is a product of this contrasting emphasis, and is integral to each drama's success. Since *King Lear* moves from the particular to the universal it is essential that the audience should become involved in the sufferings of the dramatis personae, and it is this proximity between those outside the play world and the fully realized, idiosyncratic, human beings within it that the exposition promotes. Since *Cymbeline*, by contrast, is concerned with a process, rather than personalities, it is important for the audience to remain aloof from the figures through whom the meaning is projected, and it is towards the promotion of this objective stance that the opening lines are geared. Thus, while the informal exchanges of the first scene of *Lear* are designed to draw the reader or listener into the dramatic universe, the non-naturalistic dialogue of *Cymbeline* functions to frustrate audience involvement, sustaining the spectator's awareness of the stage spectacle as art, rather than life, and calling his intellectual faculties, not his capacity to empathize, into play.

Antony and Cleopatra also opens with the entrance of two gentlemen, and its exposition appears, at first sight, to be very similar to that of *Cymbeline*:

Enter DEMETRIUS *and* PHILO.

Phi. Nay, but this dotage of our general's
    O'erflows the measure: those his goodly eyes,
    That o'er the files and musters of the war
    Have glow'd like plated Mars, now bend, now turn
    The office and devotion of their view   5
    Upon a tawny front: his captain's heart,
    Which in the scuffles of great fights hath burst
    The buckles on his breast, reneges all temper,
    And is become the bellows and the fan
    To cool a gypsy's lust.
Flourish. Enter ANTONY, CLEOPATRA, *her Ladies, the*
Train, with Eunuchs fanning her.   10
                Look, where they come:
    Take but good note, and you shall see in him
    The triple pillar of the world transform'd
    Into a strumpet's fool: behold and see.

(I.i.1–13)

The role of the two Romans here has obvious affinities with that of *Cymbeline*'s Britons. Philo's opening speech, like the First Gentleman's, defines a situation, and his comments, like the First

Gentleman's subsequent lines, endow his society with a past. The method by which information is disclosed is also similar. Philo is describing the situation at court to a newcomer, though in this instance the circumstances of the second gentleman are more clearly defined in that it is established later in the scene that he has just come from Rome (59–61). Like the First and Second Gentlemen of *Cymbeline*, Philo and Demetrius are detached from the action they introduce; they play no part in subsequent events; and exhibit an attitude rather than distinctive personalities. The overtly expositorial function of the opening lines is also comparable. Just as the First Gentleman's

> (if this be worth your hearing,
> Mark it)
>
> (57–8)

is directed towards the spectator rather than his companion, undermining the illusion that the play world is self-contained, so Philo's repeated injunctions to watch – 'Take but good note' (11), 'behold and see' (13) – are aimed at the audience, rather than Demetrius, and enhance the spectator's awareness of the speaker as a choric figure.

On closer inspection, however, major differences between this exposition and that of the romance quickly become apparent. In the first place, whereas the First Gentleman's observations are factual, and supply the members of the audience with items of information that allow them to make sense of the incidents that follow, Philo's comments, for all their superficial objectivity, soon emerge as opinions, and hence do not have the same status as the historical facts and universally accepted value judgements that the First Gentleman exists to retail. The first thirteen lines of the scene present the reader or spectator with two images of Antony and one of Cleopatra. On the one hand, Philo celebrates Antony as a great military leader and public figure. He thinks of him as another Mars (the god of war), capable of bursting the buckles on his armour by the strenuousness of his exertions in battle (4 and 6–8), and as one of the three 'pillars' (12) sustaining the Roman state. On the other hand, he laments the man his general has become. He sees him as narrowing his vision from the many to one (2–6), squandering his titanic energy on the sexual satisfaction of an insatiable woman

(6–10), and exchanging power and responsibility for servitude and indignity (11–13). The image presented of Cleopatra, by contrast, is wholly adverse. She is 'tawny' (6) – an opprobrious epithet – a mere 'gypsy' (10) and a 'strumpet' (13). These observations clearly predispose the spectators to view the play's central figures from the speaker's point of view, and his closing injunctions, 'Take but good note' (11), 'behold and see' (13), are indicative of his confidence that the appearance of the lovers will confirm the justice of his report. In fact, the entrance of Antony and Cleopatra does not fulfil the expectations that these opening lines arouse. Though the stage direction, '*Enter* . . . CLEOPATRA . . . *with Eunuchs fanning her*' appears to bear out the suggestion that Antony has become 'the bellows and the fan / To cool a gypsy's lust' (9–10) and has become emasculated in the process, the scene which follows runs counter, in many ways, to Philo's account. The initial entrance of the lovers is visually impressive. The eroticism of Cleopatra is plainly indicated, but so too is her royalty – and this is an aspect of her personality that the terms 'gypsy' and 'strumpet' manifestly fail to convey. The exchange that follows between the lovers is also significant. Where Philo regards the relationship between the two as negative, the vocabulary Antony and Cleopatra employ is positive. Both refer to 'love' rather than lust (cf. 14, 16, 24, 44), while Antony sees their embraces as 'nobleness' (36), not intemperate sensuality. Philo's strictures on his general's conduct are also countered. Antony's expressions of his love for Cleopatra imply that rather than substituting a single demeaning relationship for an exalted public role, Antony sees himself as having exchanged one kind of empire for another:

Cleo. If it be love indeed, tell me how much.
Ant. There's beggary in the love that can be reckon'd.　　　　15
Cleo. I'll set a bourn how far to be belov'd.
Ant. Then must thou needs find out new heaven, new
　earth.

(14–17)

The function of Philo's opening speech is thus much more complex than that of *Cymbeline*'s First Gentleman. Not only does it 'place' the dramatic action by establishing the point at which it begins and the premises upon which it depends, it also offers an interpretation of the central situation which is then juxtaposed against that of the principal figures. Having made one set of assumptions in the first thirteen lines, the members of the theatre audience are obliged to consider the validity of their previous position, and to assess one set of attitudes in the light of another. The exposition involves the spectator, in short, in a process of evaluation. *Antony and Cleopatra* does not trace the unequivocal 'fall' of either of its central figures. It invites those outside the play world to consider whether their progress constitutes an ascent or a descent by presenting their situation from a variety of perspectives, and it is this process of assessment that the exposition initiates.

The entrance of Philo and Demetrius also differs from that of *Cymbeline*'s gentlemen in that it contributes to a stage spectacle that is important in the projection of meaning. The expository figures are both men, and Philo's reference to 'our general' (1) implies that they are soldiers. They are clearly Romans, and their costume and bearing would suggest their military background. Cleopatra, by contrast, enters followed by her ladies and attended by eunuchs, and all that surrounds her suggests softness and fluidity. The austere masculinity of the Romans is thus in stark contrast with the opulence (cf. *'the Train'* (s.d.)), sensuousness (cf. *'with Eunuchs fanning her'* (s.d.)), and effeminacy of the Egyptians, and this visual contrast is enforced by the imagery employed by the two groups. While Philo talks of the 'files and musters of the war' (3), of 'plated Mars' (4), the 'scuffles of great fights' (7), and of Antony bursting the 'buckles on his breast' (8), Antony and Cleopatra speak of 'love' (14), 'soft hours' (44), and 'pleasure' (47), and can envisage Rome melting (33). Where *Cymbeline*'s Britain was physically at war with Augustus' Rome, Cleopatra's Egypt is conceptually opposed to the world of the Caesars, and it is this divided universe which the exposition is designed to evoke. In this respect Philo stands at the furthest possible remove from *Cymbeline*'s First Gentleman – his very appearance expressing a partisanship that is at the opposite pole from the First Gentleman's stateless objectivity.

The opposition between Rome and Egypt impressed on the audience by this opening scene is crucial to the meaning of the play. The two states are physically at war by Act III; they offer contrasting opportunities for Antony's self-fulfilment; and they represent opposing attitudes to life. In glancing from Philo to Cleopatra, the members of an audience become involved, not merely in assessing a relationship, but in evaluating the value systems between which

Antony attempts to choose, and the virtues and vices of antithetical societies. Every aspect of the play's opening scene thus contributes to the projection of a multi-layered meaning. What appears at first sight to be a very elementary kind of exposition rapidly proves to be something much more complex.

The opening scenes of *Lear*, *Cymbeline*, and *Antony and Cleopatra* (like that of *Othello* discussed in the previous chapter) all open with a conversation between two gentlemen designed to communicate information to those outside the play world, yet they differ markedly in the relationship between play and spectator that they engineer. *Lear* invites the members of the audience to make deductions about character and motive, *Cymbeline* frustrates audience involvement and draws attention to archetypal patterns, while *Antony and Cleopatra* calls the spectator's judgement into play. Together with the expositions of *The Comedy of Errors* and *Hamlet* they demonstrate the variety of ways in which Shakespeare sets his plays in motion, and the role played by the exposition in determining the mode of the ensuing action. It would be wrong to suggest, however, that the opening scenes discussed in this chapter can serve as a paradigm for Shakespearian drama as a whole. Each of the thirty-seven plays begins in a different way – and no formula can be adduced that will apply to every composition. Nevertheless, these expositions do illustrate some lines of enquiry that the interested reader might pursue when confronted with an unfamiliar work. Starting from the basic question of how information is communicated to the audience, the student should consider in what ways the pre-history of the action is unfolded; whether those outside the play world know more or less than those within it; how complex the characters are; to what extent the members of the audience become involved in individual experience; if the spectator's attention is drawn towards the dramatist's art, or away from it; how the stage spectacle contributes to the projection of meaning; and whether those disclosing information may be regarded as objective. Above all, the student should bear in mind that the opening scenes of a play do not simply convey facts to the audience, though the communication of information is obviously an important aspect of their function. They manipulate the spectator into a particular relationship to the ensuing action; they frequently dictate a mood or atmosphere; and they determine the mode in which the drama evolves. A careful study of the opening scene of a Shakespearian play can thus cast considerable light upon the meaning of the whole, while affording the reader an insight into the diversity of Shakespeare's structures. For this reason Shakespeare's expositions may be seen as the gateway to the study of the entire corpus, offering the inexperienced reader a highly rewarding way of approaching the plays.

4

Plays within Plays

The kinds of exposition described in the previous chapter all involve a pair or group of figures who belong, however tenuously, to the same world, or order of reality, as the characters upon whom the attention of the theatre audience is ultimately to focus. Egeon, in *The Comedy of Errors*, is the father of the twins upon whose resemblance the central action depends; Kent, Edmund and Gloucester play leading roles in Lear's tragedy; while the soldiers on the walls of Elsinore communicate directly with Hamlet. Renaissance playwrights did not always, however, usher their audiences as directly into their play worlds as these examples suggest. A large number of Elizabethan–Jacobean dramas open with a prologue, which may outline the events that are about to be enacted (cf. Marlowe's *Dr Faustus*), define the author's aims and intentions (cf. Jonson's *Volpone*), or apologize for the deficiencies of the coming performance (cf. Lyly's *Campaspe*). The effect of such introductory speeches is to heighten the spectator's awareness of the theatrical representation as artifice. For a short time at least after the Prologue has made his exit, the audience remains alive to the fact that the characters who succeed him on the stage are actors in a play, and a number of dramatists actively promote this awareness by direct allusion in the Prologue's speech to the machinery of the theatre, or the inability of the actors to do justice to the writer's conceptions. Conversely, the character who speaks the prologue is detached by his superior knowledge, or critical stance, from the persons of the play proper. He does not belong to the same order of reality as they do, though he forms part of the dramatic structure which is about to unfold. Shakespeare's *Henry V* affords an example of this kind of prologue. The play opens, not with the discussion between the Archbishop of Canterbury and the Bishop of Ely about the reformation in the character of the young king which could well have formed the play's starting point, but with a powerful introductory speech which, by its insistence upon such words as 'stage' (3), 'act' (3) and 'scene' (4), and its emphasis upon the limitations of the actors in relation to their subject (8–11), firmly establishes what is to follow as a play – a mere shadow of 'reality':

Enter PROLOGUE

O, for a Muse of fire, that would ascend
The brightest heaven of invention;
A kingdom for a stage, princes to act
And monarchs to behold the swelling scene!
Then should the warlike Harry, like himself,   5
Assume the port of Mars; and at his heels,
Leash'd in like hounds, should famine, sword, and fire
Crouch for employment. But pardon, gentles all,
The flat unraised spirits that hath dar'd
On this unworthy scaffold to bring forth   10
So great an object: can this cockpit hold
The vasty fields of France? or may we cram
Within this wooden O the very casques
That did affright the air at Agincourt?
O, pardon! since a crooked figure may   15
Attest in little place a million;
And let us, ciphers to this great accompt,
On your imaginary forces work.
Suppose within the girdle of these walls
Are now confin'd two mighty monarchies,   20
Whose high upreared and abutting fronts
The perilous narrow ocean parts asunder:
Piece out our imperfections with your thoughts;
Into a thousand parts divide one man,
And make imaginary puissance;   25
Think, when we talk of horses, that you see them
Printing their proud hoofs i'the'receiving earth;
For 'tis your thoughts that now must deck our kings,
Carry them here and there, jumping o'er times,
Turning th'accomplishment of many years   30
Into an hour-glass: for the which supply,
Admit me Chorus to this history;
Who prologue-like your humble patience pray,
Gently to hear, kindly to judge, our play.

(I. Prologue 1–34)

The function of this speech is complex. It invites toleration of the deficiencies of the actors, implies the magnitude of the play's subject by drawing attention to the difficulties of its representation, and involves the spectator in the performance, not by convincing him that he is watching actual events, but by stimulating his imagination, and inviting his participation in the creative act. From the very outset of this play the members of the audience are thus made aware of a variety of levels of reality. They are aware of themselves as spectators, gathered together in a particular location – the wooden O of the playhouse – to watch a specific theatrical event; they are aware of an actor, playing the part of the Prologue, who is to function as Chorus, and who can relate more than can be enacted in the play proper; and they are aware of the historical drama which the Prologue presents and which opens with the entrance of the two clerics.

The introductory material heralding the central action was not always confined to a single speech designed to convey information to the audience, or to manoeuvre its members into an appropriate state of receptivity. A large number of Renaissance plays begin with an *Induction* – or prefatory playlet – with its own cast of characters and an area of activity detached from that of the principal action but thematically related to it. Jonson's *Cynthia's Revels*, for example, opens with a quarrel between the boy actors who are to play the courtiers in the main body of the drama, their controversy over which of them should speak the prologue introducing the theme of self love which is to be the play's primary concern. Similarly, Marston's *Antonio and Mellida* is introduced by a scene in which the actors complain about the parts they have been assigned, their doubts about their ability to sustain their roles serving to alert the spectators to a major preoccupation (man's inability to live up to his pretensions) of the ensuing drama. In some instances the characters of such introductory playlets figure in more than one scene. For example, in Greene's *James IV* and Kyd's *The Spanish Tragedy* the figures of Bohan and Oberon in the former, and of Revenge and Don Andrea in the latter do not merely introduce the subject matter of the central action, they observe that action throughout, their area of activity forming a *frame plot* which enfolds the principal plot (or plots) within itself. Clearly, in a structure of this kind the audience's awareness of multiple levels of reality is much greater than in those plays in which a Prologue merely appears to speak a few lines and then disappears from the stage altogether. Throughout the performance the spectator is engaged in watching one group of characters watching another, and this inevitably heightens his awareness of the theatricality of the inset action while diminishing his involvement in it.

The Taming of the Shrew provides an example of Shakespeare's use of this kind of frame plot. Unfortunately, the history of the text is a confused one, and the original design of the drama is now unclear, but the first act of the play undoubtedly illustrates a self-conscious use of the box-within-a-box kind of structure outlined above. The play opens, not with Baptista's difficulty in finding a husband for his shrewish daughter Katherina, which is the ultimate focus of interest, but with an altercation between Sly the Tinker and a Hostess over some broken glasses. Sly then falls asleep on stage, and a Lord enters with his followers. The Lord finds the Tinker asleep, and evolves the idea of dressing him in his own clothes, treating him as a nobleman when he wakes, and watching how he responds to the alien situation in which he finds himself. At the outset of this sequence the spectator's attention is centred upon Sly. He opens the play with the Hostess, and he is left alone on stage when she exits in search of the 'third-borough' (10). With the Lord's device, however, some of the attention shifts from the Tinker himself to those who are practising on him. By scene ii the audience is watching a play about a man who has been dressed up and set to act out a part, and the responses of the internal, or on-stage audience to the Tinker's performance are as interesting to those outside the play world as the mistaken attitudes of Sly himself. The arrival of a company of players is then announced, and these actors in turn begin their play, transforming Sly, the focus of attention hitherto as a character, firstly in Shakespeare's play, and then in the Lord's, into the central member of a new internal audience. And the successive levels of actors and audiences do not end here. After the opening scene of the play-within-the-play, in which Lucentio is introduced, Baptista enters with his daughters and their suitors, and Lucentio and his servant, Tranio, in their turn, step aside to watch the 'show' (I.i.47) that is about to unfold. At this point in the action, the spectator to the Shakespearian play is no longer merely engaged in watching a play about a Lord watching a deluded Tinker. He or she is watching a Lord, watching a Tinker, watching a play about a young man, watching an old man with two daughters. Moreover, the characters of the play-within-the-play have no sooner been introduced, than they too, like the Lord and Sly, begin to assume alien roles and to play parts. Lucentio disguises himself as

Cambio, Tranio becomes Lucentio, Hortensio Litio, etc. (cf. II.i.38ff.).

Sly, together with the Lord and his servants, remain on stage for the remainder of the first scene, and may originally have been intended to do so throughout. They comment on the performance at I.i.248–53 and continue, for a short time at least, to form the principal focus of audience attention, until the complexities of the play-within-the-play establish its primacy as the central action. A reader or spectator unfamiliar with *The Taming of the Shrew* would not, therefore, be aware until the drama had been in progress for a significant length of time which group of characters would emerge as the principal persons of the play. At the outset, the comedy appears to be a farcical piece concerning the adventures of Sly the Tinker and it only gradually becomes apparent that this character functions merely to usher the play proper onto the stage. To cut the Sly scenes, as in a number of twentieth-century productions, thus involves a radical alteration in the relationship between those outside the play world and the characters of the Shrew play itself. The elaborate sequence of internal audiences that Shakespeare sets up serves to detach the spectator from the action which the frame plot enfolds, frustrating audience involvement with the figures that it presents. A spectator watching a Lord, watching a Tinker, watching a group of players perform a play, cannot but be aware of that play as a 'show', or 'game' – an entertainment to be appreciated for its wit or gusto, rather than a slice of 'real' life. From this perspective, the physical and verbal battles of the central action become much less offensive to modern sensibilities than might otherwise be the case. The frame plot ensures that the members of the audience do not equate the Kate–Petruchio relationship with day-to-day actuality, but relate it to the theatrical conventions that form the stock in trade of the travelling performer.

The complex Induction to *The Taming of the Shrew* does not simply serve to distance the spectator from the central action, and to call his attention to its theatricality, it also introduces some of the themes of the Shrew play itself. The opening exchanges of the Induction turn upon an inversion of roles, with an overbearing woman berating and abusing a cowering and resentful man, and the concept of reversal is recapitulated when the Lord dresses Sly in his own clothes, treats him as a nobleman and waits upon him as a servant. When the players begin their play, both kinds of reversal are quickly caught up. Katherina, the elder daughter of Baptista, is described in masculine terms, and is shown bullying and abusing her suitors; while Lucentio and Tranio exchange places, the lord becoming a servant, and the servant a lord. The Induction thus serves as an introduction to the concerns of the main plot. It sketches in bold outline the anarchic consequences of the disruption of the natural order implicit in each strand of the central action, and highlights the ludicrousness of those who fail to recognize, or act in conformity with, their social roles. At the same time, the similarity between the situations of the characters in the main and frame plots suggests that the deficiencies of the characters of the inset action are not idiosyncratic but universal. The world inhabited by Sly the Tinker, with its hostesses and ale houses, is merely a heightened version of the real world, while the anarchic universe evoked by the players is a heightened version of Sly's. Since the defects of the characters of the play-within-the-play are shared by the members of its (internal) audience, the spectators of the Shakespearian play share, by implication, the tendency of both sets of dramatis personae to undermine the social order by failing to comport themselves in a manner appropriate to their social status.

Slight as it may appear on first inspection, the frame plot of *The Taming of the Shrew* is clearly much more than an ingenious and entertaining device designed to set the play proper in motion. Like the prologue to *Henry V* it calls attention to the artifice of the principal action, while it introduces the themes of the comedy it frames through both its content and design. Meaning, in this instance, is derived not merely through the actions and experiences of the main plot characters, but from the relationships that are set up between events taking place on different levels of reality, with the audience keenly aware throughout the performance (or, at least, throughout the first act) that they are spectators in a theatre watching a play. The use of a play-within-a-play is not always designed, however, to emphasize the artificiality of the dramatic representation. Whereas in *The Taming of the Shrew* it is the frame plot which approximates to reality, and the overtly theatrical inset action which emerges as the principal focus of audience attention, in a large number of Renaissance dramas it is the enfolding actuality which is the primary area of interest, and the inset playlet which comments upon it. In *The Spanish Tragedy*, for example, the principal revenger, Hieronimo, designs a play, to be performed by himself and his enemies, which recapitulates the events of the main plot, while in Jonson's *Bartholomew Fair* the characters gather to watch a puppet play which caricatures the persons and events of the enfolding comedy. Shakespeare makes use of inset actions of this kind throughout his dramatic career. In *Love's Labour's Lost*, for example, a group of well-meaning citizens perform the 'Pageant of the Nine Worthies' before the King of Navarre and a visiting French princess; in *A Midsummer Night's Dream*, Bottom and his fellow mechanicals produce 'A tedious brief scene of young Pyramus / And his love Thisbe' (V.i.56–7) for Theseus and Hippolyta; Hamlet stages both a dumb show and a tragedy for the benefit of Claudius; while Prospero, in *The Tempest*, engineers a series of shows and spectacles for the courtiers shipwrecked on his island. In each of these instances the inset drama forms a crucial element of the statement that the play makes, but the nature of its contribution to the meaning of the whole varies from context to context.

Love's Labour's Lost concerns the attempt of the King of Navarre and his followers to become 'heirs of all eternity' (I.i.7) by devoting themselves to a life of study and forsaking the pleasures of the world – particularly the society of members of the opposite sex. The arrival of the Princess of France on an embassy from her father immediately establishes a tension between the King's obligations to keep his vows, and his responsibilities as a monarch, and both his problems and those of his lords, are compounded when the would-be scholars fall in love with the French ladies. At first sight, the 'Pageant' which 'The pedant, the braggart, the hedge-priest, the fool, and the boy' (V.ii.536–7) attempt to perform before the court appears to have very little to do with this sequence of events. The actors are grotesquely miscast and have failed to master their lines, and the members of the court jeer at them mercilessly for their deficiencies. Nevertheless, although the members of the theatre audience also find the discrepancies between the amateur actors and the persons that they represent amusing, they do not share the responses of Navarre and his lords. Before the entrance of the first Worthy, the following exchange takes place between the King, Berowne (his chief follower) and the French Princess:

> *King.* Berowne, they will shame us; let them not approach.
> *Ber.* We are shame-proof, my lord; and 'tis some policy
>   To have one show worse than the king's and his company.
> *King.* I say they shall not come.   510
> *Prin.* Nay, my good lord, let me o'er-rule you now.
>   That sport best pleases that doth least know how.

> Where zeal strives to content, and the contents
> Dies in the zeal of that which it presents;
> Their form confounded makes most form in mirth, 515
> When great things labouring perish in their birth.
> *Ber.* A right description of our sport, my lord.

(V.ii.507–17)

Berowne's lines serve to alert the spectator to a similarity between the actors in the pageant and the gentlemen of the court. The King and his followers have laid themselves open to ridicule in their attempts to court the ladies, and Berowne claims that the failures of the Worthies will act as a foil for their own. The Princess's reference to 'great things' that 'perish in their birth' (516) also has relevance, as Berowne notes, to the activities of the courtiers. The scholarly enterprise that Navarre and his gentlemen have undertaken has failed at its inception – perishing at the moment that the Princess of France approached the court. Once alerted by these comments to possible analogies between the Worthies and the courtiers, the members of the theatre audience become aware of a number of other parallels between the two groups. The gentlemen have aspired to become 'heirs of all eternity', 'brave conquerors' of their 'own affections', by warring against 'the huge army of the world's desires', and seeking to establish an institution that 'shall be the wonder of the world' (I.i.7–12). The terminology invites comparison with heroic figures from the past – Pompey, Alexander, or Hercules – comparison, in short, with the 'Worthies' who are represented in the play-within-the-play. The grotesque inability of 'The pedant, the braggart, the hedge-priest, the fool, and the boy' to sustain the roles that they have assumed thus parodies the failure of the King and his lords in relation to the parts they have elected to play. Just as a curate is incapable of playing the part of an Alexander because his lack of self-assertiveness runs counter to his role, so Navarre is unfitted for the part of a scholar or an ascetic since his kingly duties require him to live in the world, not to withdraw from it, and to defeat time through offspring rather than arrest it through 'art' (I.i.14).

The actors' problems with their lines also have relevance to the experience of the lords. Having fallen in love with the Princess and her ladies, the gentlemen seek to court them under the guise of Russians, only to have their spokesman, Moth, mocked out of his part, and to find their own words twisted, and their 'lines' misdirected, by the superior wit of the ladies. Once again, the events of the play-within-the-play act as a commentary upon the events of the 'real' world. The stumbling speeches, hesitations and confusions of the Worthies in the face of the jibes of those that they are seeking to please caricature the verbal defeat of the courtiers by those they had sought to impress. Polished as the gentlemen appear at first sight, their wit fails as dismally when they are confronted by the ladies as that of the Worthies when they are confronted by the lords – and the folly of one group serves to accentuate the lack of wisdom of the other.

It is important to note, however, that though Berowne alerts the members of the theatre audience to the similarities between the play-within-the-play and the conduct of the courtiers, Navarre and his followers remain oblivious, throughout the performance, of the relevance of the pageant to themselves. Despite the attempts of the Princess to encourage the actors, the gentlemen mock the luckless performers from beginning to end, making it impossible for them to sustain their parts. Though the reader or spectator is amused by these exchanges, and relishes (to a degree) the wit that the young men exhibit, he or she does not share the standpoint of the internal audience, but becomes increasingly critical of it. The interjections of the Princess (cf. V.ii.623 and 656), the similarities between the Worthies and their mockers, and, above all, the responses of the actors themselves as they valiantly attempt to present their play, all make a criticism of the gallants which is summed up when the exasperated Holofernes (representing Judas Maccabaeus) rounds upon them with, 'This is not generous, not gentle, not humble' (V.ii.621). Much as they pride themselves on their intelligence, the gentlemen of Navarre's court are lacking in understanding, and the pageant of the Worthies exposes just how limited their self-knowledge is.

The play-within-the-play thus serves to highlight the deficiencies of the play world through both its subject matter and reception. The members of Navarre's court regard the pageant as no more than a pleasant means of passing the time; they are unaware of its relevance to themselves; and learn nothing about their conduct in the course of it. The members of Shakespeare's audience, by contrast, apply the inset action to the drama which enfolds it, deducing more about the one from its relationship with the other. The 'meaning' of the play-within-the-play is not, therefore, identical for its internal and external audiences. For the first it is a ludicrous exercise by incompetent performers; for the second it crystallizes the limitations of a court seriously lacking in gentility.

The tragedy of Pyramus and Thisbe performed by the mechanicals for Theseus and Hippolyta in *A Midsummer Night's Dream* seems, at first sight, to fulfil a function very similar to that of the pageant of the Worthies in *Love's Labour's Lost*. The subject matter of the drama – the tribulations of lovers – is clearly related to that of the framing action, while the internal audience, once again, is made up of a group of lords and ladies who are highly conscious of the deficiencies of the performers. The contribution made by the play-within-the-play to the meaning of the whole is very different, however, from that made by the inset action of the earlier play. It extends the themes of the drama, rather than presenting the concerns of the framing action in heightened form, while it stands in a different structural relationship to the action which enfolds it.

On the most superficial level, *A Midsummer Night's Dream* presents an anatomy (or analysis of the nature) of love. The play opens with a pair of royal lovers – Theseus and Hippolyta – a mature, rational, sexually experienced couple (cf. II.i.68–80) anxious for their wedding night, but content to while away the time that must elapse before the consummation of their marriage 'with pomp, with triumph, and with revelling' (I.i.19). A second group of lovers, Hermia, Helena, Demetrius and Lysander, is then introduced who form a contrast, in every respect, with the royal couple. They are young, sexually inexperienced, passionate, and wholly opposed to the sovereignty of reason in amatory affairs. The flight of Lysander and Hermia, pursued by Helena and Demetrius, to the wood outside Athens, and the coincidental decision of a group of workmen to rehearse the play they hope to perform before the Duke in the same place, allows for the introduction of yet another couple, Oberon and Titania, the King and Queen of the fairies, who contrast with Theseus and Hippolyta in a different way. Whereas the human rulers were formerly at war and have now formed a harmonious alliance, the fairy potentates are at odds with one another, and have thrown their world into disorder. The conflict between the King and Queen of the fairies produces, in turn, another pairing. Oberon, in order to revenge himself upon Titania, causes her to fall in love with one of the workman-actors, Bottom the weaver, whom he has appropriately endowed with an ass's head. The lack of rationality implicit in the relationship between Bottom and Titania represents a

heightened version of the repudiation of the sovereignty of reason
in love by Hermia, Helena, Demetrius and Lysander, while the
conduct of both groups is linked with that of the youthful Theseus
by Oberon's account of Titania's role in the Duke's previous
amorous adventures:

> *Obe.* Didst not thou lead him through the glimmering night
> From Perigouna, whom he ravished;
> And make him with fair Aegles break his faith,
> With Ariadne and Antiopa?
>
> (II.i.77–80)

Rape constitutes the ultimate rejection of reason in love, and it is a
potentiality of all the play's amatory relationships. Theseus declares
that he 'woo'd' Hippolyta with his sword and won her love by doing
her 'injuries' (I.i.16–17); Demetrius suggests he might rape Helena
in the wood (II.i.214–19); while Titania has her lover's tongue tied
up, and comments upon 'enforced chastity' (III.i.191–4). The play
thus represents the entire spectrum of love from affection to
ungoverned appetite, and presents a diversity of lovers ranging
from immortals to bestial human beings.

The play which Bottom and his companions perform before the
Duke, and which constitutes the finale of *A Midsummer Night's
Dream* itself, draws together the strands of the previous amorous
encounters, while affording the members of the theatre audience a
fresh perspective upon the nature of love. Pyramus, like Theseus, is
a figure from the legendary past; he is subject to the opposition of a
parent, like Lysander; he exhibits a high degree of irrationality, like
the young lovers; and falls victim, like Titania, to sensory delusion.
Prior to the performance of the play-within-the-play, the responses
of the theatre audience to the lovers gathered in and around Athens
are complex. The couples function on a scale of ludicrousness, from
Theseus and Hippolyta at one extreme to Titania and Bottom at the
other, but at every point their ridiculousness is modified by some
other element. Titania's grotesque misalliance with Bottom, for
example, is pathetic as well as amusing, while the passionate
exuberance of the young lovers is delightful as well as comic.
Pyramus and Thisbe permit the spectator to perceive the humorous
aspect of amatory experience uncomplicated by any other
consideration. The extravagant gestures, impetuosity, and
irrationality of the lover are all caricatured in the playlet, while the
self-conscious theatricality of the performance ensures that the

theatre audience does not become sympathetically involved in the passions that are displayed. The inset action of *A Midsummer Night's Dream* thus draws attention, like the pageant of the Worthies in *Love's Labour's Lost*, to the themes of the principal action, but, unlike the earlier playlet, it also extends the implications of the drama as a whole. Love takes many forms and elicits a variety of responses. It may be rational, impulsive, sensual, perverse – and it may evoke respect, admiration, pity, or amusement. The mechanicals' play contributes to the analysis of this complex state by affording the theatre audience the 'Lord, what fools these mortals be' (III.ii.115) viewpoint of love unmodified by other responses. Viewed with sufficient detachment, human passions are ridiculous in the extreme, and the play-within-the-play allows the audience to see love from this perspective.

A Midsummer Night's Dream is not, however, simply an anatomy of love. It also explores the nature of reality, and it is in this context that the structural differences between this play and *Love's Labour's Lost* are important. *Love's Labour's Lost* is essentially episodic. The phases of the action are largely self-contained, each one principally consisting of a 'set of wit' (V.ii.29) played by one character, or group of characters, against another. Thus the lords debate whether to devote themselves to study (I.i.1–159), decide to infringe their vows (IV.iii.281–369), woo the ladies disguised as Muscovites (V.ii.158–265), deride the pageant of the Worthies (V.ii.518–704), etc. *A Midsummer Night's Dream*, by contrast, is much more complex in its organization. Rather than one action simply following another, like a series of railway carriages, the events enfold, or enclose, one another, as in the party game 'pass the parcel'. The members of the theatre audience watch Oberon and Puck, Oberon and Puck watch the human lovers, while the human lovers watch the tragedy of Pyramus and Thisbe. The situations projected on all of these levels of perception are strikingly similar, in that all the dramatis personae are concerned with love and estrangement, while the participants themselves exchange roles. Bottom, for example, is a self-conscious performer in Peter Quince's play, but he has been an unconscious actor in Oberon's; Lysander is a spectator to Bottom's play, but has taken part, unknowingly, in Puck's; Theseus, who comments magisterially upon the mechanicals' play, and dismisses the world of the imagination as fiction, has his nuptials superintended and his happiness promoted by Oberon; while Oberon himself, the supreme stage-manager, is an element of a larger design, organized by a different consciousness for the theatre audience. In short, all those who are members of an audience on one level of reality are simultaneously players upon another – the puppets of powers, or forces, beyond their control. Like *The Taming of the Shrew*, but to a much greater extent, *A Midsummer Night's Dream* unsettles the spectator's grasp upon what constitutes actuality by enmeshing him in a series of plays within plays. Since all those who conceive of themselves, at some point, as spectators, are merely players in a drama of which they are unaware, the members of the theatre audience, by implication, may be merely actors, manipulated by a consciousness beyond the parameters of their experience. Thus the tragedy of Pyramus and Thisbe, rather than merely affording a fresh context, like the pageant of the Worthies, in which the deficiencies of the dramatis personae may be exposed, is a major instrument in the projection of theme in that it multiplies the levels of reality upon which the drama as a whole functions.

The attitude of the internal audience to the mechanicals' 'tragedy' is also important in relation to the meaning of the play. Whereas Navarre and his followers disconcert the Worthies by their mockery, and effectually destroy their pageant, Theseus and Hippolyta are much more generous in their stance towards the performers, though they are equally conscious of their limitations. When the play is first declared unfit for performance before the Duke, Theseus is quick to maintain that it is the intentions of the actors that dignify the event, while Hippolyta is concerned that the performers should not be humiliated:

> *The.* We will hear it.
> *Phil[ostrate].*   No, my noble lord,
>   It is not for you: I have heard it over,
>   And it is nothing, nothing in the world;
>   Unless you can find sport in their intents,
>   Extremely stretch'd and conn'd with cruel pain   80
>   To do you service.
> *The.*   I will hear that play;
>   For never anything can be amiss
>   When simpleness and duty tender it.
>   Go bring them in; and take your places, ladies.
> >   [*Exit Philostrate.*]
> *Hip.* I love not to see wretchedness o'er-charg'd,   85
>   And duty in his service perishing.
> *The.* Why, gentle sweet, you shall see no such thing.

Hip. He says they can do nothing in this kind.
The. The kinder we, to give them thanks for nothing.
　Our sport shall be to take what they mistake: 90
　And what poor duty cannot do, noble respect
　Takes it in might, not merit.

(V.i.76–92)

The Duke's position here is fundamentally different from Navarre's.
Though he, too, is ready to derive 'sport' (90) from the deficiencies
of the would-be actors, he sees the performance as a vehicle by
means of which the social roles of the two parties may be realized.
While on the one hand it enables the mechanicals to exhibit their
'duty' (91), on the other hand it allows the Duke to display his
magnanimity – and thus strengthens the social bond between the
two groups. In the course of the ensuing performance, though the
courtiers laugh among themselves at the ineptitude of the
representation, their remarks are not intended to discountenance
the actors, who are offered every encouragement. Even at the point
at which the conduct of the courtiers comes closest to that of
Navarre's followers, when the exuberance of the spectators gets the
better of them and Moonshine is disconcerted, Hippolyta is quick to
recover the situation in the barrage of compliments that succeeds
Thisbe's encounter with the Lion:

Dem[etrius]. Well roared, Lion!
The. Well run, Thisbe!   255
Hip. Well shone, Moon! Truly, the moon shines with a
　good grace.

(V.i.254–7)

Clearly, unlike the pageant of the Worthies, which exposes a lack of
understanding on the part of the play's aristocrats, and projects a
vision of social discord, the tragedy of Pyramus and Thisbe (for all its
subject matter) projects an image of social harmony. The concord
which Titania and Oberon design for the royal lovers is shown in
operation in the joyous but responsible exercise of authority on the
part of the rulers, and the eager exhibition of goodwill and respect
on the part of the ruled. Thus, although the contexts in which the
inset actions occur are broadly similar, their meaning in relation to
the enfolding comedy is radically different.

The pageant of the Worthies and the tragedy of Pyramus and Thisbe do, however, share one important characteristic that sets them aside from the play performed before Claudius in *Hamlet*, or the shows and spectacles organized by Prospero in *The Tempest*. In both *Love's Labour's Lost* and *A Midsummer Night's Dream* the members of the internal audience are oblivious of the relevance of the play-within-the-play to themselves, and thus do not share in the enlargement of understanding that the inset action affords the theatre audience. Though in *Love's Labour's Lost* the conduct of the Worthies relates in a variety of ways to the conduct of the lords, Navarre and his followers see only the inadequacies of the actors and are blind to the implications of their performance; while in *A Midsummer Night's Dream* none of the lovers betrays any recognition of the relationship between the folly of Pyramus and Thisbe and his or her own. The play-within-the-play thus functions in very different ways for its immediate and secondary audiences. For the former it is merely a spectacle designed for their entertainment, while for the latter it is a means of apprehending more about the nature of the protagonists, and, in the case of *A Midsummer Night's Dream*, more about the nature of love and the universe in which both the dramatis personae and those outside the play world exist. In *Hamlet*, by contrast, the significance of the inset action depends, in large measure, upon the perception by the members of the internal audience of the analogy between the fictional world and their own. As a result, the play's emphasis upon the function of art is much greater than in the early comedies, while references to theatrical concerns are much more extensive.

The theme of role-playing, and the relationship between seeming and being, are introduced in the first scene in which Hamlet appears. Asked by his mother why the death of his father appears to affect him so deeply, Hamlet replies:

Seems, madam? . . . I know not 'seems'.
'Tis not alone my inky cloak, good mother,
Nor customary suits of solemn black,
Nor windy suspiration of forc'd breath,
No, nor the fruitful river in the eye,   80
Nor the dejected haviour of the visage,
Together with all forms, moods, shapes of grief,
That can denote me truly. These indeed seem,
For they are actions that a man might play;

But I have that within which passes show,   85
These but the trappings and the suits of woe.

(I.ii.76–86)

These lines do more than merely assert that Hamlet's grief is deeply
felt. They serve to alert the audience to a possible discrepancy
between appearance and reality in the world of Denmark, and they
imply that some members of the court may be playing parts. In Act
II, the validity of these inferences becomes apparent. Hamlet
himself is now acting a role in order to conceal his knowledge of
Claudius' responsibility for his father's death from his uncle, while
those around him conceal their true motives from him in order to
probe the causes of his supposed madness. It is into this world of
counterfeits that the Players are introduced in II.ii. Asked by Hamlet
to recite a speech from a play on the Trojan war, the First Player
enters so fully into the feelings of those he impersonates that he is
moved to tears, prompting Hamlet to comment upon the
discrepancy between the Player's passionate response to a
hypothetical situation, and his own more restrained reactions to a
real one:

O what a rogue and peasant slave am I!
Is it not monstrous that this player here,   545
But in a fiction, in a dream of passion,
Could force his soul so to his own conceit
That from her working all his visage wann'd,
Tears in his eyes, distraction in his aspect,
A broken voice, and his whole function suiting   550
With forms to his conceit? And all for nothing!
For Hecuba!
What's Hecuba to him, or he to her,
That he should weep for her? What would he do
Had he the motive and the cue for passion   555
That I have? He would drown the stage with tears,
And cleave the general ear with horrid speech,
Make mad the guilty and appal the free,
Confound the ignorant, and amaze indeed
The very faculties of eyes and ears.   560
Yet I,
A dull and muddy-mettled rascal, peak

Like John-a-dreams, unpregnant of my cause,
And can say nothing.

(II.ii.544–64)

Up to this point, the actors have fulfilled a function very similar
to that performed by the amateur thespians of earlier plays. The
speeches that the First Player recites reflect upon the action of the
main plot in that they concern the exaction of vengeance (see below
pp. 117ff.), while the histrionic ability of the actor highlights that
difficulty in distinguishing between appearance and reality which is
one of the central problems that Hamlet confronts. At this point,
however, the acting motif takes on a further significance. Hamlet has
enquired whether the players are capable of performing a tragedy
entitled *The Murder of Gonzago*, and decides that a version of the
play, adapted by himself, shall be performed before Claudius. His
motive is not a desire to please the King, but a belief that some
interaction takes place, in the course of representation, between a
drama and the members of a theatre audience:

> I have heard
> That guilty creatures sitting at a play   585
> Have, by the very cunning of the scene,
> Been so struck to the soul that presently
> They have proclaim'd their malefactions.
> For murder, though it have no tongue, will speak
> With most miraculous organ. I'll have these players   590
> Play something like the murder of my father
> Before mine uncle. I'll observe his looks;
> I'll tent him to the quick. If a do blench,
> I know my course . . . .
> . . . . The play's the thing   600
> Wherein I'll catch the conscience of the King.

(II.ii.584–601)

In the following act, the nature and function of drama are even
more overtly discussed. III.ii opens with a dialogue between Hamlet
and the Players in which the Prince stresses the importance of
naturalism of movement and gesture on the part of the performer
asserting that the purpose of playing is to:

hold as 'twere the mirror up to nature; to show virtue
her feature, scorn her own image, and the very age
and body of the time his form and pressure.

(III.ii.22–4)

These lines serve a double purpose. On one level, Hamlet's emphasis upon the relationship between drama and life, and his reiteration of his belief that a play stimulates the moral imagination of its spectators, heightens the expectations of the theatre audience in relation to the play-within-the-play that is to follow. It ensures that the spectator's attention will be divided between the internal audience and the inset action, and generates expectation of some interaction between the two. At the same time, the insistent emphasis upon the techniques of theatrical representation, and the function of the dramatist's art, draws the attention of those outside the play world to the artifice of *Hamlet* itself. Listening to the Prince's disquisition upon the nature of acting, the spectator cannot but consider the degree to which the actor speaking the lines complies with his own dicta, while he or she is led to speculate upon the nature of the mirror which the Shakespearian play itself holds up to actuality.

The performance of *The Murder of Gonzago* turns Hamlet's theory into practice. The death of Hamlet's father is re-enacted not once, but twice, before Claudius, and the responses of the members of the court to the theatrical event vary considerably. The performance begins with a dumb show which recapitulates the events leading up to, and immediately following, the King's death:

Enter a KING *and a* QUEEN, *the Queen embracing him and he her. She kneels, and makes show of protestation unto him. He takes her up, and declines his head upon her neck. He lies him down upon a bank of flowers. She, seeing him asleep, leaves him. Anon comes in another* Man, *takes off his crown, kisses it, pours poison in the sleeper's ears, and leaves him. The* QUEEN *returns, finds the King dead, makes passionate action. The* Poisoner *with some* Three *or* Four *comes in again. They seem to condole with her. The dead body is carried away. The Poisoner woos the Queen with gifts. She seems harsh awhile, but in the end accepts his love.*

(III.ii.s.d.133)

Ophelia is the only character who makes any comment on this

performance, and her remarks reveal her total ignorance of what it portends. She asks what the dumb show means, and speculates that it may be 'the argument of the play' (III.ii.136). The Players then enter and embark on a series of exchanges that act out the events that have been mimed. At the end of the first scene, Hamlet asks his mother whether she likes the play, eliciting a response, 'The lady doth protest too much, methinks' (III.ii.225), that suggests that her attention has been focused upon the character whose situation corresponds most closely with her own. Claudius' question, 'Have you heard the argument? Is there no offence in't?' (227–8), also indicates that he senses the relevance of the playlet to himself, and this implication is confirmed at the end of the second scene in which the murder is enacted. As the poisoner pours the unction in the sleeping man's ear, and Hamlet rapidly recounts the events that are still to come, Claudius abruptly rises from his seat, calls for lights, and leaves the room, Guildenstern revealing, a moment later, that he is 'marvellous distempered' (293). Gertrude, by contrast, seems unmoved by this scene of the drama. She enquires, 'How fares my lord?' (261) in evident surprise when Claudius rises, and makes no comment upon the events that have been portrayed. *The Murder of Gonzago* thus serves, as Hamlet had hoped, to trigger the consciences of its audience. It reveals Ophelia's innocence, Gertrude's sensitivity in relation to her second marriage, and Claudius' responsibility for his brother's death. Rather than merely highlighting the concerns of the principal action for the benefit of the theatre audience, the play-within-the-play holds up a mirror to its immediate spectators, inducing the dramatis personae to recognize the relationship between the fictional characters and themselves.

The act of recognition that takes place between the internal audience and the play-within-the-play has important implications for the evolution of the action. Whereas in *A Midsummer Night's Dream* and *Love's Labour's Lost* the inset playlets are interludes, or diversions, that contribute to the meaning of the drama but do not advance the progress of the plot, in *Hamlet* the performance of *The Murder of Gonzago* has important implications for all the dramatis personae. Claudius' responses to the play, for example, convince Hamlet of his uncle's guilt and confirm the Prince's obligation to exact vengeance, while Hamlet's running commentary on the action, and his responsibility for the entire performance, alert Claudius to the real causes of his nephew's melancholy, and the threat that he poses to him. Claudius' decision to send Hamlet to his death in England is thus a direct consequence of the play-within-the-play, while the moral impact of the drama upon its guilty spectators is revealed in the latter half of Act III in Claudius' attempted repentance (III.iii) and Hamlet's successful onslaught upon his mother's conscience (III.iv). In a world of players, it is highly appropriate that it should be through a drama that the characters come to know more about one another, and themselves.

Both the tragedy of Pyramus and Thisbe and *The Murder of Gonzago* re-enact, in heightened form, the events of the actions which enfold them. Nevertheless, it will be apparent from the above that their functions are very different. The mechanicals' play extends the implications of the main plot by allowing the audience a fresh perspective upon the subject of love, while it simultaneously contributes to an exploration of the nature of reality. *The Murder of Gonzago*, by contrast, advances the action of the main plot; it explores the function of play-acting; and asserts the positive value of art as an instrument for expanding the moral understanding. Though the members of the theatre audience may be uncertain, when Claudius rises to disrupt the play, whether it is fear, anger or conscience that motivates him, they are in no doubt that the spectacle has meant something very different to him than the play of the Worthies meant to Navarre or the tragedy of Pyramus and Thisbe to Theseus – and the repentance scene that follows makes clear one aspect, at least, of the impact it has made.

The Tempest draws together the concepts of the play as a metaphor for life and the play as an educational instrument. The comedy is unique in the Shakespearian canon in that the action is dictated by a single figure who exists on the same level of reality as the remainder of the dramatis personae, but who has the power to control others through magic. Prospero, banished from his dukedom by his brother, and now lord of an island inhabited only by his daughter, his bestial and spiritual servants and himself, has taken advantage of the providential proximity of his enemies to shipwreck his former foes on his own shores. Since he has the power through his art to control their actions, he is in a position analogous to that of the dramatist himself: he has assembled a cast, and is preparing to have his actors perform a play. The events that take place on the island may thus be seen as a kind of play-within-a-play. The members of the theatre audience watch a Shakespearian comedy, while the principal figure within that comedy organizes another play for purposes of his own. In addition to governing the actions and observing the responses of the courtiers, however, Prospero also produces a series of plays or shows for their benefit. He stages a masque of Juno and Ceres for his daughter and her lover, and provides a magic banquet, disrupted by a Harpy, for his usurping brother and his allies. The members of the theatre audience are thus presented with a structure similar to that of *A Midsummer Night's Dream* with its successive layers of actors and spectators. Here, the external audience watches Prospero, who watches the courtiers, watching the shows that the spirits perform.

For all the structural similarities between *A Midsummer Night's Dream* and *The Tempest*, however, the responses of the latter's spectators to the playlets they witness have more in common with those of Claudius to *The Murder of Gonzago* than with those of Theseus to the tragedy of Pyramus and Thisbe. Prospero's brother, Antonio, for example, together with Alonso (the King of Naples), Sebastian (Alonso's brother), and a group of courtiers, are all presented with a series of shows culminating in the appearance of a Harpy. A number of *'strange Shapes'* appear with a banquet; they *'dance about it with gentle actions of salutations'*; and invite the King to eat (s.d. III.iii.17). The responses of the internal audience, like those of the spectators to *The Murder of Gonzago* are significantly varied. Alonso, and a faithful lord named Gonzalo, are struck by the harmonious music accompanying the spectacle, and by the 'excellent dumb discourse' (39) of the actors, whereas Antonio and Sebastian see only the extraordinary nature of the spirits and are eager to eat the food (21 and 41–2). The difference of nature implicit in these responses is accentuated when the Harpy appears. The part is performed by Prospero's instrument, Ariel, who recapitulates the sins of the courtiers against the banished Duke:

> You are three men of sin, whom Destiny, –
> That hath to instrument this lower world
> And what is in't, – the never-surfeited sea   55
> Hath caus'd to belch up you; and on this island,
> Where man doth not inhabit, – you 'mongst men
> Being most unfit to live. . . . .
> . . . . But remember, –
> For that's my business to you, – that you three
> From Milan did supplant good Prospero: 70
> Expos'd unto the sea, which hath requit it,

Him and his innocent child: for which foul deed
The powers, delaying, not forgetting, have
Incens'd the seas and shores, yea, all the creatures,
Against your peace. Thee of thy son, Alonso,　　　　　75
They have bereft; and do pronounce by me
Ling'ring perdition – worse than any death
Can be at once – shall step by step attend
You and your ways; whose wraths to guard you from, –
Which here, in this most desolate isle, else falls　　　80
Upon your heads, – is nothing but heart-sorrow
And a clear life ensuing.

(III.iii.53–82)

Alonso responds immediately to the meaning of the Harpy's words. He acknowledges his guilt, and concurs with the judgement that his son's death is a consequence of his own misdeeds (95–102). Sebastian and Antonio, by contrast, give no indication of accepting responsibility for their former actions or repenting of them. They resort instantly to violence, seeing the spirit as a 'fiend' (102), and drawing their swords to confront it. The faithful Gonzalo, who had succoured Prospero as far as he was able, understands the meaning of the show but does not experience the violent emotions of his companions. His response –

All three of them are desperate: their great guilt,
Like poison given to work a great time after,　　　　105
Now 'gins to bite the spirits. I do beseech you,
That are of suppler joints, follow them swiftly,
And hinder them from what this ecstasy
May now provoke them to –

(III.iii.104–9)

is indicative of the loyalty and compassionate concern that formerly activated his conduct towards the banished Duke.

Like *The Murder of Gonzago*, then, the inset action works upon the moral understanding of its spectators, but the nature of its impact is not determined solely by the extent of the onlooker's guilt. Antonio, Sebastian and Alonso were equally involved in the initial act of deposition, yet, though the words of the Harpy produce a violent reaction from all three (analogous with Claudius' call for lights and abrupt exit), two of them exhibit neither remorse nor contrition. At the close of the play, when the three conspirators stand before the man they have abused, it is evident that whereas the 'enchanted trifle[s]' (V.i.112) Alonso has witnessed have served to heighten his moral awareness, the spectacles that Antonio and Sebastian have observed have merely enraged and bewildered them. While Prospero embraces Alonso, he repudiates Antonio as a 'most wicked sir, whom to call brother / Would even infect my mouth' (V.i.130–1).

In this instance the play-within-the-play both advances the action (in that it promotes reconciliation between Prospero and Alonso), and contributes to the spectator's understanding of the dramatis personae. The contrast between Alonso's responses to the shows that Prospero presents and those of Antonio and Sebastian suggests that the aberrant behaviour of the King was merely a lapse, while that of his fellow conspirators was symptomatic of natures fundamentally impervious to goodness. At the same time, the relationship between the inset action and its immediate audience initiates an investigation into the nature and function of art itself. Art, it is implied, can illuminate life, but its capacity to enlarge the understanding is dependent upon the receptivity of the consciousness upon which it works. There are some natures, to quote Prospero, upon which nurture can never stick (IV.i.188–9).

The responses of Prospero to the larger drama that unfolds at his instigation confirms the educative function of art, while contributing, once again, to the evolution of the action. At the outset of the play his attitude towards those whom he has brought to the island is negative in the extreme. Such words as 'perfidious', 'false', 'enemy', 'treacherous', 'foul' crowd every phase of his account of his usurpation (I.ii.66–174) leading the audience to anticipate the exaction of vengeance for what has taken place in the past. In the following scenes, although his more positive attitude towards Alonso's son, Ferdinand, is soon made apparent, his anger and resentment towards those who have abused him continues to be stressed. In III.iii, for example, he applauds Ariel's performance of the banquet scene, and speaks of the 'enemies' (89) who are now in his power. At the same time, however, the speech of the Harpy gives some indication that his ultimate purposes may be constructive. The spirit promises not only 'Ling'ring perdition' (77) for the play's sinners, but the possibility of 'a clear life ensuing' (82) for the penitent. The theatre audience, in short, is led to suspect that Prospero may be punishing his enemies with distraction in order to bring them to contrition, employing his art as an instrument to promote soul-searching, and to trigger repentance. The opening of Act V draws these strands of perception together. Prospero asks Ariel how the King and his followers are – and the following exchange takes place:

> *Pros.* How fares the King and 's followers?
> *Ari.*   Confin'd together
>   In the same fashion as you gave in charge,
>   Just as you left them; all prisoners, sir,
>   In the lime-grove which weather-fends your cell;   10
>   They cannot budge till your release. The King,
>   His brother, and yours, abide all three distracted,
>   And the remainder mourning over them,
>   Brimful of sorrow and dismay; but chiefly
>   Him you term'd, sir, "The good old lord, Gonzalo";   15
>   His tears runs down his beard, like winter's drops
>   From eaves of reeds. Your charm so strongly works 'em,
>   That if you now beheld them, your affections
>   Would become tender.
> *Pros.*   Dost thou think so, spirit?
> *Ari.* Mine would, sir, were I human.
> *Pros.*   And mine shall.   20
>   Hast thou, which art but air, a touch, a feeling
>   Of their afflictions, and shall not myself,
>   One of their kind, that relish all as sharply
>   Passion as they, be kindlier mov'd than thou art?
>   Though with their high wrongs I am struck to th' quick,   25
>   Yet with my nobler reason 'gainst my fury
>   Do I take part: the rarer action is
>   In virtue than in vengeance: they being penitent,
>   The sole drift of my purpose doth extend
>   Not a frown further. Go release them, Ariel: 30
>   My charms I'll break, their senses I'll restore,
>   And they shall be themselves.

                                        (V.i.7–32)

Two points are of particular importance here. The spectacle of the courtiers' afflictions has moved Ariel to such an extent that he claims that if he were a human being he would show compassion, while Prospero elects, in view of his enemies' sufferings, to renounce vengeance in favour of 'virtue' (28). Just as the magic spectacles that Alonso has witnessed have stimulated the nobler side of his nature and produced an act of contrition, so the play of the courtiers has produced a change in Prospero that is to lead to an act of clemency. It should be noted, however, that at this stage Prospero's benevolence is conditional. He declares that he will restore his enemies' senses if they are penitent – as, at this point, he appears to believe them to be. When Alonso, Antonio and Sebastian make their next entrance, however, it is clear to both Prospero and the theatre audience that two of the three are far from contrite. Antonio and Sebastian have not responded positively to Prospero's redemptive art but remain locked in the viciousness and cynicism that have characterized them throughout. Nevertheless, although fully aware of their degeneracy, Prospero proceeds to forgive them:

Pros.   Welcome, my friends all!   125
   [*Aside to Seb. and Ant.*] But you, my brace of lords,
     were I so minded,
   I here could pluck his highness' frown upon you,
   And justify you traitors: at this time
   I will tell no tales.
Seb.   [*Aside*] The devil speaks in him.
Pros.   No.
   For you, most wicked sir, whom to call brother   130
   Would even infect my mouth, I do forgive
   Thy rankest fault, – all of them.

                                 (V.i.125–32)

The magnanimity displayed here is at a considerable remove from the negative attitudes of I.i, or even the conditional human kindness of V.i.20–32. Just as Alonso has distinguished himself from Antonio and Sebastian by his capacity to respond to aesthetic experience, so Prospero elevates himself here above the courtiers by the degree to which he has been enriched by the drama that he has initiated and watched unfold.

It is at this point in the action that the play-within-the-play motif acquires a yet deeper resonance. Prospero, who has functioned as

an internal audience throughout, while being changed by the play
he has witnessed, now turns to the external audience to deliver an
epilogue:

> Now my charms are all o'erthrown,
> And what strength I have's mine own,
> Which is most faint: now, 'tis true,
> I must be here confin'd by you,
> Or sent to Naples. Let me not,   5
> Since I have my dukedom got,
> And pardon'd the deceiver, dwell
> In this bare island by your spell;
> But release me from my bands
> With the help of your good hands: 10
> Gentle breath of yours my sails
> Must fill, or else my project fails,
> Which was to please. Now I want
> Spirits to enforce, Art to enchant;
> And my ending is despair,   15
> Unless I be reliev'd by prayer,
> Which pierces so, that it assaults
> Mercy itself, and frees all faults.
>   As you from crimes would pardon'd be,
>   Let your indulgence set me free.   20

                                            (1–20)

Superficially the speech is a conventional plea for a round of
applause to conclude the performance, but it also serves a much
more important purpose. In the first eight lines, Prospero places the
members of the theatre audience in the same relation to himself as
he stood in relation to the play of the courtiers. He urges the
spectators not to confine him on his island by a 'spell' (as he could
have confined Alonso) now he has 'pardon'd the deceiver' (7–8), or
reached, like the King, a higher plane of awareness. By implying
that the external audience will determine his ultimate destiny, he
transforms its members from passive spectators of the play into
active director-producers of it, and thus draws them into that
process of interaction between spectators and performers that is
characteristic of the dramatic structure throughout. The final lines of
the epilogue are equally significant. At first sight, the plea,

As you from crimes would pardon'd be
Let your indulgence set me free,

(19–20)

seems merely to reiterate the assertion that those outside the play world stand in the same relationship to the Shakespearian comedy that Prospero stood to the play of the sinners, and that, just as Prospero pardoned those who offended him and was enriched in the process, so the members of the theatre audience will benefit in personal terms if they exhibit similar magnanimity towards him. But, in fact, the implications of the passage run deeper than this. The phrase '*As you from crimes would pardon'd be*' (19) suggests the existence of a power to whom the spectators must ultimately refer their own conduct – a power observing the little play of man's life, as the theatre audience has watched Prospero, and Prospero has watched the play of the courtiers. In these final lines the play-within-the-play is not simply an instrument by means of which the understanding of the percipient spectator may be enlarged, it is also a metaphor for human life, each member of the theatre audience being merely a player in an arena in which ultimate success or failure depends upon the development of the capacity to comprehend and forgive.

The Renaissance stage delighted in artifice, and Renaissance dramatists were intensely interested in the nature of their own art. By creating dramatic structures that function on more than one level of reality, Shakespeare and his contemporaries evolved an instrument that allowed them to explore the relationship between art and life, and to assert the positive value of the medium in which they worked. Though a play-within-a-play may appear, at first sight, to be merely an entertaining diversion for those inside and outside the play world, it will invariably have some bearing upon the meaning of the drama as a whole, and may crystallize or extend its themes. The reader or spectator presented with a multi-layered structure should enquire whether the concerns of the play-within-the-play reflect those of the principal action; whether the perspectives of the external and internal audiences on the performance coincide; whether the inset action contributes to the evolution of the plot which enfolds it; and whether it forms part of a series of inset actions, literal or implied, which serve to undermine the audience's grasp on the nature of reality, or which reflect on the nature and function of art. The epilogue to *The Tempest* and the prologue to *Henry V* may seem, to the modern theatre-goer, to be mere flourishes designed by the artist to ornament the play proper, but the figures which speak them, occupying as they do a universe between those of the spectator and the dramatis personae, help to dictate the relationship between the audience and the dramatic fiction – and it is on the nature of this relationship that one dimension of the dramatist's meaning ultimately depends.

5

Parallel Actions

It will be apparent to the least experienced reader or theatre-goer that Shakespeare's plays, even those which do not overtly 'frame' one action within another, usually trace not one sequence of events but two, or even three, each with its own 'cast' of characters the members of which may, or may not, come into contact with one another. In the comedies, for example, the courtship of Hero and Claudio in *Much Ado About Nothing* is paralleled by that of Beatrice and Benedick, while that of Rosalind and Orlando in *As You Like It* is complemented by those of Phebe and Silvius, Touchstone and Audrey, Celia and Oliver. Similarly, in the histories, the social dislocation produced by the disruptive attitudes of the nobility in *1 Henry IV* is re-enacted in the tavern scenes involving Falstaff, while, in the tragedies, Antony's oscillation between Rome and Egypt (*Antony and Cleopatra*) is echoed by that of Enobarbus. The function of multiple plotting varies from play to play. The secondary actions may duplicate the events of the main plot, universalizing the issues involved, or they may contrast with the principal action to allow the main plot's concerns to be viewed from a different perspective. In every instance, however, the subsidiary actions contribute to the meaning of the whole, not simply through the ramifications of the events that are enacted, but through the relationship between those events and the experience which forms the principal focus of audience attention.

The most notable parallel plot in Shakespearian drama is that of *King Lear*. Here the events of the main plot are broadly repeated on a slightly lower social level. Thus in the main plot the King, Lear, is deceived by his two treacherous daughters into placing his trust in them, and banishes his loyal daughter, Cordelia; while in the sub-plot the Earl of Gloucester is deluded into placing his faith in his disloyal son, Edmund, and has his loving son, Edgar, banished. In both cases, the unnatural offspring then turn on their fathers, driving them from the seeming security of human society onto the heath, where they undergo a period of physical and mental suffering before being succoured by their loyal children, and reaching some understanding, prior to their deaths in the final act, of the experience they have undergone. These parallels are then reinforced by a more complex web of correspondences. Just as Lear, for example, is most deceived when he is sane and comes to fuller understanding through madness, so Gloucester comprehends or 'sees' least when he has his sight, and comes to perceive most when he is blind. The mental torture Lear experiences through the conduct of his daughters becomes physical torture in the sub-plot, with Gloucester blinded through his son's agency, while the animality which appears to Lear, during his madness, to be the essence of human nature is given physical form in Edgar's disguise as Poor Tom, a lunatic beggar living a life no different from that of a beast.

The function of this systematic process of duplication is complex. On the very simplest level it universalizes the events of the main plot. Lear's experience alone is one man's experience. When that experience is paralleled by that of another man in the same society that experience is generalized and becomes applicable to all fathers. At the same time the conduct of Lear as king is perverse, and the unnatural dislocation of family relationships in the sub-plot world is felt to be a product of the unnatural state brought into being by the abnormal conduct of the king. In this way the events of the Gloucester plot constitute the first steps towards the disturbance of the entire cosmos through Lear's act, elevating the stature of the central figure. The meaning of Lear's actions too is made more fully comprehensible through the Gloucester parallel. For example, the concept of false appearance, presented through the hypocritical speeches of Lear's unnatural daughters, becomes literal, and thus more readily grasped, in the sub-plot with the forged letter through which Edmund deceives his father. In short, the implications of the main plot are enlarged, and its significance clarified by the complementary action, with the audience deducing the meaning of the whole from the interaction between the parts of the design.

The use of parallel action is not exclusive to Shakespeare. It is one of the principal methods of plot construction in Renaissance drama as a whole, with three plots frequently interlacing to produce a complex composition projecting meaning through contrast or by analogy rather than through the unfolding of a single sequence of events. While the diagrammatic nature of many plays makes it impossible to overlook such correspondences, in some the relationships that are set up are less obtrusive and may escape a

reader unfamiliar with Elizabethan–Jacobean theatrical conventions. This is most likely to occur where other aspects of the
dramatic technique appear to approximate to those of our own age,
and this is particularly true of Shakespeare's tragedies in which the
use of the soliloquy, and emphasis on the personal experience of the
central figure, invite a psychologically based interpretation focused
upon the world view of the hero himself. Of all Shakespeare's plays
Hamlet lends itself most readily to this kind of approach, with the
introspection of the hero seemingly encouraging the play-goer to
view the world exclusively through his eyes, and to assess him in his
own terms. The Prince, shocked by his mother's marriage to his
uncle within weeks of the death of his father, and then faced by the
obligation to avenge that father's murder, regards the world he
inhabits as diseased, and sees his lack of impetuosity in taking his
uncle's life as dilatoriness or cowardice, arising from an over-
cerebral response to experience and a sense of the futility of life. An
interpretation of the play based solely upon what Hamlet himself
says and does prompts such questions as 'What is the central flaw in
his character which inhibits Hamlet from fulfilling the injunctions of
the Ghost?' and it leads to a view of the Prince as a potentially noble
man, tainted by the world he inhabits, and thus incapable of acting
coherently in it.

To view the play as a psychological case history is, however, to
distort it. In common with Elizabethan–Jacobean drama in general
the revenge play characteristically evolved through a multiplicity of
plots, with the vengeance of one individual precipitating plot and
counter-plot throughout the social group. In *The Spanish Tragedy* for
example, the starting point for the genre in England, the vengeance
arranged by Revenge for Don Andrea leads to violent action on the
part of Lorenzo, Bel-imperia and Hieronimo, while in *Antonio's
Revenge* (closely related in terms of both date and incident to *Hamlet*)
five revengers finally combine to exact vengeance upon the villain,
Piero. Shakespeare's play relies heavily on the traditions of the
revenge genre, and its organization is no exception. Four revengers,
not one, are set before the audience in the course of the play, all
concerned with the death of a father and subject to some delay in the
execution of their purpose. In I.i, before Hamlet himself has
appeared, the spectator learns from Horatio that young Fortinbras is
in arms against Denmark and is determined to recover the lands lost
to Norway when his father was slain by Old Hamlet. In the same act
Old Hamlet reveals the manner of his own death and exhorts his son

to avenge him, while in the following act, not only is the Norwegian interest caught up, but a third revenger, Pyrrhus, is introduced in the speeches from a play on the Trojan war spoken by Hamlet himself and the First Player. In Act III Polonius is killed while spying, providing the motive for a fourth revenger, Laertes, who first seeks vengeance in Act IV and finally kills Hamlet at the close of the play. Hamlet himself comes into contact with all three of his fellow revengers and reflects upon the contrast between their conduct and his own, usually to his own disadvantage. But the judgements made by the audience are not always identical with those of the Prince, and it is in the discrepancy between the two that much of the play's meaning lies.

The revenger most readily overlooked by a twentieth-century reader is Pyrrhus. His role in the Trojan war is no longer widely understood, while the play-within-a-play technique by which he is presented diminishes his 'reality' within the dramatic structure. The briefest examination of II.ii, however, reveals the prominence that Shakespeare gives to the revenge that he exacts. II.ii is 601 lines long. The players are first mentioned approximately half way through at line 315. The competition they are experiencing from the boy actors is then discussed (328–58); their trumpets are heard off stage (s.d. following 364); and Polonius enters with the news that they have come to court, and enumerates the various classes of production in which they excel (376–98). The players themselves then enter and Hamlet asks the First Player to 'give us a taste of your quality' (427–8), finally proposing that he recite a passage from Aeneas' tale to Dido. So far the lengthy introduction to the players can be justified in relation to the performance of *The Murder of Gonzago* in the following act, through which Hamlet hopes to make Claudius reveal his guilt (see above pp. 102ff.), but the same cannot be said for the seventy lines of recitation which follow. Hamlet begins to quote at line 446. The First Player picks up the speech at line 464 and continues, with interjections from Polonius, for another fifty lines – after which Hamlet, having dismissed his companions, comments for a further forty lines on the performance he has just witnessed. If these speeches had no relevance except to suggest a means of catching the conscience of the King, the spectator would be obliged to concur with Polonius' judgement that 'This is too long' (494).

The speeches themselves, however, are of considerable significance in relation to the themes of the play, though they in no way advance the central action. In them the members of the theatre audience are presented with a complete revenge play in miniature, and the actors in that play correspond to those of *Hamlet* itself. An outraged son, Pyrrhus, whose father was treacherously slain, is about to exact vengeance upon a king, Priam, and upon his queen, Hecuba, who, like Gertrude, is primarily seen in her maternal role. The recitation, broken as it is by Polonius' interjections, falls into three sections, each of which focuses upon one of the three figures involved. Since Hamlet is obliged to remind the Player of the lines he wishes him to speak, it is he who recites the opening passage in which the revenger, Pyrrhus, is described, heightening the audience's awareness of the parallel between the persons of the play world and those of the play-within-the-play, and inviting comparison between the two.

Up to this point in the Shakespearian play the audience has been presented with a situation that appeared relatively clear cut. Objective evidence has been supplied that, morally, Claudius is not above reproach. He has undoubtedly embarked upon an incestuous relationship with his brother's wife, and he is given to drunkenness, while his antagonist, the Prince, has been defined as inherently noble, like his father before him. If the Ghost's accusation should prove well-founded, no moral obstacle would appear to prevent Hamlet from sweeping to a fully justified revenge. The vengeance of Pyrrhus complicates this assessment. Significantly, Hamlet, searching his memory for the lines he wants to hear, begins with a false start: 'The rugged Pyrrhus, like th' Hyrcanian beast' (446). The effect is naturalistic, but the misquotation also initiates image strands that are caught up in the passage that follows. A Hyrcanian beast is a tiger – a predatory animal – and its colours are black and red. In the speech which Hamlet then quotes these two aspects of the image are developed to terrifying effect. The ruthlessness of the tiger is recalled by the word 'rugged' (448) and by an emphasis on blood. Pyrrhus himself is described as having 'sable' (the heraldic term for black) arms (448); his purpose is 'Black' (449) and resembles 'night' (449); while his complexion is 'black' and inspires 'dread' (451). The blackness is relieved, however, by 'heraldry more dismal' (452). He is (453) 'total gules' (the heraldic term for red); 'horridly trick'd / With blood' (453–4); and pasted with 'gore' (458). By the end of the passage the violence and the two colours take on a deeper significance. The black and red represent the darkness and flames of Hell. The light in the Trojan streets is now described as '*damned*'

(456); Pyrrhus is *'Roasted in wrath and fire'* (457); his stature superhuman by virtue of the *'coagulate gore'* (458) with which he is encrusted; his eyes are *'carbuncles'* (459), suggesting he is a fiend; and he is explicitly described as *'hellish'* (459).

At the same time that the bestial and diabolic nature of the revenger is being suggested, the human worth of his victims is also being implied. Instead of referring to the slaughtered as 'men, women, and children', Shakespeare uses the words *'fathers, mothers, daughters, sons'* (454), stressing natural bonds, and the loss involved through death, not merely for the victim, but for the whole family group. Similarly, the principal target of the revenge, the King, is not seen in terms of power and authority, but age and kinship. He is *'Old grandsire'* (460) Priam.

Clearly, the passage which Hamlet himself speaks serves to alienate the audience from the revenger, and this process is continued when the First Player takes up the recitation. The focus is now on the King, the object of vengeance, and once again the impotence and dignity of ageing majesty are simultaneously stressed. On the one hand he strikes *'too short at Greeks'* (465); his sword is *'antique'* (465); and *'Rebellious to his arm'* (466). Facing Pyrrhus he is *'Unequal match'd'* (467), *'unnerved'* (470), and quickly *'falls'* (470). At the same time, however, his antique sword suggests his ancient, inherited office. He is a *'father'* (470), his head is *'milky'* (474), and he himself *'reverend'* (475). The third segment of the playlet, which centres on Hecuba, also stresses the violation of natural bonds, and human vulnerability. Hecuba is seen as a wife and a mother. Her loins are *'all o'erteemed'* (504), and she laments the sight of Pyrrhus mincing *'her husband's limbs'* (510). Though she is a queen, she has none of the outward signs of majesty. She is *'barefoot'* (501); has a cloth on her head instead of a diadem (502–3); a blanket clasped about her (504–5); and can oppose the flames only with her tears (501–2). Not only does she arouse pity in the audience, but the spectators are told that the *'burst of clamour that she made'* (511) when she witnessed the death of her husband was such that it *'Would have made milch the burning eyes of heaven'* (513) if the gods were responsive to human suffering.

So far it will be apparent that one function of the Trojan playlet is to act out in the simplest terms the kind of single-minded vengeance that Hamlet could take – and frequently urges himself to take. The correspondences between the dramatis personae of *Hamlet* itself and of the play-within-the-play invite the audience to consider the relationship between the two, or to apply deductions about one to the other. The rights and wrongs of the situation presented in the recited speeches are not explored. The motive for Pyrrhus' conduct is not stated and no indication is given of the former attitudes of Priam and Hecuba. What is implied is that the course of action that Pyrrhus pursues is wholly vicious. It turns man into beast; creates a hell on earth; and leads to the butchery, not merely of human beings, but of humane values. The significance of the relationship between play and playlet is given a further dimension, moreover, by an additional point of correspondence between the two. Precipitate as Pyrrhus' vengeance appears to be, like Hamlet's, it is not accomplished without delay. At the very moment the Greek seems poised to take his revenge, he pauses:

> *Unequal match'd,*
> *Pyrrhus at Priam drives, in rage strikes wide;*
> *But with the whiff and wind of his fell sword*
> *Th'unnerved father falls. Then senseless Ilium,*   470
> *Seeming to feel this blow, with flaming top*
> *Stoops to his base, and with a hideous crash*
> *Takes prisoner Pyrrhus' ear. For lo, his sword,*
> *Which was declining on the milky head*
> *Of reverend Priam, seem'd i'th'air to stick;*   475
> *So, as a painted tyrant, Pyrrhus stood,*
> *And like a neutral to his will and matter,*
> *Did nothing.*
> *But as we often see against some storm*
> *A silence in the heavens, the rack stand still,*   480
> *The bold winds speechless, and the orb below*
> *As hush as death, anon the dreadful thunder*
> *Doth rend the region; so after Pyrrhus' pause*
> *Aroused vengeance sets him new awork,*
> *And never did the Cyclops' hammers fall*   485
> *On Mars's armour, forg'd for proof eterne,*
> *With less remorse than Pyrrhus' bleeding sword*
> *Now falls on Priam.*

(II.ii.467–88)

What the audience is presented with here is an emblematic representation of Hamlet's posture in the Shakespearian play. In both, the capacity to exact vengeance exists, but the will of the revenger seems momentarily paralysed. And once again, the significance of the parallel lies in the wholly negative terms in which Pyrrhus' conduct is presented. He is seen as a *'tyrant'* (476), towering above a *'reverend'* (475) old man. His hesitation leads neither to an act of clemency nor divine intervention, as the audience hopes, but forms the prelude to an act of violence performed with machine-like pitilessness in the presence of his victim's wife.

As noted above, prior to the entrance of the players, the audience is inclined to accept that, if the Ghost's accusation against Claudius proves to be valid, Hamlet has a duty to avenge his father's death. By the end of Act II the issue has become much more complex. Private retribution is now seen as potentially degrading, and the ruthlessness it demands as bestial or diabolic. Confronted with the Trojan war episode the audience is brought to recognize that the task before Hamlet is no easy one if he is to avoid becoming a Pyrrhus, and that to postpone an act of violence might, in some circumstances, constitute a virtue.

It is important to note, however, that Hamlet himself does not view the player's speeches from the same perspective as the audience. While the reader or spectator has been appalled by a horrific act and is led to consider the morality of revenge, Hamlet has been impressed by the degree to which the First Player is moved by his own performance, and reflects on the discrepancy between his own responses to an actual experience, and the Player's response to a hypothetical one:

> O what a rogue and peasant slave am I!
> Is it not monstrous that this player here,   545
> But in a fiction, in a dream of passion,
> Could force his soul so to his own conceit
> That from her working all his visage wann'd,
> Tears in his eyes, distraction in his aspect,
> A broken voice, and his whole function suiting   550
> With forms to his conceit? And all for nothing!
> For Hecuba!
> What's Hecuba to him, or he to her,
> That he should weep for her? What would he do
> Had he the motive and the cue for passion   555
> That I have? He would drown the stage with tears,

And cleave the general ear with horrid speech,
Make mad the guilty and appal the free,
Confound the ignorant, and amaze indeed
The very faculties of eyes and ears.   560
Yet I,
A dull and muddy-mettled rascal, peak
Like John-a-dreams, unpregnant of my cause,
And can say nothing.

                                        (II.ii.544–64)

What is notable here is that the adverse judgement the Prince passes
on himself is not endorsed by the audience. While, on the one
hand, those outside the play world understand *why* Hamlet
upbraids himself for his apparent indifference, on the other they
cannot but recognize the fallacy of his position. The Player's
emotion is self-generated. It is not a response to experience. It is
play-acting, like Claudius' seeming grief for his brother's death. As
Hamlet himself pointed out in a soliloquy in the preceding act, his
mother followed her husband's coffin 'Like Niobe, all tears' (I.ii.149)
only to re-marry within a month. External shows of emotion are
clearly not to be equated with true grief, and Hamlet, for all his
self-dissatisfaction, is not necessarily culpable for failing to react
histrionically to his father's death.

The second half of the soliloquy widens the gulf between the
spectator's perceptions and those of the speaker. Hamlet sees his
inability to respond incisively to his father's murder in terms of
cowardice, or reprehensible lack of resolution:

Yet I,
A dull and muddy-mettled rascal, peak
Like John-a-dreams, unpregnant of my cause,
And can say nothing – no, not for a king,
Upon whose property and most dear life   565
A damn'd defeat was made. Am I a coward?
Who calls me villain, breaks my pate across,
Plucks off my beard and blows it in my face,
Tweaks me by the nose, gives me the lie i'th'throat
As deep as to the lungs – who does me this?   570
Ha!
'Swounds, I should take it: for it cannot be

But I am pigeon-liver'd and lack gall
To make oppression bitter, or ere this
I should ha' fatted all the region kites   575
With this slave's offal.

(II.ii.561–76)

Without the playlet which precedes this soliloquy the audience
might well have been inclined to accept this conclusion. Inaction in
such a situation, coupled with a failure to exhibit the customary
symptoms of concern, would appear to suggest a lack of moral fibre
in the face of filial obligation. But the Player's lines have
undermined both the simplistic concept of courage and the
conventional course of conduct to which Hamlet appeals. The
vengeance of Pyrrhus is not courageous, but animalistic, and the
audience has been induced to question whether fattening kites with
an enemy's offal does indeed testify to greatness of spirit. Once
again, though the spectator is encouraged to appreciate the reasons
for Hamlet's frustration, he or she views the situation from a
perspective that is larger than that of the central figure.

The Trojan war passage, then, has a dual function. On the one
hand it acts out one potentiality of Hamlet's situation, allowing the
theatre audience to appreciate the possible implications of what
might, in theory, appear a desirable course to pursue, while on the
other it supplies an objective means of assessing that which Hamlet
has to say about himself, allowing those outside the play world to
perceive more than he perceives, while participating, through his
soliloquy, in his experience.

The episodes involving Fortinbras have a comparable function.
The Norwegian prince is introduced very early in the play and the
similarities between his situation and that of the Danish prince are
quickly established. Fortinbras, like Hamlet, is the son of a king who
has recently lost his life by an act of violence (I.i.83ff.). His uncle has
succeeded to his father's throne (II.ii.70), and he burns for action in
the face of injury (I.i.98ff.). His conduct is discussed before Hamlet
himself is first mentioned, and his reported responses to his father's
death therefore act as a yard-stick against which those of the Danish
prince may be measured.

Once again, the image that is projected of the parallel revenger is a
negative one. The death of the elder Fortinbras is dealt with very
fully in I.i and the circumstances surrounding it are described by a

character upon whose objectivity the audience can rely – Horatio. Old Fortinbras was slain in single combat with Old Hamlet (I.i.83–9); the conflict was instigated by Fortinbras himself (I.i.83–9); and the lands which Young Fortinbras seeks to recover were lost by a due process of law as a result of an agreement drawn up before the combat took place (I.i.89–98). Young Fortinbras' proceedings against Denmark are thus unwarranted and unlawful. The Prince's followers are described as 'lawless resolutes' (101), and the youth himself as 'Of unimproved mettle, hot and full' (99). The function of this account becomes clear in I.v when Hamlet is confronted by his father's ghost. The process of the Elder Hamlet's death, if the Ghost is to be believed, was very different from that of his former adversary. Though both die at another man's hand, the Norwegian was slain honourably, the Dane dishonourably, by an act of treachery (I.v.59–75). The Elder Hamlet, unlike the Elder Fortinbras, had no reason to suspect that his death was imminent, and therefore had no opportunity to prepare himself for it (I.v.76–9), while the fall of Old Hamlet, unlike that of Old Fortinbras, involved the overthrow, not of a single man, but of the natural order, in that he died at his brother's hands (cf. I.v.25–41). On the most superficial level, the contrast between the violent ends of the two kings suggests that vengeance for the death of a father is not necessarily morally justifiable, and it provides an implicit justification for the need that Hamlet expresses at the close of II.ii to put the Ghost's accusation against Claudius to the test. Were the Danish prince to proceed against his mighty opposite on insufficient grounds, he, like his Norwegian counterpart, would become a mere 'lawless resolute' (I.i.101) of 'unimproved mettle, hot and full' (I.i.99).

The second mention of Fortinbras occurs in II.ii and once again his reported relationships and decisions counterpoint those of the central figures. Voltemand and Cornelius, returning from Norway, report that representations made by Claudius to the Norwegian king have induced him to deflect his nephew from his purpose against Denmark, and that the troops levied by Fortinbras are now to be employed against Poland. A number of points of correspondence serve to link these events with Hamlet's situation. Claudius has made an approach to a foreign power to avert a danger to his throne, as he is later to do when he sends Hamlet to England. Fortinbras and his uncle are shown in a relationship not unlike that between Hamlet and Claudius (II.ii.61–8), while, more tenuously, the turning aside from an initial purpose links the Norwegian prince with both Pyrrhus, who pauses during the exaction of vengeance, and Hamlet, who delays.

It is in IV.iv, however, that the relationship between the Scandinavian princes is most fully exploited. The structure of the scene resembles that of the latter half of II.ii (in which Pyrrhus is presented), in that it consists of an encounter between Hamlet and an otherwise unimportant figure who gives him an account of a fellow revenger's conduct, after which the Prince soliloquizes on what he has seen and heard. IV.iv begins with the passage of Fortinbras, with his army, across the stage. The visual image suggests the strength of purpose of the Norwegian leader, while initiating the concept of violent action upon which the rest of the scene is to turn. The Captain of the army, who is left alone on stage, is then joined by Hamlet, who questions him about the reasons for the military preparations the members of the audience have just witnessed. Though the Captain is in Fortinbras' service, and might therefore be expected to be enthusiastic about his cause, the account which he gives is remarkably negative. He sees the land Fortinbras is about to fight for as having 'no profit but the name' (19), as being worthless as farm land (20), and valueless on the open market (20–2). Hamlet's initial response to this information contrasts sharply with what he says a moment later in soliloquy. Dispassionately observing the situation, and not yet moved to relate Fortinbras' behaviour to his own, he develops the Captain's economically based criticism of the Polish adventure into a moral indictment of it. He sees the issue for which the Norwegian leader is fighting as a mere 'straw' (26), the thousands jeopardized by his cause not as soldiers but as 'souls' (25), and his whole expedition as symptomatic of a diseased society (27). Moreover, the image which he uses to express the corruption which he sees as issuing in Fortinbras' enterprise –

This is th'impostume of much wealth and peace,
That inward breaks, and shows no cause without
Why the man dies,

(27–9)

serves to link the Norwegian prince with the 'strange eruption[s]' (I.i.72) consequent upon the accession of Claudius and thus to distance him from Hamlet himself. By the close of the exchange the audience is in no doubt of the worthlessness of the expedition or of the moral bankruptcy of the 'resolution' that has given rise to it.

Hamlet is then left alone on the stage and begins to meditate upon what he has witnessed. The audience has shared the combined viewpoints of Captain and Prince in the previous exchange and for the first eight lines of the soliloquy the spectator continues to accept Hamlet's judgements. He argues that a man who merely responds to physical impulses is no more than an animal, that human beings differ from beasts by virtue of their capacity for rational thought, and that it is incumbent on all men to employ that capacity to the full. As Hamlet's mind circles around the inadequacy of his response to his own predicament, however, and he reflects upon the contrast between his conduct and that of the Norwegian prince, the judgements of speaker and listener begin to diverge. Lines 39–46 initiate this process. Hamlet offers two possible explanations for his delay in exacting vengeance – 'Bestial oblivion' (40), and cowardice born of 'thinking too precisely on th'event' (41). Neither explanation can be fully endorsed by the audience. In this play it is action, rather than inaction, that has so far proved bestial, while, as Hamlet himself has just pointed out, it is the extent to which man applies his reason that is the measure of his 'godlike' (38) nature. By line 46 Hamlet's mind has returned to Fortinbras, and the terms in which he now refers to him no longer correlate those he employed earlier. He sees him as a 'delicate and tender prince' (48), 'puff'd' with 'divine ambition' (49), engaged in an act of daring 'Even for an eggshell' (53). As in his earlier exchange with the Captain, he describes the issue for which the Norwegian leader is to risk his life as a 'straw' (55), but the repetition of the word serves merely to highlight the contrast between his objective and subjective responses to what he has witnessed. When speaking to the Captain, he uses the word negatively:

> Two thousand souls and twenty thousand ducats   25
> Will not debate the question of this straw!
> This is th'impostume of much wealth and peace –
>
> (25–7)

but when he contrasts Fortinbras' conduct with his own the context is positive:

Rightly to be great
Is not to stir without great argument,
But greatly to find quarrel in a straw   55
When honour's at the stake.

(53–6)

The final phase of the speech follows logically, for the Prince if not
the audience, from this shift of perspective. Hamlet contrasts his
inaction in a worthy cause with the 'imminent death of twenty
thousand men' (60), who, for 'a fantasy and trick of fame' (61) will
'Go to their graves like beds' (62), and resolves that from 'this time
forth' (65) his thoughts will 'be bloody or be nothing worth' (66).

Taken out of context this soliloquy is unproblematic. It sets up a
straightforward contrast between high-minded valour and
cowardly inaction and it operates to the speaker's discredit.
Juxtaposed against the exchanges between Prince and Captain
which precede it, however, its significance changes. Having
witnessed the previous encounter and accepted the disinterested
judgements of the two speakers, the audience is aware, on one
level, throughout the soliloquy that Fortinbras' expedition is
worthless, that the loss of twenty thousand men for a 'fantasy' (61) is
a reflex of a diseased society, not a noble one, and that having
bloody thoughts does not necessarily indicate a praiseworthy state
of mind. In short, through the relationship between the two phases
of the scene, the audience is led, once again, not merely to
appreciate Hamlet's responses, but to assess them. By the close,
though those outside the play world fully sympathize with his
desire to emulate a fellow prince whose conduct appears more
worthy than his own, they do not automatically endorse either his
self-disgust or his final resolve. To embrace Fortinbras' example
might well be to act in violation of 'godlike reason' (38), the faculty
which distinguishes man from beast.

The third outraged son whose situation corresponds with
Hamlet's is, of course, Laertes. Laertes acts exactly as Hamlet urges
himself to do throughout. On hearing of his father's death he
returns immediately to Denmark, determined to exact vengeance
for Polonius' murder. In IV.v, convinced that Claudius is
responsible for what has occurred, he rushes to the court and
confronts him in the presence of the Queen, as Pyrrhus confronted

Priam and Hecuba in II.ii and Hamlet is later to confront Claudius before Gertrude in V.ii. The scene reflects in a host of ways on the predicament of the central figure and on the course he elects to pursue. Hamlet, though he censures himself for inaction, has tested the truth of the Ghost's accusation and is therefore assured that the man he is seeking to bring down is, in fact, his father's murderer. Laertes, rushing, by contrast, to the headlong vengeance that Hamlet longs to take, mistakes the source of the wrong that has been done to him and is poised to commit not merely an unjust act in killing an innocent man, but a rebellious one in unlawfully overthrowing the head of state. The anarchic nature of his conduct is stressed from the very outset. The terms in which the messenger describes his coming recall the speech describing Pyrrhus quoted by Hamlet in II.ii. He is 'impetuous' (100), the Elizabethan spelling of the word, 'impitious', suggesting his ruthlessness and impiety as well as his haste. He heads a 'riotous' (101) rabble, who 'O'erbear' (102) the officers of state. Just as Priam's antique sword is ineffectual against Pyrrhus, so 'Antiquity' and 'custom' (104) are brushed aside at Laertes' coming, the tumult he occasions being suggested by the 'Caps, hands, and tongues' (107) which applaud the cry of 'Laertes shall be king' (108).

The effect of Laertes' action also provides an implicit comment upon Hamlet's more guarded pursuit of vengeance. His eruption into the court serves, like that of Pyrrhus in the Trojan playlet, to elevate the monarch he opposes and to generate sympathy for his queen. Though the members of the audience are aware that Claudius is far more corrupt than the man who confronts him, it is he, ironically, not Laertes, who commands their respect. He is referred to consistently as the 'king' (112, 115, 123); he himself suggests that his person is hedged about by a 'divinity' (123) that disables aggression; while he demonstrates considerable courage in facing his attacker (120ff.). Gertrude's anxiety for her husband similarly serves to attract the sympathy of the audience towards the couple. She tries physically to restrain Laertes (122 and 126), and interjects anxiously in order to convince him of her husband's innocence (128). Laertes, by contrast, in a blind fury, explicitly allies himself with the powers of darkness, and asserts his readiness to hazard his soul in the pursuit of vengeance:

How came he dead? I'll not be juggled with.   130
To hell, allegiance! Vows to the blackest devil!

Conscience and grace, to the profoundest pit!
I dare damnation. To this point I stand,
That both the worlds I give to negligence,
Let come what comes, only I'll be reveng'd   135
Most throughly for my father.

(130–6)

Asked by Claudius whether it is his father's friends or foes that he
pursues, he alienates the audience still further by the blasphemous
connotations of the image with which he responds:

To his good friends thus wide I'll ope my arms,   145
And, like the kind life-rend'ring pelican,
Repast them with my blood.

(145–7)

The lines draw on the belief that the adult pelican fed its young on its
own blood, but for an Elizabethan audience they would have carried
a more profound significance. The bird traditionally represented
self-sacrificing parental love, and it was frequently used as an image
of Christ upon whose blood the souls of mankind depend. In
spreading wide his arms and employing the image of the pelican,
while dedicating himself to violent retribution rather than Christian
forgiveness, Laertes is enacting a parody of the crucifixion,
repudiating Christianity, and perverting Holy Communion. It is
significant that Claudius whom Hamlet describes as a 'damned
villain' (I.v.106), applauds the speech:

Why, now you speak
Like a good child and a true gentleman.

(147–8)

IV.vii, in which Laertes next appears, spells out even more clearly
the viciousness to which the precipitate and unthinking pursuit of
vengeance leads. Claudius and Laertes enter together, confirming
the alliance between the younger, inherently noble man, and the
older, inherently corrupt one, and the dominance of the latter over
the former is quickly established. Like Fortinbras before him,

Laertes has now been deflected from his initial purpose through Claudius' agency, and his anger is now directed towards Hamlet rather than the King. Claudius, however, queries his resolution before broaching his own plot to destroy the Prince:

> *King.* Laertes, was your father dear to you?
>   Or are you like the painting of a sorrow,
>   A face without a heart?
> *Laer.*   Why ask you this?
> *King.* Not that I think you did not love your father,
>   But that I know love is begun by time,   110
>   And that I see, in passages of proof,
>   Time qualifies the spark and fire of it.
>   There lives within the very flame of love
>   A kind of wick or snuff that will abate it;
>   And nothing is at a like goodness still,   115
>   For goodness, growing to a pleurisy,
>   Dies in his own too-much. That we would do,
>   We should do when we would: for this 'would' changes
>   And hath abatements and delays as many
>   As there are tongues, are hands, are accidents,   120
>   And then this 'should' is like a spendthrift sigh
>   That hurts by easing.
>
>   (106–22)

The passage has an obvious application to Hamlet. Not only are the situations of the young men identical in that both have lost a father by violent means and seek vengeance upon the murderer, but Hamlet has constantly censured himself for those 'abatements and delays' (119) which Claudius feels may qualify the 'spark and fire' (112) of Laertes' filial piety. As noted above, the unqualified assent the audience might otherwise have given to Hamlet's self-deprecatory stance is modified by the interplay between the speculative discourses of the Prince and the actions of his fellow revengers but up to this point in the play it is upon the compromising nature of action that attention has been focused, rather than upon the positive value of delay. In this speech, the situation is reversed. Claudius is concerned to employ Laertes as an instrument to remove Hamlet from his path. He wishes him to perform a highly dishonourable act, and is seeking to manipulate his blind fury for his own ends. What he fears is that Laertes might pause, might think, might change course. He fears, in fact, that he might become a Hamlet. In this context 'delay' cannot be seen in negative terms. If Claudius, the prime source of evil in the play world, advocates unthinking, precipitate action, then the extent to which unthinking precipitate action is resisted becomes a measure of moral awareness.

The closing lines of Claudius' speech, and Laertes' response to them, are equally significant. Claudius asks:

> what would you undertake
> To show yourself in deed your father's son
> More than in words?
> *Laer.* To cut his throat i'th'church. 125

> (123–5)

Once again, the application to Hamlet is clear. In III.iii, on his way to confront his mother with her guilt, the Prince had come upon Claudius at prayer, and had debated whether to take his life. Here, Laertes is quick to declare his readiness to commit sacrilegious murder, while Claudius applauds his resolution:

> No place indeed should murder sanctuarize;
> Revenge should have no bounds.

> (126–7)

The reader or spectator can have little doubt where true morality lies when the propriety of a course of action is asserted by a man who has seduced his brother's wife, committed one murder, and is about to propose a stratagem to assassinate the heir to the throne.

The final phase of the exchange, before the entrance of Gertrude, sets up yet another contrast between those pursuing private retribution. Claudius proposes a fencing match between Hamlet and Laertes, and suggests that the latter should employ an unbuttoned rapier as a means of engineering the death of the Prince through a seeming accident. Not only does Laertes welcome the proposal, but he suggests that he should poison his sword to ensure the success of the device revealing that he has already purchased an 'unction' from a 'mountebank' (140) that would be suitable for the purpose. His readiness to embrace a dishonourable vengeance and the revelation of his interest in poisonous substances diminish him still further in the eyes of the audience, while his treacherousness is thrown into relief by the account which Claudius gives, in the same passage, of Hamlet's character. He describes the Prince as,

Most generous, and free from all contriving,

(134)

contemptuously contrasting the trustfulness of the Prince with their capacity for 'shuffling' (136). Spoken as it is by Claudius, this testimony to Hamlet's generosity of spirit is peculiarly objective, serving to direct the sympathy of the audience towards the central figure and away from his alter ego.

The parallels that the dramatist establishes between the play's principal revengers in IV.v and IV.vii thus serve a double purpose. On the one hand, like the Pyrrhus/Fortinbras episodes, they expose the viciousness of the pursuit of private vengeance, while, on the other, they elevate the stature of the Prince, undermining the charges he levels against himself and helping to justify his conduct. The prompt revenge Hamlet blames himself for failing to execute is shown in these scenes to be anarchic. The fury into which he seeks to lash himself leads here to misdirected action, and dignifies, rather than degrades, its object. The proposition that revenge should have no bounds, to which Hamlet fails to adhere, is exposed as blasphemous, while the pursuit of vengeance through guile is seen as despicable. Above all, the delay to which Hamlet's revenge is pre-eminently subject, is redefined through its condemnation by Claudius, and may no longer be viewed unequivocally as a symptom of the disease which pervades the play world.

The closing scenes of the drama emphasize the proximity and distance between Hamlet and Laertes through two physical confrontations. Throughout the play Hamlet is preoccupied by the relationship between appearance and reality – in particular the outward show of grief and the inner experience of it. In II.ii he blames himself for responding to his loss with words rather than deeds,

> I, the son of a dear father murder'd,
> Prompted to my revenge by heaven and hell, 580
> Must like a whore unpack my heart with words
> And fall a-cursing like a very drab,
>
> (579–82)

and his public statements on his father's death are restrained in the extreme. Laertes, by contrast, is given to rant. His hyperbolic speeches in IV.vii lead Claudius to question the relationship between his words and his actions (123–5), and he weeps openly when he hears of his sister's death (184ff.). In V.i, when Ophelia is buried, he is entirely carried away by his emotions, leaping into her grave and expressing his sorrow in the most extravagant terms. Hamlet, who has come to regard all demonstrative emotion as suspect, responds to his unrestrained passion as to a challenge, self-consciously out-mouthing, and out-ranting him as they grapple over the coffin (278–9). Their shared object of grief and extravagant protestations of emotion heighten the audience's awareness of the similarities between then, but the comparison serves only to emphasize the typicality of the ungoverned conduct of the one and the untypicality of the behaviour of the other, exposing the shallowness of Laertes, and obliging the spectator to recognize that Hamlet would be a lesser man were he to model his conduct consistently upon his.

The last scene of the play witnesses the final confrontation between the two men and the vengeance of both, with the contrast between their behaviour again operating to Hamlet's advantage. Laertes has planned the death of his enemy in advance. The means he employs are doubly treacherous, involving both an unbuttoned rapier and the use of poison, and at the last he regrets what he has done:

> Hamlet, thou art slain.
> No medicine in the world can do thee good; 320
> In thee there is not half an hour's life.
> The treacherous instrument is in thy hand,
> Unbated and envenom'd. The foul practice
> Hath turn'd itself on me. Lo, here I lie,
> Never to rise again. Thy mother's poison'd. 325
> I can no more. The King – the King's to blame.
>
> (V.ii.319–26)

The words 'treacherous' (322), 'foul' (323), 'practice' (323), 'blame' (326) all point to the revulsion of the speaker from the deed he has performed, and it is notable that at his death he feels it necessary to ask forgiveness of the man who has murdered his father (334–6), and refers to him as 'noble' (334). Hamlet's vengeance, though it too is accomplished with a poisoned, unbuttoned rapier, differs from that of Laertes in every possible respect. The Prince does not plan or contrive Claudius' death. Though he feels the compulsion to avenge his father's murder as strongly as Laertes, he does not rush into headlong action but broods upon the ramifications of his situation, testing the truth of the Ghost's assertions and neglecting the opportunity to kill Claudius when he is praying. On his return from Denmark, after the abortive journey to England, he is increasingly content to see himself as part of a providential plan rather than as an instigator of action, seeing Heaven as 'ordinant' (V.ii.48) in the deaths of Rosencrantz and Guildenstern and attributing his own escape from the trap set for him by Claudius to 'a divinity that shapes our ends, / Rough-hew them how we will' (V.ii.10–11). Though he feels a sense of disquiet when the fencing match is proposed, he rejects both fear of what is to come and the need to shape it:

> . . . We defy augury. There is a special provi-   215
> dence in the fall of a sparrow. If it be now, 'tis not to
> come; if it be not to come, it will be now; if it be not
> now, yet it will come. The readiness is all.   (V.ii.215–18)

The vengeance that he finally executes is planned not by him but by Claudius, or, as the sounding trumpets (cf. s.d. V.ii.285) and ironic turn of events imply, by providence acting through him. It is Claudius who suggests the fencing match, the unbuttoned rapier, and the poisoned wine. And it is Claudius, not Hamlet, who brings about the deaths of Laertes and Gertrude, enabling Hamlet to fulfil the injunction of the Ghost not to take action against his mother. At the last, Hamlet merely responds with an appropriate 'readiness' (V.ii.218) to the occasion that is presented to him. He is thus freed from both blame and self-reproach for Claudius' death, and succeeds in killing his adversary without diminishing himself or elevating his opponent. His conduct throughout the scene is that of a 'noble' prince (334), not an animal or a devil, and it is hoped by those that survive him that 'flights of angels' (365) will accompany his soul to rest.

It should be clear, by this stage, that a reading of *Hamlet* which takes cognizance of the relationships that are set up between strands of action generates a very different set of responses from one which concentrates solely upon the Prince's psychological state. The character-orientated approach, as noted at the outset, prompts such questions as, 'What is the basic flaw in Hamlet's character which inhibits him from fulfilling the injunctions of the Ghost?' and it leads to a view of the central figure as an inherently noble man, tainted by the world he inhabits and thus incapable of acting coherently in it. An awareness of the interplay between main and subsidiary actions casts a very different light upon Hamlet's predicament. With the examples of Pyrrhus, Fortinbras and Laertes before him the reader or spectator cannot regard Hamlet's failure to sweep to his revenge as a flaw, when those who embrace this course of action are presented as animalistic and diabolic; nor can he regard an inability to act precipitately as symptomatic of a diseased will, when the precipitate actions that are performed are presented in negative terms.

The significance of the play as a whole is considerably enriched by this level of audience awareness. While on the one hand the reader or spectator is encouraged to participate in Hamlet's self-disgust through his soliloquies, and to share his desire to extirpate the evil which Claudius embodies, on the other he or she is made aware of the danger to the individual implicit in the exaction of vengeance, and feels concern for the moral safety of the Prince. The members of the audience are thus led to confront a series of issues independent of those with which Hamlet consciously wrestles, and with which they wrestle through him. They are faced with the problem of reconciling the need to fulfil the injunctions of the Ghost with the viciousness of private vengeance, and they ponder the attributes which distinguish the central figure from the subsidiary revengers, and which thus, by implication, differentiate a man from a beast or a devil. As a result, Hamlet's progress through the play answers more questions than the Prince himself is aware of. For example, his resignation to the will of providence at the close frees him, personally, from the intolerable pressure to initiate action to which he had been subject throughout, but it also resolves the problems faced by the audience regarding the means by which revenge can be exacted without detriment to the actor. At the same time, though Hamlet censures himself for 'thinking too precisely on th'event' (IV.iv.41), it is the capacity for thought which emerges, for the spectator, as the prime distinguishing feature between the Prince, Pyrrhus, Fortinbras and Laertes. Faced with the task imposed upon him by the Ghost, Hamlet does not rush for an unbuttoned rapier, or buy poison from a mountebank, he embarks upon a thought journey that ultimately leads him to a recognition of the inevitability of death, the incomprehensibility of human life, and, above all, to the existence of a divinity that 'shapes our ends, / Rough-hew them how we will' (V.ii.10–11). The significance of that thought journey is made clear, though he is unaware of it, by Hamlet himself. In IV.iv, having discussed Fortinbras' expedition against Poland with the Captain and remarked upon the diseased nature of the enterprise, the Prince comments:

> What is a man
> If his chief good and market of his time
> Be but to sleep and feed? A beast, no more.   35
> Sure he that made us with such large discourse,
> Looking before and after, gave us not
> That capability and godlike reason
> To fust in us unus'd.

(IV.iv.33–9)

In the course of the lines that follow, the speaker, driven by the need to avenge the murder of his father upon his uncle, comes to equate the process of thinking with the avoidance of action, and hence with a species of cowardice. The members of the audience, by contrast, faced with an unthinking Pyrrhus, Fortinbras and Laertes, recognize reason to be the attribute which associates man with the divine, and which distinguishes him from the beast. Thus the extent to which Hamlet looks 'before and after' (IV.iv.37) – the source of his notorious 'delay' – becomes the measure of the distance between the Prince and his fellow revengers, emerging as the prime index, not of the diseased will of the protagonist, but of his human greatness.

   The use of parallel actions in Shakespearian drama is not exclusive (as noted at the outset of this chapter) to the tragedies. The comedies, histories and 'problem plays' all feature complementary plots which, like the subsidiary revenges of *Hamlet*, contribute to the definition of character, while helping to broaden the scope of the drama from the individual to the issue. The relationship between these primary and secondary areas of interest does not, however, remain constant from play to play. As demonstrated above, *King Lear* exemplifies a kind of structure in which the themes of the main plot are universalized by a process of repetition, whereas *Hamlet* contrasts the conduct of a series of figures placed in a similar situation. *Measure for Measure*, a play written soon after *Hamlet* (and not long before *King Lear*) also generates meaning by contrastive means, but in this instance the relationship between main and sub plot characters evolves in a different direction. Whereas *Hamlet* starts from a point of likeness (in that the Prince, Laertes, Fortinbras and Pyrrhus have all suffered the death of a father by violent means), and moves towards the revelation of difference, *Measure for Measure* begins from a point of difference, and moves towards the recognition of likeness.

An immeasurable gulf appears at the outset of *Measure for Measure* to separate the play's most, and least idealistic figures. Angelo, whose name is indicative of his apparent sanctity, is a man of rigid self-discipline (cf. I.iv.57–61), who is so little the slave of passion his blood is described as 'very snow-broth' (I.iv.58), and whose public virtue is such he is entrusted (by the Duke) with the task of purging Vienna of vice. The aim Angelo elects to pursue is, moreover, as absolute as his nature. He is determined to administer strict, impartial justice in the interests of the whole community, believing that both society and the individual are best served by the unflinching enforcement of the law. His response to a plea for mercy is indicative of the uncompromising idealism he embodies:

> Isab[ella].   Yet show some pity.   100
> *Ang.* I show it most of all when I show justice;
>   For then I pity those I do not know,
>   Which a dismiss'd offence would after gall,
>   And do him right that, answering one foul wrong,
>   Lives not to act another.   105

(II.ii.100–5)

The law Angelo is shown attempting to uphold is an edict against fornication. Two groups of characters fall victim to the enforcement process – a pair of lovers, Claudio and Juliet, and the associates of a bawd, Mistress Overdone. Claudio and Juliet, although already betrothed, have not waited to consummate their marriage until the church had publicly bestowed her blessing on it, and Juliet is expecting a child when the action opens. Claudio, though he has exhibited a greater susceptibility to the temptations of the flesh than Angelo, nevertheless shares some of the attitudes of the man who condemns him, in that he regards his arrest as a logical consequence of his lack of self-discipline:

> *Lucio.* Why, how now, Claudio? Whence comes this
>   restraint?
> *Cla.* From too much liberty, my Lucio. Liberty,
>   As surfeit, is the father of much fast;
>   So every scope by the immoderate use
>   Turns to restraint. Our natures do pursue,   120
>   Like rats that ravin down their proper bane,
>   A thirsty evil; and when we drink, we die.
>
>   (I.ii.116–22)

By contrast, Lucio (one of Mistress Overdone's principal customers), whose name, like Angelo's is indicative of his moral status, embraces the promptings of the flesh with no sense of guilt. Not only would he be sorry if Claudio's life were 'foolishly lost at a game of tick-tack' (I.ii.180–1), but he has himself fathered an illegitimate child (cf. III.ii.193–6), and maintains that lechery cannot be extirpated until 'eating and drinking be put down' (III.ii.99).

The distance between Angelo, Claudio and Lucio is narrowed when Isabella, Claudio's sister, is induced to plead with Angelo on her brother's behalf. Angelo is promptly fired by the beauty and sanctity of the intercessor, and attempts to blackmail her into exchanging her virginity for her brother's life. Through the agency of the Duke, Angelo's former betrothed, Mariana, takes Isabella's place in Angelo's bed, but he persists in ordering Claudio's execution, even though he believes that the terms of his ransom have been met.

It will be apparent that by this stage in the play the positions of Angelo, Claudio, and Lucio have drawn closer together. All three men have now committed fornication, and this development serves a number of purposes. In the first place the progress of Angelo subverts the spectator's initial preconceptions about the nature of the play world. At the outset of the drama a simple opposition appeared to exist between reformers and those in need of reformation, but once Angelo succumbs to his passion for Isabella this simplistic division of mankind into good and bad is rapidly overthrown. Once having given his 'sensual race the rein' (II.iv.159) Angelo moves swiftly from fornication to perjury, finally endangering the innocent in the play's closing scene by denying his whole course of conduct before the Duke (cf. V.i.232–7). By the end of the play the fallibility of the most self-disciplined and most idealistic of men has thus been exposed, and the failings common to all human beings – lust, mendacity, cowardice – the failings that link an Angelo to a Lucio, have been revealed. At the same time, the positive aspects of the less virtuous characters have also emerged. Claudio, though he is guilty both of anticipating his nuptials and attempting to persuade his sister to exchange her virginity for his life, displays a capacity for repentance (cf. I.ii.117–22 and III.i.170) which Angelo only belatedly exhibits (cf. V.i.364–72), while Lucio, for all his degeneracy, treats Isabella with greater respect than his moral superiors (cf. I.iv.30–6) and goes to considerable lengths to save her brother's life (cf. I.iv.16–84 and II.ii.25–162). In short, the pure and the impure emerge, by the final act, as mere mortal men, compounded of both vices and virtues, and with a capacity for both good and evil.

The complementary actions of *Measure for Measure* do not, however, simply help to define the progress of Angelo by exposing his affinity with other men. Like the parallel vengeances of *Hamlet*, the careers of Angelo's fellow fornicators contribute to the exploration of a central problem – in this case the administration of justice. Angelo, Claudio and Lucio have all committed the same crime, and, according to the strict letter of Venetian law, all three should die. As the action progress, however, it very quickly becomes apparent, to the members of the audience, if not to Angelo, that though the offences the three men commit are technically similar, the attitudes and intentions of those that commit them are radically different. Angelo blackmails a woman who has devoted herself to a life of chastity (Isabella is in the process of entering a convent) into going to bed with him. He is thus involved in the gross abuse of both his office and another person, and is instrumental (in intention, at least) in the violation of a religious commitment. He is motivated not by love, but by lust, and his attitude are violent and unhealthy; cf.

Fit thy consent to my sharp appetite;   160
Lay by all nicety and prolixious blushes
That banish what they sue for. Redeem thy brother
By yielding up thy body to my will;
Or else he must not only die the death,
But thy unkindness shall his death draw out   165
To ling'ring sufferance.

(II.iv.160–6)

Claudio, by contrast, loves and is loved by Juliet. The two are married in the eyes of God in that they are betrothed, while their union is naturally fruitful in outcome. The imagery surrounding their relationship thus contrasts forcibly with that employed by Angelo:

Fewness and truth; 'tis thus:
Your brother [i.e. Claudio] and his lover have embrac'd,   40
As those that feed grow full, as blossoming time
That from the seedness the bare fallow brings
To teeming foison, even so her plenteous womb
Expresseth his full tilth and husbandry.

(I.iv.39–44)

Lucio's attitudes have more in common with Angelo's than Claudio's in that he too is motivated by lust, but for him the offence is casual. Where Angelo acts with a consciousness of sin, Lucio has no sense of the moral significance of his sexual activities, and has nothing but contempt for his partner in them; cf.

Lucio. I was once before him [the Duke] for getting a wench with child.
Duke. Did you such a thing?
Lucio. Yes, marry, did I; but I was fain to forswear it;   170
they would else have married me to the rotten
medlar.   (IV.iii.167–72)

The parallel offences of Angelo, Claudio and Lucio thus expose the limitations of Angelo's proposition that every crime should have its allotted punishment – a proposition with which the members of the audience may, initially, be tempted to concur. Though the three men have given evidence of human fallibility in the same way, the degree of culpability inherent in the actions that they perform is radically different. Angelo intends to violate; Lucio exploits; while Claudio wishes to establish an enduring (and sanctified) relationship. The superficially similar misdemeanours of the three men are thus distinguished by the intentions that underlie them, and it is the nature of these intentions which determines, for the members of the audience at least, the gravity of the offence. The failings of the play's sinners thus call for a much more subtle concept of justice than that propounded by Angelo at the outset. It is the problem that this poses, the problem of administering justice in a fallen world – a world in which all men are culpable and no man inveterately vicious – that the Duke confronts in the final scene, and the spectator ponders after the close of the play.

The Claudio/Juliet, Lucio/Mistress Overdone interests could be readily detached from *Measure for Measure*. The main plot of the play is coherent in its own right, tracing the fall of an outstanding individual from the pinnacle of social esteem to public humiliation and disgrace through a temptation to which, like Macbeth, he proves unequal. But without the parallel actions *Measure for Measure* would be a different kind of play. It would focus on one, idiosyncratic experience, and might be seen as the tragedy of Angelo. The seething background supplied by Lucio and his associates, together with the attachment between Claudio and Juliet, ensures that the career of Angelo is not perceived in these terms. These figures define the nature of human beings, and expose the failings common to all men, allowing those outside the play world to perceive that the deputy's downfall is the product, not of his exposure to a unique set of circumstances, but of his attempt to suppress an aspect of his humanity. He falls, in short, not because he has failed to grapple with an exceptional circumstance, but because he has failed to recognize (or refuses to accept) what man is. At the same time, the prominence of Claudio and Lucio in the design draws the spectator's attention away from the 'potential hero' towards the affinities between the dramatis personae, and the problem that these affinities expose. Whereas Hamlet dominates the drama that bears his name from first to last, ensuring that it is on his predicament that the members of the audience focus throughout, Angelo shares the stage with a series of offenders, and consequently enjoys a smaller proportion of audience attention. As a result, the centre of interest shifts away from the outstanding individual and the problem he confronts to the problem itself, which the careers of a number of figures serve to illuminate. *Measure for Measure* is thus a play about justice rather than a play about Angelo, Claudio, or Lucio, with a network of correspondences ensuring that it is on the issue, rather than the individual that the mind of the spectator ultimately comes to rest.

The relationship between strands of action cannot be said to carry the entire meaning of any play, however obtrusive or systematic the correspondences the dramatist sets up. The significance of a drama arises from the interaction between all the elements of the dramatic composition, and cannot be extrapolated from any single aspect of it. Nevertheless, the richness of Shakespeare's designs, like those of the majority of his contemporaries, owes much to the variations that are woven around a central theme, and an awareness of the pattern of relationships the dramatist unfolds can considerably enhance the student's understanding and enjoyment of the whole. Of the three plays discussed in the course of this chapter *Hamlet* is the one which, as modern productions have shown, can best survive the loss of its parallel plots. *King Lear* without the Duke of Gloucester is an impressive, but much less horrifying work, while *Measure for Measure* without Lucio is far less intellectually challenging. Nevertheless, though *Hamlet* read as a play which centres on the private agony of a uniquely sensitive individual is a much more rewarding play than *Measure for Measure* viewed as the tragi-comic progress of Angelo, it too becomes a far more important composition when viewed in its entirety. Seen as a drama which not only explores a unique sensibility, but simultaneously holds up a series of mirrors to the seeming irresolution of its central figure – mirrors which reverse conventional assumptions about action and retribution, and transform a culpable failure of will into a towering moral achievement – it becomes a much more profound and original work. There can surely be no better case for urging the value of studying Shakespeare's parallel plots.

6

The Treatment of Character

To many readers it may come as some surprise that the discussion of Shakespeare's characters should be reserved for Chapter 6 of this book, rather than being the subject of Chapter 1. Throughout the history of Shakespearian criticism it has been upon the dramatist's ability to create vital and convincing human beings that attention has principally been focused, and it is the characters of Shakespeare's plays – Hamlet, Falstaff, Lady Macbeth – rather than his plots which live in the popular imagination, transcending, in the fullness of their conception, the dramatic context from which they derive. For many students of Shakespearian drama the character is synonymous with the play, and the meaning of the drama co-extensive with the experience of its central figures. It is for this reason that the discussion of Shakespeare's handling of his dramatis personae, has been postponed until this relatively late stage. The earlier chapters of this book have been designed to demonstrate that the meaning of a Shakespearian play does not derive exclusively from the progress of its central figures; it is also a product of the kind of dramatic language that is employed, the disposition of the characters on the stage, the degree of distance between play and spectator, and the relationship between levels of action. The characters of a drama, however fully realized, are only one element of a complex structure, and an awareness of the context in which they function is crucial to an understanding of the meaning that they help to project.

The popular belief that the significance of a Shakespearian play is to be equated with the experience of its central figures is not, however, the only fallacy to bedevil the study of Shakespeare's characters. Equally damaging is the assumption that it is in the extraordinary realism of his creations that the dramatist's distinction as an artist resides. This proposition is misleading in two respects. In the first place, Shakespearian drama is rarely 'realistic' in the sense of holding up a mirror to day-to-day actuality. The situations in which Shakespeare's protagonists find themselves, and the decisions that they are called upon to make, are remote from those of everyday life, and frequently have their origins in folk tale or romance. In *The Winter's Tale*, for example, the Queen, Hermione, a moving and vividly realized figure, allows the husband who has accused her of adultery to believe that she is dead for sixteen years, before pretending to be a statue in order to be re-united with him; while in *The Merchant of Venice*, the capable Portia secures a husband, not by means of a conventional courtship, but through a species of lottery devised by her father. Shakespeare's stage is certainly crowded with a gallery of differentiated individuals, and these individuals frequently create the illusion of being complex men and women by (among other things) their fluctuating purposes, inconsistencies, and contradictory impulses, but their world is not a mirror image of our world, nor do they act as we do. The equation of Shakespeare's achievement with the creation of articulate character is also unhelpful in a second respect. It implies that the success of any given play depends upon the complexity of the figures that it exhibits and thus constructs a hierarchy of dramatic works based upon this criterion alone. Judged from this standpoint, Shakespeare's early plays become mere stepping stones towards the plays of the middle period because their characters are relatively undeveloped; the problem plays become problems because (in part) of the inconsistencies of their heroes and heroines; while the late plays puzzle and confuse because of their lack of a central focus and seeming neglect of motivation. In short, by employing one single criterion as a measure of success, the character-orientated reader reduces the major oeuvre of the world's foremost dramatist to a handful of plays, and is in danger of equating the achievement of *Henry IV, Part I* with the creation of Falstaff.

In fact, to ground Shakespeare's pre-eminence as a dramatist upon the creation of a galaxy of figures valid 'not [for] an age, but for all time' is, paradoxically, to limit his achievement. Shakespeare did not write the same sort of play throughout his dramatic career, he constantly experimented with his medium, and with the elements that go to make up a dramatic composition. The degree to which his characters are differentiated varies from play to play, as do the techniques by which they are presented, and these variations arise, not from the relative maturity or senility of the playwright, but from the kind of statement about human life that he was attempting to make. This is not to deny, of course, that in the space of his theatrical career Shakespeare succeeded in creating the most vividly realized, endearing, and terrifying figures yet to emerge on the European stage. The responses of generations of readers and theatre-goers is sufficient testimony to the simultaneous individuality and universality of Viola and Rosalind, Bottom and Falstaff, Goneril and Regan. Nevertheless, to approach a Shakespearian play in the expectation that its meaning will necessarily be projected through the experience of complex characters is to don a critical straitjacket that will inevitably inhibit appreciation, not merely of one specific play or group of plays, but of the richness and complexity of Shakespeare's art.

The Comedy of Errors is the play that probably lies at the furthest remove from the work of the Shakespeare of the popular imagination. The plot of the play is founded upon that of the *Menaechmi*, a comedy by the Roman dramatist Plautus, in which confusion is created by the arrival of a young man in a city in which, unknown to him, his identical brother lives. In taking up the plot of the Roman play, Shakespeare increased the scope for comic confusion by giving his identical masters identical servants, while he placed the events relating to the two brothers within an encircling frame action concerning their father, Egeon, whose life has been endangered by his search for his lost sons (see above pp. 62ff.). The frame plot and the main plot contrast forcibly both in terms of pace and the treatment of character. The frame plot evolves slowly and deliberately, allowing the audience time to dwell on its central figure. The play opens with the entrance of the Duke of Ephesus accompanied by Egeon under guard, and most of the first scene is taken up (as noted in Chapter 3) by the prisoner's lengthy account of the way in which his twin sons, and those of a servant, came to be separated from one another, of the decision of the twin remaining to him to seek his brother, and of his own search for both sons that has brought him to a city in which his life is forfeit unless ransomed for a thousand marks. The scene is 158 lines long, and over 100 of those lines are spoken by Egeon, ensuring that the attention of the audience is focused on him; while the length of his speeches, together with the absence of incident, make the scene a slow one, establishing a sense of the dragging hours of Egeon's captivity. The tempo of the action changes dramatically, however, in the subsequent scenes, which are devoted to the humorous consequences of the arrival of Egeon's son, Antipholus of Syracuse, in Ephesus, where his brother is a prominent citizen. Antipholus of Syracuse, and his servant, Dromio, are promptly mistaken for their Ephesian counterparts, while the masters confuse the servants with one another, and the servants mistake their masters. Throughout this section of the play not only is the pace increasingly hectic as the confusion grows, but very little emphasis is placed upon the idiosyncracies of the human personality. At the start of the play, Antipholus of Syracuse and Antipholus of Ephesus, together with the two Dromios, have a clear understanding of who and what they are, but as the action progresses, this awareness is undermined by the onslaught upon their sense of selfhood that their community makes. Adriana, for example, Antipholus of Ephesus' wife, has no hesitation in claiming Antipholus of Syracuse as her husband, while her sister, Luciana, rebukes the Syracusan Antipholus, in the belief that he is her brother-in-law, for making amorous advances to her. Similarly, the two Dromios, who have served the Antipholus brothers throughout their lives, bring the products of the errands upon which they are sent to the wrong masters, while the masters berate the wrong servants for failing to carry out their injunctions. In these scenes both the complexity of the action and the humour of the situation depend upon the overwhelming likeness that exists between two sets of human beings, and hence there can be no place for the kind of treatment of character that highlights the infinite complexity and variety of human nature. Indeed, it is man's inability to be other than that which society believes him to be that these central acts stress. Dromio of Syracuse is claimed by the fat cook regardless of his own wishes in the matter, while Antipholus of Ephesus finds himself shut out of the house of which he firmly believes himself to be the master.

Considered in the abstract, the kind of plot outlined above, depending as it does upon a lack of correlation between the individual's perception of himself and that of the society in which he functions, is potentially tragic. Divorced of their treatment, the central episodes of *The Comedy of Errors* are painful rather than funny, involving not only wrongful arrest, and a wife's conviction that her husband has deserted her for another woman, but the threatened incarceration of an intelligent and respected citizen in a madhouse – the logical product of a divorce between individual and collective notions of reality. Every character in the play undergoes a degree of suffering, either physical or mental – and all experience the breakdown of the stable fabric of their lives. In the central section of the play, however, the tragic implications of the situation are not allowed to obtrude upon the audience's attention. Not only does the action move too swiftly to allow the spectators to dwell upon the uncomfortable positions in which the protagonists find themselves, but the dramatic language that the characters are assigned frustrates involvement in their predicaments, rather than encouraging those outside the play world to participate in their experience. Adriana's lament over her husband's supposed infidelity illustrates the point:

> His company must do his minions grace,
> Whilst I at home starve for a merry look.
> Hath homely age th'alluring beauty took
> From my poor cheek? then he hath wasted it.   90
> Are my discourses dull? barren my wit?
> If voluble and sharp discourse be marr'd,
> Unkindness blunts it more than marble hard.
> Do their gay vestments his affections bait?
> That's not my fault, he's master of my state.   95
> What ruins are in me that can be found
> By him not ruin'd? Then is he the ground
> Of my defeatures; my decayed fair
> A sunny look of his would soon repair;
> But, too unruly deer, he breaks the pale   100
> And feeds from home; poor I am but his stale.

(II.i.87–101)

This speech manifestly does not reflect the way that the mind of an injured wife works, nor does it convey the accents of the human voice at a moment of crisis. The use of rhyme, for example, works against the passion and disorder that the content of the speech implies, as do the heavily end-stopped lines, and the regular rhythm of the blank verse, cf.

> Unkínd|néss blúnts | ĭt móre | thăn már|blĕ hárd.

Similarly the evolution of the speech through question and answer suggests a degree of intellectual control that is incompatible with the speaker's mental state; while the metaphor of the deer (100–1), together with the pun upon which it depends, functions as a pleasing idea, rather than affording the listener an insight into an idiosyncratic mental state. This does not mean that the speech is an artistic failure – quite the reverse. The formal, or overtly 'poetic', structure of the passage serves to erect a kind of plate glass window between the speaker's world and that of the theatre audience, distancing the 'injured wife' from the spectators, and thus enabling them to perceive the ludicrousness of her situation. And a host of allied techniques are employed to sustain the distance that the speed of the action and relatively stylized dramatic language promote. The superior awareness of the theatre audience is deployed to explode the seriousness of confrontation scenes (cf. IV.i.15–85), while the extravagant responses of the dramatis personae to the situations in which they find themselves help to rob those situations of their gravity (cf. IV.ii.17–22). In short, throughout the central section of the play, rather than sharing in the experience of the protagonists and pondering the significance of their psychological progress, the spectator laughs *at* the dramatis personae and deduces a meaning from what happens to them.

The distinction between the conduct of main and frame plots is most evident in the final scene. Up to this point it has been the humorous aspect of mistaken identity that the dramatist has exploited, with the situations produced by the plot, rather than the complexities of the characters, engaging the attention of the audience. In the final scene, however, with the re-entrance of Egeon, the focus shifts. Having failed to raise the sum required for his release, Egeon is being led to execution when he believes he recognizes the son who can save his life. The man he addresses is the wrong Antipholus, however, and the following exchange takes place:

> *Egeon.* Why look you strange on me? you know me well.
> *Eph. Ant.* I never saw you in my life till now.
> *Egeon.* O! grief hath chang'd me since you saw me last,
>   And careful hours with time's deformed hand
>   Have written strange defeatures in my face;   300
>   But tell me yet, dost thou not know my voice?
> *Eph. Ant.* Neither.
> *Egeon.* Dromio, nor thou?
> *Eph. Dro.*   No, trust me sir, nor I.
> . . . .
> *Egeon.* Not know my voice? O time's extremity,
>   Hast thou so crack'd and splitted my poor tongue
>   In seven short years, that here my only son
>   Knows not my feeble key of untun'd cares?   310
>   Though now this grained face of mine be hid

In sap-consuming winter's drizzled snow,
And all the conduits of my blood froze up,
Yet hath my night of life some memory;
My wasting lamps some fading glimmer left;   315
My dull deaf ears a little use to hear –
All these old witnesses, I cannot err,
Tell me thou art my son Antipholus.
Eph. Ant. I never saw my father in my life.

(V.i.296–319)

These speeches are very different from Adriana's lines quoted
above. The passage is in blank verse, rather than rhyming couplets,
and thus approximates more closely to natural speech, while the use
of enjambement (as in lines 308–10) and variations in the regular
iambic pattern, cf.

Knóws nót | my fée|blĕ kéy

(310)

mŷ blóod | fróze ŭp

(313)

Tell mĕ | thou árt

(318)

heighten the illusion of the speaking voice. Where Adriana employs
conventional analogies (e.g. 'marble hard', 'sunny look' (II.i.93 and
99)), the imagery that Egeon uses is idiosyncratic, convincing the
listener that he has something personal to say – that he is an
individual, not a dramatic type. Time is personified, for example,
not as an old man with a scythe and an hour-glass, but as the
possessor of a deformed, and hence distorting, hand, that disfigures
all that it touches (299–300), while the temporal process is seen as
violent and destructive in its effects, cracking and splitting the
tongue of the speaker (307–10), whose face has become 'grained' (in
the sense of furrowed) by long hours of anxiety (311). The
commonplace adjectives employed by Adriana, which help the

audience to recognize her generic role as the injured wife (e.g. 'merry look', 'alluring beauty' (II.i.88 and 89)) have also given place to a much more highly charged vocabulary. Egeon's memory, together with his eyes and ears, are 'old' (317) witnesses of the truth of what he says, not merely because they are called upon to recollect a man that the speaker has not seen for seven years, but because Egeon himself is old, and his faculties have the imperfections of age. The words that Egeon employs, too, are, in the main, simpler, and hence closer to everyday speech, than those used by Adriana. Though both characters employ the unfamiliar term 'defeatures' (cf. II.i.98 and V.i.300), for example, the linguistic context in which they do so is very different. Adriana's speech is rich in latinate vocabulary (cf. 'company' (87), 'minions' (87), 'alluring' (89), 'voluble' (92), 'discourse' (92), 'vestments' (94)), minimizing the impact of the unusual term, whereas Egeon's first two speeches are predominantly monosyllabic, highlighting the action of an alien and disfiguring force by the contrast between 'strange defeatures' (300) and the homely context in which the latinate phrase occurs.

The kind of dramatic language that Egeon is assigned here places the audience in a very different relationship to him from that in which they stood towards the central figures. Up to this point in the play (excluding the opening scene) the basic premise that the principal figures are interchangeable, the speed of the action, ludicrous situations, and stylized dialogue have combined to project human beings stripped of their complexity, and man as an amusing victim of a universe beyond his control. With the encounter between Egeon and Antipholus of Ephesus the perspective changes. Where Adriana and the Antipholus brothers expostulate, enabling those outside the play world to view their predicaments with detachment, Egeon enacts his pain and confusion, convincing the listener of his humanity by his highly personal response to the events that have befallen him. At this point in the play, loss of identity ceases to be a matter for laughter. Whereas the lack of emphasis upon articulate character in the main plot permitted the spectator to perceive the humorous aspect of being mistaken for someone else, the fuller realization of Egeon allows the reader to glimpse the nightmare potentiality of the whole situation, before the frame plot is swallowed up in the main plot and all is resolved. Egeon has blundered into a world in which his own sense of familiarity is no guarantee of an answering response in others. Antipholus of Ephesus, as he confronts him, is in the reverse situation; he has stepped into a universe in which he is recognized, but does not recognize, the universe his brother has inhabited throughout the play. Both situations are akin to madness and conducive to madness – as the fate almost thrust upon Antipholus of Ephesus demonstrates. In the moment that Antipholus fails to recognize his father, the darker implications of the main plot rise to the surface, and the audience perceives, not only how funny it is to be mistaken for someone else, but how fragile man's sense of self-hood is, and how dependent human happiness and security are upon an acknowledged status within the social group.

The reader or theatre-goer who approaches *The Comedy of Errors* with the assumption that the play will either explore the workings of a specific consciousness, or act as a vehicle for the exhibition of a number of idiosyncratic individuals, will be sadly disappointed. The single character who is conceived in any depth appears in only two scenes, the first of which is formal in the extreme; while the central figures are 'two-dimensional' in that they lack psychological depth. Nevertheless, the play is extremely effective in the theatre, and it is upon Shakespeare's handling of character that this success, in part, depends. The distance between play and spectator, and the lack of differentiation between the central figures, allows the audience to enjoy the uncomfortable situations in which the Syracusans and Ephesians find themselves without an accompanying sense of concern, while the contrast in mode between main and frame plots affords the spectator two perspectives upon the central situation, and thus enriches the play's meaning. The presence of a Hamlet or a Viola among the citizens of Ephesus would not only increase the anxieties of an audience in the later acts, but would reduce the shock of Egeon's encounter with his son in V.i, through which the sinister undertones of the comedy are released.

The Comedy of Errors is a useful starting point for the study of Shakespeare's treatment of character in that a number of important points about the dramatist's work may be exemplified from it. In the first place, the play demonstrates that Shakespeare did not always seek to draw those outside the play world into the consciousness of his creations, and that the success of his plays does not necessarily depend upon the degree to which he does so. In the second place, it illustrates that the meaning of a drama is not always co-extensive with the perceptions of the central figures. It is the members of the audience who find confusion amusing in the main body of the play, not the characters, who become increasingly enmeshed and unhappy; and it is the spectator, not Egeon, who perceives that it is not time which confounds man but chance. In the third place, the play reveals that the characters of a Shakespearian drama are not always consistent in their presentation from scene to scene. The Egeon who appears in I.i. has an expositorial function. He is entrusted with communicating background information to the audience, and the means by which he does so make few concessions to naturalism (see above, pp. 62ff.). The Egeon who appears in Act V is much more firmly integrated into the play world. He responds to an evolving situation, and his speeches enact the anguish of a specific individual. At this moment, the Egeon who functioned as Prologue disappears, and a suffering human being, for the briefest of moments, takes his place.

The Comedy of Errors, modelled as it is upon a Roman comedy, stands aside, to some extent, from the main body of Shakespearian drama, and is often regarded as untypical of it. Its differences from an assumed norm, however, can help to alert the student or inexperienced reader to the variety of Shakespeare's work, and hence encourage an open-minded approach to other plays within the canon. *Julius Caesar*, for example, becomes a much less difficult, and much more original play when the reader's preconceptions about the nature of tragedy in general, and of Shakespearian tragedy in particular, are laid aside. Consideration of the play in the study or the classroom is apt to be dominated by an attempt to identify a 'hero' or central figure, through whose experience the action evolves, and the number of potential candidates for the role – Caesar, Brutus, Antony – can lead to a sense of dissatisfaction with the work, and confusion about its concerns. In fact, the structure of the play is quite different from that of *Hamlet*, for example, or *Macbeth*, in which one principal figure is foregrounded throughout. The focus of attention in *Julius Caesar* shifts from act to act, with the character to whom the members of the audience relate in one scene being distanced from them in the next. The play thus affords the spectator a variety of perspectives upon the situation, rather than exploring a single experience, and involves the theatre audience in a constant process of revaluation as the focal point of the action shifts.

The richness and complexity of the play's design can be appreciated only by a careful study of the handling of character in the drama as a whole – though it is experienced in the theatre as the action unfolds – but three scenes may serve to illustrate in broad outline the kinds of technique that are employed throughout. Act II scene i might be said to 'belong' to Brutus. The scene is a long one – over 330 lines – and in the course of it Brutus is seen both on his own and in a variety of relationships. The first 85 lines are taken up by an extended soliloquy, interrupted at a number of points by a young servant, whose brief appearances serve to trigger new ideas in the speaker's mind. The passage is too lengthy to quote in full, but the first 34 lines are particularly important in establishing the relationship between the spectator and the central figure:

Bru. What, Lucius, ho!
    I cannot, by the progress of the stars,
    Give guess how near to day. Lucius, I say!
    I would it were my fault to sleep so soundly.
    When, Lucius, when? Awake, I say! What, Lucius!   5
            Enter LUCIUS
Luc. Call'd you, my lord?
Bru. Get me a taper in my study, Lucius:
    When it is lighted, come and call me here.
Luc. I will, my lord.   [*Exit.*]
Bru. It must be by his death: and for my part,   10
    I know no personal cause to spurn at him,
    But for the general. He would be crown'd:
    How that might change his nature, there's the question.
    It is the bright day that brings forth the adder,
    And that craves wary walking. Crown him? – that; –   15
    And then, I grant, we put a sting in him,
    That at his will he may do danger with.
    Th'abuse of greatness is when it disjoins
    Remorse from power; and, to speak truth of Caesar,
    I have not known when his affections sway'd   20
    More than his reason. But 'tis a common proof,
    That lowliness is young ambition's ladder,
    Whereto the climber-upward turns his face;
    But when he once attains the upmost round,
    He then unto the ladder turns his back,   25
    Looks in the clouds, scorning the base degrees
    By which he did ascend. So Caesar may;
    Then lest he may, prevent. And since the quarrel
    Will bear no colour for the thing he is,
    Fashion it thus: that what he is, augmented,   30
    Would run to these and these extremities;

And therefore think him as a serpent's egg,
Which, hatch'd, would, as his kind, grow mischievous,
And kill him in the shell.

(II.i.1–34)

The first five lines of this scene convey a great deal of information to the audience in a highly economical way. Brutus alternates here between calling to this servant and talking to himself, and his brief comments not only set the scene, but give some indication of his state of mind. His reference to the 'progress of the stars' (2) establishes that the action is taking place at night, and that he is out of doors, while his injunction to Lucius to light a taper in his study (7) makes clear that the scene is set in close proximity to his own house – and thus, presumably, in his garden. His regret that he is unable to sleep as soundly as the boy (4) is indicative of his mental unrest, while his inability to 'guess how near [it is] to day' (3) implies that the night may be far advanced, and that he has been walking in his garden for some considerable time. The soliloquy that begins at line 10 is thus set in the context of a thought process that has been in progress for much of the night, and the illusion that the reader or theatre-goer has intruded upon a man in the course of thinking is heightened by the line with which the speech opens, 'It must be by his death' (10). Here, the members of the theatre audience are obliged to identify imaginatively with the speaker, supplying 'the frustrating of Caesar's ambitions', or 'the preservation of the republic' in order to make sense of a statement that refers back to thoughts to which those outside the play world have not been privy. The proximity between speaker and listener produced by this process of imaginative involvement is sustained in the ensuing lines in a variety of ways. The movement of the verse follows the rhythms of natural speech, with enjambement (cf. 26 and 28), variation in the position of the caesura (cf. 12, 15, 25), metrical irregularities (cf. 26, 30), and the use of light and feminine endings (cf. 11, 13, 19) all helping to diminish the listener's awareness of the iambic pattern, and to create the illusion of the speaking voice. At the same time, the necessity for the members of the audience to participate in the process of thinking, rather than merely listening to what the speaker has to say, is continued to the close. The enigmatic opening 'It' (1) is followed, at line 15, by 'Crown him? – that –', the final word not merely emphasizing the crucial importance of the act of coronation, but encapsulating all the possible implications of Caesar's ascent to the throne. Line 31, 'Would run to these and these extremities', involves an even closer engagement with the mind of the speaker. Brutus does not spell out the abuses of power that could succeed Caesar's elevation. He envisages them in a mental flash, expressed in terms of a species of shorthand – 'these and these extremities' – which every member of the audience expands in a different way, according to his or her own conception of ultimate tyranny.

While the kind of dramatic language employed by Brutus is designed to involve those outside the play world in his experience, the content of his speeches, and in particular his difficulty in determining what constitutes right action, convinces the spectator of his humanity. Far from being a two-dimensional figure, embodying a single attitude or attribute, Brutus is a complex creation, divided between conflicting impulses, and caught up in a process of reasoning that he himself recognizes to be spurious. While he is aware, on the one hand that Caesar has not been guilty of abusing his position, he fears, on the other, that a further access of power might corrupt him, and consequently resolves that he must die, not for what he is, but for what he might become. His concern with the logic of his position (cf. 'And since the quarrel / Will bear no colour for the thing he is, / Fashion it thus' (28–30)) reveals that he is far from indifferent to moral considerations, yet his justification of a hypothetical good by a dubious process of reasoning is highly disturbing in its implications. The Brutus presented here has laudable intentions, but the situation in which he finds himself is far from clear cut, and the difficulty he finds in reconciling morality and pragmatism contributes to the spectator's perception of him as a credible, and comprehensible, human being.

Whereas the first 85 lines of II.i are designed to reveal the motives that impel Brutus towards the murder and involve the spectator in his experience, the remaining 249 lines are directed towards establishing his social and familial role. Lines 86–228 are taken up by his meeting with his fellow conspirators, and the respect in which he is held by them is quickly apparent. At three points in the scene it is his voice which is crucial in determining the conduct of the enterprise. He resists Cassius' suggestion that the conspirators should bind themselves to the murder by oath (112–40); he rejects the proposition that Cicero should be included in the enterprise (141–52); and he refuses to allow Antony to die with Caesar (154–83). All three decisions may be interpreted as a product of his idealism.

He resists the taking of an oath because he believes that the worth of the enterprise is sufficient guarantee of their devotion to it; he rejects Cicero because he dislikes his thirst to lead rather than co-operate; while he desires to spare Antony from a reluctance to vitiate their cause by a tyrannical act. The three decisions, however, are all impolitic. By refusing to allow the conspirators to swear an oath, Brutus is neglecting the need to bind together a group of people acting from disparate motives; by rejecting Cicero he is putting a private aversion before the success of the conspiracy; and in sparing Antony he is jeopardizing the enterprise by underestimating his opponents. Once again, it is a complex figure that is projected here. Probity and political judgement do not go hand-in-hand in this scene, and the members of the audience are torn between according Brutus the respect that the majority of the conspirators show towards him, and censuring him for his lack of judgement.

Lines 233–309 transfer the focus of attention from Brutus' public role to his relationship with his wife. Finding that her husband has risen from his bed, Portia comes to seek him, and the encounter between the two affords an insight into Brutus' private life. A number of points are important here. In the first place, Portia reveals that the mental unrest that the audience has witnessed is symptomatic of the disturbing effect upon Brutus that the contemplation of the assassination has produced:

> Y'have ungently, Brutus,
> Stole from my bed; and yesternight at supper
> You suddenly arose, and walk'd about,
> Musing, and sighing, with your arms across;   240
> And when I ask'd you what the matter was,
> You star'd upon me with ungentle looks.
> I urg'd you further; then you scratch'd your head,
> And too impatiently stamp'd with your foot;
> Yet I insisted, yet you answer'd not,   245
> But with an angry wafture of your hand
> Gave sign for me to leave you.

(II.i.237–47)

Portia's surprise at Brutus' conduct is also important in that it suggests a contrast between his current behaviour and his customary manner. She is clearly unused to 'ungentle' (242) behaviour, to being excluded from her husband's confidence (241ff.), and dismissed from his presence (245–7). The relationship between husband and wife is evidently a close one, and the scene as a whole reveals how strong the bond between the two is. Portia is not a mere handmaid to her husband. She is a woman of strong and noble mind, and the devotion of such a woman to Brutus enlists the sympathies of the audience on his behalf.

The last 25 lines of the scene are also designed to demonstrate Brutus' capacity to inspire devotion, but it is the charismatic aspect of his personality that is stressed here, rather than his 'gentleness'. Lucius enters once again to announce the arrival of a visitor, the infirm Caius Ligarius, and the following exchange then takes place between Brutus and the sick man:

Bru.   Would you were not sick!   315
Cai. I am not sick if Brutus have in hand
    Any exploit worthy the name of honour.
Bru. Such an exploit have I in hand, Ligarius,
    Had you a healthful ear to hear of it.
Cai. By all the gods that Romans bow before,   320
    I here discard my sickness. Soul of Rome!
    Brave son, deriv'd from honourable loins!
    Thou, like an exorcist, hast conjur'd up
    My mortified spirit. Now bid me run,
    And I will strive with things impossible,   325
    Yea, get the better of them . . .
    . . . . Set on your foot,
    And with a heart new-fir'd I follow you,
    To do I know not what; but it sufficeth
    That Brutus leads me on.

                                        (II.i.315–34)

It will be apparent from the above that Act II scene i is dominated by a single character. Brutus is on stage from first to last, and he is shown from a variety of standpoints – as a private individual, the co-leader of a conspiracy, a husband and an admired associate. The members of the audience are allowed an insight into both the way his mind works and the inner uncertainty underlying his public confidence, while they are conscious of limitations of which he himself is unaware. This kind of treatment of character is

comparable in its complexity with that afforded to the central figures
of a number of Shakespeare's plays, and the scene has strong
analogies with I.vii of *Macbeth* in which, once again, a prominent
member of the play's society examines his reasons for a projected
murder, can find no adequate motive for the deed, and discusses his
situation with his wife (see below, pp. 185–90). What is remarkable
about *Julius Caesar* is that the intimacy engineered by the dramatist
between Brutus and the theatre audience is largely confined to this
scene, subsequent acts encouraging those outside the play world to
view events, not through Brutus' eyes, but through those of other
actors in Caesar's drama. For example, just as Act II might be said to
'belong' to Brutus, Act III 'belongs' to Antony. His first major
entrance is preceded by a piece of stage business that effectively
alienates the spectators from the conspirators, and hence paves the
way for a transference of sympathies to Brutus' political opponents.
Having struck the last blow at the dying Caesar, Brutus calls upon
his fellow republicans to stoop with him, and to bathe their hands in
the dead man's blood:

> Stoop, Romans, stoop,   105
> And let us bathe our hands in Caesar's blood
> Up to the elbows, and besmear our swords:
> Then walk we forth, even to the market-place,
> And waving our red weapons o'er our heads,
> Let's all cry, 'Peace, freedom, and liberty!'   110
>
> (III.i.105–10)

The contrast between Brutus' words and the spectacle that he
presents is highly disturbing, and it is at this point that Antony's
servant enters to herald the arrival of his master. Though Brutus
welcomes Antony, it is not to him but to the dead man that Antony
speaks first, and his tone when he turns to the conspirators is
impressive, both in its dignity, and in the controlled emotion that it
evinces:

> O mighty Caesar! dost thou lie so low?
> Are all thy conquests, glories, triumphs, spoils,
> Shrunk to this little measure? Fare thee well.   150
> I know not, gentlemen, what you intend,
> Who else must be let blood, who else is rank:
> If I myself, there is no hour so fit

As Caesar's death's hour; nor no instrument
Of half that worth as those your swords, made rich   155
With the most noble blood of all this world.

(III.i.148–56)

Like Brutus' soliloquy in II.i, Antony's lines here follow the rhythms
of the speaking voice, convincing the members of the theatre
audience that they are witnessing an idiosyncratic response to
experience, rather than listening to a set piece speech. The nature of
Antony's response, moreover, is diametrically opposed to that of
the conspirators. Caesar is seen now, not as a potential tyrant, but a
man of unparalleled nobility, and Antony's willingness to die with
him swings the sympathies of the spectators away from the
murderers, and towards the dead man and his grieving friend. This
response is not confined furthermore, to this speech. By way of
answer to Brutus' assertion that the assassination can be justified,
Antony takes each of the conspirators by the hand, only to
jeopardize the politic role he has elected to assume as his eyes fall on
the dead man, and his feelings rise to the surface:

Let each man render me his bloody hand.
First, Marcus Brutus, will I shake with you;   185
Next, Caius Cassius, do I take your hand;
Now, Decius Brutus, yours; now yours, Metellus;
Yours, Cinna; and, my valiant Casca, yours;
Though last, not least in love, yours, good Trebonius.
Gentlemen all – alas, what shall I say?   190
My credit now stands on such slippery ground,
That one of two bad ways you must conceit me,
Either a coward, or a flatterer.
That I did love thee, Caesar, O, 'tis true!
If then thy spirit look upon us now,   195
Shall it not grieve thee dearer than thy death,
To see thy Antony making his peace,
Shaking the bloody fingers of thy foes,
Most noble, in the presence of thy corse?
Had I as many eyes as thou hast wounds,   200
Weeping as fast as they stream forth thy blood,
It would become me better than to close
In terms of friendship with thine enemies.

Pardon me, Julius! Here wast thou bay'd, brave hart;
Here didst thou fall; and here thy hunters stand,   205
Sign'd in thy spoil, and crimson'd in thy lethe.

(III.i.184–206)

The latter half of this speech is clearly impolitic. It reveals the
bitterness, grief and hostility that underlie the wary self-control of
the opening lines, and thus allows the audience to glimpse the
private man beneath the politic facade. The Antony presented in
this scene thus emerges not as a role ('Caesar's friend', for example),
but as an individual, caught up, like Brutus, in a situation
generating conflicting needs and impulses.

Act III scene i focuses upon the Antony who admired Caesar
passionately, and whose grief at the assassination modifies the
spectator's assessment of the dead man. By III.ii, however, this
Antony has almost wholly disappeared. The man who appears now
is a manipulator, engaged in rousing the mob against the
conspirators (cf. III.ii.75–262), while in IV.i he is seen as a ruthless
pragmatist, locked in a struggle for political power. His
contemptuous attitude towards his fellow triumvir, Lepidus (cf.
IV.i.12–40), and readiness to condemn his own nephew to death
(IV.i.1–6), alienate the audience from him, while the brevity of his
appearances in the last two acts, when he is seen only in
conversation, preclude participation in his experience.

The distancing of Antony from the audience in the course of IV.i
prepares the way for the play's most remarkable shift of focus – that
from Antony to Cassius. Scenes ii and iii of Act IV swing back to the
conspirators, but it is not Brutus now but his fellow commander to
whom the members of the audience relate. Up to this point in the
play, Cassius has figured as the most arid and the most calculating
of the conspirators, opposed to Caesar, not because of the threat
that he posed to Rome, but from resentment that any man should be
regarded as superior to himself. In IV.iii, however, the 'lean and
hungry' Cassius (I.ii.191) of earlier acts becomes a much more
complex figure. The scene turns upon a quarrel between the two
leaders of the conspiracy over Cassius' apparent refusal to send
Brutus money to maintain his army, and at every stage of the
discussion it is Cassius who has the better of the argument, and who
emerges, to the audience's surprise, as in some respects the more

admirable man. The quarrel is initiated in IV.ii in terms which immediately overturn the spectator's assumptions about the characters of the two men. Cassius, whom the members of the audience have come to regard as the more circumspect of the joint leaders of the conspiracy, enters at the head of his army, and greets Brutus, before their troops, in the most heated terms, cf.

> Most noble brother, you have done me wrong,

(IV.ii.37)

and

> Brutus, this sober form of yours hides wrongs.

(IV.ii.40)

It is Brutus who reminds Cassius, in this scene, of the need to preserve a facade of unity before their followers, and who urges that the argument be continued in private, and it is with this private discussion that IV.iii deals. What takes place in this scene bears out the second of Cassius' accusations. Brutus roundly condemns his fellow commander for selling 'offices for gold' (11), but he also blames him for failing to send him 'gold to pay [his] legions' (76), claiming that he is unable to raise money by 'vile means' (71) himself. The double standard Brutus is seeking to maintain here serves to align the audience with Cassius, and this alignment is strengthened by the contemptuous tone in which Brutus speaks. When Cassius attempts, for example, to argue that he is the more experienced soldier of the two, and hence better fitted to manage their affairs, Brutus responds by challenging him to single combat, asserting initially that the other man has claimed to be his military superior, rather than his senior, and then brushing aside Cassius' repudiation of the charge with arrogant petulance:

> *Bru.* You say you are a better soldier:
>   Let it appear so; make your vaunting true,
>   And it shall please me well. For mine own part,
>   I shall be glad to learn of noble men.
> *Cas.* You wrong me every way; you wrong me, Brutus.   55

I said, an elder soldier, not a better:
Did I say better?
Bru.   If you did, I care not.

(IV.iii.51–7)

IV.iii is remarkable, moreover, not merely because it muddies the audience's perception of the relative worth of the principal conspirators but because it generates an emotion that appears, at first sight, to be in excess of that which the immediate situation warrants. Though this emotion is partly attributable to the pressures to which the two commanders are now subject, its deeper causes are shown to lie in personal relationships. From line 82 onwards these deeper causes begin to emerge through an exchange that throws an entirely fresh light upon the character of Cassius:

Cas.   I denied you not.
Bru. You did.
Cas.   I did not. He was but a fool.
    That brought my answer back. Brutus hath riv'd my heart.
    A friend should bear his friend's infirmities;   85
    But Brutus makes mine greater than they are.
Bru. I do not, till you practise them on me.
Cas. You love me not.
Bru.   I do not like your faults.
Cas. A friendly eye could never see such faults.
Bru. A flatterer's would not, though they do appear   90
    As huge as high Olympus.
Cas. Come, Antony, and young Octavius, come,
    Revenge yourselves alone on Cassius,
    For Cassius is aweary of the world:
    Hated by one he loves; brav'd by his brother;   95
    Check'd like a bondman; all his faults observ'd,
    Set in a note-book, learn'd and conn'd by rote,
    To cast into my teeth. O, I could weep
    My spirit from mine eyes! There is my dagger,
    And here my naked breast; within, a heart   100
    Dearer than Pluto's mine, richer than gold:
    If that thou be'st a Roman, take it forth.
    I, that denied thee gold, will give my heart:
    Strike, as thou didst at Caesar; for I know,

> When thou didst hate him worst, thou lov'dst him better 105
> Than ever thou lov'dst Cassius.

(IV.iii.82–106)

The cool, manipulating Cassius of the play's opening scenes gives place here to a highly emotional man. Whereas, up to this point, he appeared to be using Brutus in order to lend probity to the assassination, he now reveals an emotional dependence upon the other man that reverses the spectator's assumptions about their relative status in the conspiracy. Where Brutus appeared, in Acts I and II to be the pawn of Cassius' more acute intellect, Cassius now emerges as the victim of Brutus' personal magnetism – and the remainder of the scene makes plain that this flaw in his intellectual armour is to bring about his downfall. Unable to stand out against Brutus after their reconciliation (106–22), he agrees to engage Antony at Philippi (cf. 195–224), and thus commits the army to a battle that he knows has little chance of success. The Cassius who appears from this point is not the calculating master of political events who had figured in earlier scenes. He talks of his birthday (V.i.71–3), of his new belief in omens (V.i.77–89), of his short-sightedness (V.iii.21), and his friendship for Titinius (V.iii.34–5). All these details contribute to an image, not of an adroit public figure, but of a private individual, one with personal anxieties, limitations, and affections, to whom the members of the audience are encouraged to relate.

The shift of focus that Shakespeare engineers from scene to scene in this play is productive of a highly rewarding theatrical experience. Rather than allowing those outside the play world an insight into the factors governing the rise or fall of a single individual, or aligning the spectators with a 'cause', the play explores the ramifications of Caesar's death from a number of standpoints, undermining in the process the simplistic moral and political judgements that it invites. The assassination of Caesar emerges as both sacrifice and butchery depending upon the standpoint from which it is viewed, and the battle of Philippi as both a triumph and a disaster. Conspirators and avengers alike are revealed to be neither wholly good men, nor wholly bad, but complex human beings whose actions are shaped by a variety of pressures, rather than by consistent impulses towards good or evil. At the close of the play, it is not one human soul, or individual psyche, that has been explored, but the problem of defining right action in both public and private spheres, and the difficulty of passing judgement upon human beings.

A number of points about Shakespeare's projection of meaning through character may be extrapolated from a study of *Julius Caesar*. In the first place, the play demonstrates that the statement made by a dramatic work is not always to be equated with the experience of its titular 'hero'. Here a number of characters move into the spotlight as the action progresses, and it is from their different perspectives upon events that the meaning of the drama arises. In the second place, it is apparent from this play that the members of the audience are not always encouraged to relate to the characters of a Shakespearian drama in the same way throughout. Antony, for example, is presented as a young athlete in Act I, as a grieving individual in Act III, and as a hardened pragmatist and successful military leader in Acts IV and V. This progress is not, however, one in which the audience is encouraged to participate. Antony's inner self is revealed only in Act III, and the attachment to Caesar he exhibits there serves to prompt a re-consideration of the assassination, rather than to illuminate one phase of a psychological journey.

The technique of spotlighting characters who subsequently recede into the shadows, or have been presented externally at an earlier point, is used even more daringly in the late plays, and often occasions criticism of their structure. The first three acts of *The Winter's Tale*, for example, are dominated by the figure of Leontes, King of Sicilia, who accuses his innocent wife of adultery, brings about her (supposed) death, and that of his son, and orders his new-born daughter to be exposed on a foreign shore. The kind of dramatic language Leontes is assigned involves the reader or theatre-goer in his experience (see above, pp. 20ff.), while affording those outside the play world an insight into destructive impulses of which those around him are, initially, unaware. With Act III scene iii, however, the scene shifts from Sicilia to Bohemia, an entirely fresh group of characters is introduced, and it is not until V.i that the action returns to Sicilia and Leontes re-appears. The prominence of the Sicilian King in the first half of the play and his disappearance from the stage in later acts can be unsettling to the student of Shakespeare whose expectations are shaped by the study of *Hamlet* or *Macbeth*, but in fact, a careful reading of the opening scenes of *The Winter's Tale* reveals that Leontes is not foregrounded in quite the way that a summary of the plot, or a consideration of his soliloquies out of context, might seem to imply. The play opens, as demonstrated in Chapter 1, not with a naturalistic conversation designed to root the dramatis personae in the world of day-to-day experience, but with a highly formal exchange between two courtiers that is so super-polite it is extremely difficult to follow. Similarly, scene ii opens with an elaborate image of the comity of princes, enacted through a courteous interchange between a king and his hosts – the idiom of the two scenes combining to distance the play world from that of the spectator, and hence to frustrate dramatic involvement (see above, pp. 17ff.). At the same time, the information that is conveyed to the audience is of a highly unusual kind. Whereas in the majority of Shakespeare's plays the childhoods of the protagonists are rarely touched on, here the boyhood relationship and subsequent friendship between Leontes and Polixenes is emphasized (I.i.21–32), the former's courtship of his queen is recalled (I.ii.89–105), while his death is anticipated through an encomium upon his son, Mamillius (I.i.34–40). In the course of scenes i and ii, the members of the audience are thus presented not with a single Leontes but with a series of vignettes of the Sicilian King – the innocent child, frisking, like a lamb, in the sun; the earnest young suitor begging for Hermione's hand; the loving husband (the role in which he appears at the start of scene ii); and the jealous, middle-aged man, insanely tarnishing his relationship with his wife and his friend. These separate personae, moreover, effectively appear on stage simultaneously. Seeking, for example, to excuse to Hermione and Polixenes the perturbation his jealousy occasions, Leontes claims to have been moved by the likeness between himself and his son, completing a process of identification between man and boy that has been in train from the outset of the scene:

> How sometimes nature will betray its folly,
> Its tenderness, and make itself a pastime
> To harder bosoms! Looking on the lines
> Of my boy's face, methoughts I did recoil
> Twenty-three years, and saw myself unbreech'd, 155
> In my green velvet coat; my dagger muzzl'd
> Lest it should bite its master . . .
> . . . .
> How like, methought, I then was to this kernel,
> This squash, this gentleman. 160

(I.ii.151–60)

Here, the members of the audience are conscious of three Leontes-figures – Leontes the child, embodied in the boy, Mamillius; Leontes the devoted husband and friend (the role the King continues to play before Polixenes and Hermione); and Leontes the insanely jealous man (the persona so far revealed to the audience alone).

Like the formality of the dialogue, the presentation of individuals in terms of a succession of roles helps to distance the spectator from the passions displayed. While the tortured rhythms and idiosyncratic development of Leontes' soliloquies involve those outside the play world in the speaker's experience (see above, pp. 20ff.), the framework within which these speeches are set ensures that the audience remains aware that the experience of jealousy does not constitute the totality of Leontes' experience, but is merely one phase in the history of his life. The imagery employed in these scenes also contributes to this awareness. References to the visual and performing arts occur throughout the play, particularly at moments of tension. In I.ii, for example, Leontes remarks to his son:

> Go, play, boy, play: thy mother plays, and I
> Play too; but so disgrac'd a part, whose issue
> Will hiss me to my grave: contempt and clamour
> Will be my knell. Go, play, boy, play.   190

> (I.ii.187–90)

It is quite impossible for the members of an audience not to be aware, on hearing these lines, that they are spoken by an actor, and that the events that they are witnessing take place on a stage, and not at the court of Sicilia. The sudden disruption of 'the willing suspension of disbelief' helps to sustain the distance between play and spectator dictated by other aspects of the structure, while the emphasis on 'playing' contributes to the perception that sour middle age is one of the roles man plays in the course of his life. Imagery drawn from the natural world has a similar function. The rhythm of human life is assimilated to the cycle of the year, and the disruptive passions of Leontes thus emerge, not as an idiosyncratic response to a specific experience, but as one manifestation of a universal process.

The abrupt revelation discussed in Chapter 1 (see above pp. 20ff.) of the corrupt mind underlying the courtly facade is also important in determining the reader's or play-goer's response to the Sicilian

King. The members of the audience do not witness or participate in the growth of Leontes' jealousy. They are presented with his diseased opinions abruptly – and in full flower. The unexpected disclosure of his sexual obsessions serves to dislocate the dramatic action and thus helps to isolate the King's present stance from the other 'parts' or 'roles' enacted or recalled in the course of the scene. The Leontes who fulminates against his wife and his friend is not therefore seen as 'Leontes' in the absolute sense that a Lear or a Hamlet might be regarded as absolutes. The jealous man is one of the parts that the King plays in the course of his life, and the lack of a context for his suspicions helps to direct attention away from his psychology to the larger pattern of growth, decay and renewal which is the play's ultimate concern.

The opening scenes of *The Winter's Tale* are thus very different in their effect from the later acts of *Othello* in which, once again, a major character falls victim to sexual jealousy. The spectators remain aloof, to a much greater extent, from the passions that are exhibited, while the action as a whole is not 'now-centred' but enacts a cyclical process. Rather than serving to chart the disintegration of a personality, the tortured speeches of Leontes supply an explanation for one stage in a process; while the presentation of character in terms of a series of parts leaves scope for the role played by one character to be taken over by another. Seen from this perspective, the disappearance of the Sicilian King in Act IV ceases to be a problem. His consciousness is not the principal area of the action, and the recapitulation of his disruptive attitudes by Polixenes (IV.iv.418–42) enforces the cyclical structure of the drama rather than destroying its integrity.

Both *Julius Caesar* and *The Winter's Tale* depend for their effects upon the manipulation, by the dramatist, of the audience's stance towards the dramatis personae. In *Julius Caesar*, a shift of sympathy from one character to another allows those outside the play world to view the assassination of Caesar from a variety of perspectives, while the remarkable alternation between proximity and distance in *The Winter's Tale* enables the spectators to participate in a specific experience, while remaining aware of a universal process. Both plays are at a considerable remove from the kind of drama that focuses on a single psychology and can thus pose problems for a reader armed with a set of ready-made critical assumptions. *Coriolanus* – probably Shakespeare's most elaborate 'point of view' structure – can present even greater difficulties for the unwary student in that it appears to conform to conventional notions about the nature of tragedy. The play turns upon the career of the soldier, Caius Martius Coriolanus, who is banished from Rome for his arrogance towards the common people. Returning at the head of an army of Volsces, he is dissuaded from the sack of his native city by his mother, and consequently killed by his new-found allies who claim he has betrayed them. Considered in broad outline, the play appears to follow a familiar tragic pattern, in that it centres upon a single, exceptional figure who falls from the height of fortune through a 'fatal flaw' in his character, and learns something about his priorities before meeting a violent death. The experience of the play does not, however, bear out the expectations that a summary of the plot raises. Though Caius Martius is the focal point of the action throughout, the members of the audience are not encouraged to view events through his eyes, and are seldom implicated in his experience. He is rarely alone on stage; soliloquies are few; and the kind of dramatic language that he is assigned is expressive of an attitude, rather than indicative of the workings of a mind. At the same time, the significance of Coriolanus' career is far from clear cut. Where Macbeth's murder of Duncan is patently an onslaught upon the moral order of the universe, and Lear's division of his kingdom and banishment of his daughter are unequivocally misguided acts, Coriolanus' refusal to flatter the common people may be seen either as arrogance or a species of idealism, and this ambivalence is characteristic of the responses that the hero's conduct generates throughout. Similarly, whereas the members of a theatre audience have no difficulty in recognizing the desired goal of the action in *Hamlet*, *Lear*, or *Macbeth*, they have little sense of what constitutes an appropriate end for Coriolanus, and no means of assessing the degree of his success or failure. His death at the hands of his former allies is the product of a decision that the members of the audience can neither wholly commend nor wholly condemn; while his fall is instantly regretted by those who have occasioned it. Rather than experiencing a sense of pity and fear in the closing scenes, and leaving the theatre 'all passion spent', the spectator thus departs with a divided mind, unsure of the significance of what he or she has witnessed.

The distance between conventional notions about the nature of tragedy, and the experience of *Coriolanus* in the study or the theatre, is often taken as a measure of the play's failure. Once again, however, many of the problems that the play poses evaporate once

preconceptions are laid aside. The opening scene of the drama
plunges the audience into a divided world. The initial stage
direction, '*Enter a company of mutinous Citizens, with staves, clubs, and
other weapons*', implies a city divided against itself, and the opening
exchanges establish the degree to which concord has broken down.
Not only are plebians in arms against patricians, but the common
people themselves lack a single voice:

> *First Cit.* Before we proceed any further, hear me speak.
> *All.* Speak, speak.
> *First Cit.* You are all resolved rather to die than to
>   famish?
> *All.* Resolved, resolved.   5
> *First Cit.* First, you know Caius Martius is chief enemy
>   to the people?
> *All.* We know't, we know't.
> *First Cit.* Let us kill him, and we'll have corn at our own
>   price. Is't a verdict?   10
> *All.* No more talking on't; let it be done. Away,
>   away!
> *Second Cit.* One word, good citizens.
> *First Cit.* We are accounted poor citizens, the patricians
>   good. What authority surfeits on would relieve us.   15
>   If they would yield us but the superfluity while it
>   were wholesome, we might guess they relieved us
>   humanely; but they think we are too dear: the
>   leanness that afflicts us, the object of our misery, is
>   as an inventory to particularise their abundance;   20
>   our sufferance is a gain to them. Let us revenge
>   this with our pikes, ere we become rakes. For the
>   gods know, I speak this in hunger for bread, not in
>   thirst for revenge.
> *Second Cit.* Would you proceed especially against Caius   25
>   Martius?
> *All.* Against him first. He's a very dog to the com-
>   monalty.
> *Second Cit.* Consider you what services he has done for
>   his country?   30
> *First Cit.* Very well, and could be content to give him
>   good report for't, but that he pays himself with
>   being proud.

Second Cit. Nay, but speak not maliciously.

First Cit. I say unto you, what he hath done famously,   35
    he did it to that end: though soft-conscienced men
    can be content to say it was for his country, he did it
    to please his mother, and to be partly proud, which
    he is, even to the altitude of his virtue.

Second Cit. What he cannot help in his nature, you   40
    account a vice in him. You must in no way say he is
    covetous.

First Cit. If I must not, I need not be barren of accusa-
    tions. He hath faults, with surplus, to tire in
    repetition.   45

                                  (I.i.1–45)

The impression of unanimity created by the opening lines of this
scene is quickly undercut by the intervention of the Second Citizen.
The two principal speakers hold very different positions, and their
exchange complicates, rather than clarifies, the situation with which
the spectator is presented. For the First Citizen, the patricians in
general, and Caius Martius in particular, are exploiters of the
populace. Caius Martius is 'chief enemy to the people' (6–7), a 'dog to
the commonalty' (27–8), intoxicated with pride (38–9), and
motivated by devotion to his mother and lust for glory (35–9). The
Second Citizen, by contrast, sees Caius Martius as a notable public
servant (29–30), one whose pride cannot be accounted a vice (40–1),
and who is far from being covetous (41–2). The members of the
audience have no means of assessing these positions. It is disunity
that the scene enforces, and the nature of the dramatic language
contributes to the impression of a divided universe. The prose style
that is employed is heavily antithetical, both within and between
speeches, cf.

    I speak this in hunger for bread, not in
    thirst for revenge

                                 (23–4)

All.   He's a very dog to the com-
    monalty.

Second Cit. Consider you what services he has done for
    his country?   (27–30)

while negatives accumulate as the debate evolves:

> *Second Cit.* You must in no way say he is
>   covetous.
> *First Cit.* If I must not, I need not be barren of accusa-
>   tions. (41–4)

The entrance of Menenius Agrippa extends this image of disunity. Just as the plebians are divided in their estimate of the patricians, so, it appears, are the patricians in their estimate of the plebians. Menenius is hailed as,

> Worthy Menenius Agrippa, one that hath
> always loved the people,
>
> (I.i.50–1)

and the placatory tone in which he speaks appears to ally him with the citizens rather than with his own class. The entrance of Caius Martius at line 162 seems to confirm this judgement. He salutes the plebians not as 'good friends, . . . honest/neighbours' (I.i.61–2), like Menenius, but as 'dissentious rogues' (163), castigating them, in the most out-spoken terms, for what he regards as their vices:

>   What would you have, you curs,
>   That like nor peace nor war? The one affrights you,
>   The other makes you proud. He that trusts to you,
>   Where he should find you lions, finds you hares;   170
>   Where foxes, geese: you are no surer, no,
>   Than is the coal of fire upon the ice,
>   Or hailstone in the sun. Your virtue is,
>   To make him worthy whose offence subdues him,
>   And curse that justice did it. Who deserves greatness,   175
>   Deserves your hate; and your affections are
>   A sick man's appetite, who desires most that
>   Which would increase his evil. He that depends
>   Upon your favours, swims with fins of lead,
>   And hews down oaks with rushes. Hang ye! Trust ye?   180
>   With every minute you do change a mind,
>   And call him noble that was now your hate,
>   Him vile that was your garland. What's the matter,

That in these several places of the city,
You cry against the noble Senate, who   185
(Under the gods) keep you in awe, which else
Would feed on one another?

(I.i.167–87)

At this point in the scene some objective truths about the situation appear to have emerged. The citizens seem to have a legitimate grievance against Caius Martius, who manifestly abuses them, while Menenius appears to be a moderate man, attempting to mediate between opposed positions. The First Citizen, in short, seems at this stage, to be vindicated. What follows, however, completely overturns this assessment. Menenius reveals that his conciliatory stance towards the populace was merely a means of defusing a dangerous situation, and that his attitude to the plebians is as dismissive as that of his fellow patricians (I.i.200–2). He thus emerges as a much less honest man than Caius Martius, if a somewhat more politic one. Conversely, the news that the Volsces are in arms against Rome elicits a response from Caius Martius that bears out the Second Citizen's account of his character. Far from displaying overweening pride, he is content to take second place in the war to Cominius (I.i.235–8), while he displays a courage that commands respect. The plebians, by contrast, who appeared recklessly valiant at the start of the scene, 'steal away' (s.d. following 250) as soon as the possibility of fighting for Rome, rather than within it, is broached, undermining their hold on the audience's esteem, and validating Caius Martius' assessment of their corporate character. In brief, the scene as a whole not only exhibits a divided world, it elicits divided responses from the audience. The Rome that is presented here is at war, internally and externally, literally and metaphorically. The lack of consensus within and between classes implies an absence of shared values, and hence an environment in which stable judgements cannot be formulated, and 'truth' is reduced to a point of view.

The opening scene of the play establishes, therefore, that like Lear, Othello, or Macbeth, Caius Martius is a dominant figure in his community, but that unlike these characters he does not function in a world in which right action is clearly defined. Though he embraces war as a theatre for the exhibition of the masculine virtues, and dedicates himself to the service of Rome, his actions fail to win him the unqualified approval of his compatriots since courage and patriotism are no longer universally accepted ideals. *Corialanus* does not, however, focus upon the problems of decision-making that this lack of consensus poses for the protagonist. Unlike *Hamlet* which centres upon the mental processes of the Prince as he threads his way through a universe of dubiety and deceptive appearance, *Coriolanus* largely frustrates involvement with its central figure, who is presented reacting to events, rather than pondering their significance. Thus in I.i he is shown berating the mob and responding to the threat from the Volsces; in I.iv and I.vi he performs heroic actions on the battlefield; and in III.ii and V.iii he succumbs to his mother's persuasions. In all these instances the attitudes of the dramatis personae to the stances assumed by the central figure are as important as the reactions of Coriolanus himself, and as in I.i these responses prove to be highly divergent. The career of Coriolanus thus functions as a catalyst for the exposure of the relativity of truth, and the ambiguity of supposed absolutes, in a society lacking shared ideals and common aspirations. The point might be illustrated from virtually every scene, but V.iii affords a particularly striking example in that it deals with the most significant decision that Coriolanus makes – his renunciation of the sack of Rome. Here, Volumnia's successful attempt to persuade her son to place his family before his desire for vengeance should, theoretically, command the unqualified approbation of the audience, and elicit a sigh of relief, but in fact the spectator's response to what takes place is highly ambivalent. Volumnia herself is far from being a sympathetic figure. She has bred her son as a fighting machine, and her appeal to him to forgo his conquest is based on expediency, and represents the abrogation of the ideals she has inculcated, rather than the positive assertion of humane values. The Rome for which she pleads has shown itself to be an anarchic city devoid of courage or principle, and its deliverance is not therefore to be equated with the preservation of a centre of moral or spiritual values. Aufidius' silent presence throughout the interview between mother and son reminds those outside the play world that in saving Rome Coriolanus is breaking his word, and is thus both dishonouring himself and betraying the Volsces, while the participants in the scene respond in diametrically opposed ways to what has taken place. For Volumnia the preservation of Rome is the means whereby Coriolanus sustains his position as an honourable man (cf. V.iii.145–8 and 154–5), whereas for Aufidius it is the means by which he loses it (cf. V.iii.200–1). Similarly, both Volumnia and Aufidius leave the stage triumphant, the former because Rome is saved, the latter because Coriolanus is effectively destroyed. By the close of this scene it is neither the hero's personal triumph nor his defeat that the audience has experienced, but the difficulty of passing judgement on a world in which order has broken down, and the ambiguity of man's most cherished abstractions when brought into contact with specific situations.

To attempt to interpret *Coriolanus* in the light of *Hamlet*, or *Hamlet* in the light of *Julius Caesar* is a frustrating and unrewarding endeavour. Though all three plays are tragedies, in that they involve the deaths of their central figures and generate a sense of waste or loss, the theatrical experiences that they afford are radically different. The treatment of character varies from play to play, and an understanding of the way in which the dramatis personae function is crucial to the elucidation of meaning. In *Hamlet*, as shown in the previous chapter, the spectator is encouraged to participate in the Prince's experience throughout, while simultaneously judging the issues raised by his situation through a series of actions paralleling the events of the main plot. In *Julius Caesar*, by contrast, no single figure dominates the stage from beginning to end of the drama. A series of characters attract the sympathies of the audience as the action evolves, allowing those outside the play world to view the central situation from a variety of perspectives. In *Coriolanus*, though the play turns upon the career of one major character, it is not his psychological or spiritual progress that is the focus of attention, but the abstract ideas – ethical and political – which are raised by his interaction with the society in which he functions. Seen as a record of a personal experience, *Coriolanus* is an unyielding and problematic work; viewed as an exploration of unyielding problems, it is a satisfying experience.

No single paradigm can be adduced for the study of Shakespeare's characters. In the course of his theatrical career Shakespeare peopled his stage with a series of figures unparalleled in their diversity and complexity, and each of these creations constitutes one fragment of the meaning of his work. Nevertheless, some general observations can be extrapolated from the handful of characters considered above that might be useful to a student or relatively inexperienced reader confronted with an unfamiliar play for the first time. The most important point to bear in mind is that Shakespeare's plays do not conform to a single pattern. The dramatist constantly experimented with his medium, and this is as true of his handling of his characters as it is of every other aspect of his compositions. Faced with an unfamiliar work, the reader or theatre-goer should attempt to lay aside preconceptions about what constitutes a successful play, and should consider the way in which the composition is structured. A number of issues are important here. The degree to which the human personality is simplified is important in determining the degree of distance between the play world and the spectator, while the alignment of sympathy[1] dictates the perspective from which the events of the drama are viewed. Hence the spectator should ask him (or her) self whether the characters are stereotypes or idiosyncratic 'three-dimensional' creations, and whether those outside the play world are encouraged to observe them or to participate in their experience. He should consider whether the angle from which events are perceived remains constant throughout, and whether it is the individual or the process that is ultimately foregrounded. Above all, he should be aware that the whole burden of the meaning is never born by a single character. Shakespearian drama is structured upon a pattern of contrasts, and what a character is not is as important as what he is. Just as the precipitancy of Pyrrhus and Laertes illuminates Hamlet's procrastination, so Menenius' diplomacy highlights Coriolanus' out-spokenness, and the plebians' cowardice his courage. Though Rosalind, Falstaff and Macbeth haunt the imaginations of theatre-goers, the significance of those figures is not a product of their words and actions alone, but of what others are and do. Rosalind's worth is attested by the fact that she is neither Phebe on the one hand, nor Audrey on the other; Falstaff and Henry IV are very different tutors to an aspiring prince; and Macbeth is the antithesis of Duncan and Edward. In brief, the student should bear in mind that Shakespeare was a dramatist, not a portrait painter or a psychoanalyst, and that where meaning is concerned, the pattern may well be as important as the personality.

---

1. The term 'sympathy' in literary criticism is not synonymous with compassion but denotes involvement in a character's experience. The members of a theatre audience may thus be sympathetically aligned with a character for whom they feel no compassion.

7

The Use of the Soliloquy

There can be very few students of Shakespearian drama who have
not been alerted, at some point in their literary careers, to the
importance of soliloquies. School children are required to learn
them by heart; examination entrants are encouraged to base the
interpretation of entire plays upon them; while the close up camera,
in modern television productions, ensures that they are accorded
their full measure of audience attention and histrionic expertise. A
strict set of conventions is held to govern their use: they enact a
process of self-appraisal or introspection, and thus involve the
reader or spectator in the speaker's experience; they tell the truth as
far as the character concerned is able to perceive it; and they are
'overheard' by the spectators, rather than being overtly addressed
to them. The psychologically based handling of character and event
implicit in these 'rules' appeals, as noted in Chapter 5, to the
twentieth-century sensibility, fostering a character-orientated
approach to the plays, and affording the supreme illustration, for
many lovers of Shakespeare, of the dramatist's continuing relevance
or modernity.

In fact, though the use of the soliloquy is often seen as the means
whereby Shakespeare communicates most successfully across the
generations, the device itself was not a Shakespearian innovation.
In common with blank verse, thematic imagery, and parallel or
complementary action, the soliloquy formed part of the stock in
trade of the Renaissance dramatist, and was employed throughout
Elizabethan–Jacobean drama for a variety of effects. Like other
aspects of the dramatic composition, it was subject to a continuous
process of experimentation, and the 'conventions' popularly
supposed to circumscribe its use are not, therefore, universally
applicable. In common with his fellow playwrights, Shakespeare
employed the device in a variety of ways, and the attempt to
interpret his set-piece speeches in the light of a single set of criteria
can obscure the extraordinary range of speaker/listener
relationships that he engineers in the course of his career.

In the first place, paradoxical as it might appear at first sight, not

176

all monologues are soliloquies in the sense in which that term is generally understood. A character may enter, or remain alone on stage, in order to make observations that are designed to place those outside the play world in possession of information which is necessary to an understanding of the ensuing action, but which has no relevance to the personal situation of the speaker. Time, for example, in *The Winter's Tale*, opens Act IV with a speech that bridges a sixteen-year gap in the action, while Gower, in *Pericles*, punctuates the life-history of the play's eponymous hero with a series of speeches that transport the spectators from one location to another, and narrate events that cannot be enacted (see above, pp. 26–7). The opening lines of Act V of *Pericles* are typical of such passages:

> Marina thus the brothel 'scapes, and chances
> Into an honest house, our story says.
> She sings like one immortal, and she dances
> As goddess-like to her admired lays.
> Deep clerks she dumbs, and with her needle composes   5
> Nature's own shape, of bud, bird, branch, or berry,
> That even her art sisters the natural roses;
> Her inkle, silk, twin with the rubied cherry:
> That pupils lacks she none of noble race,
> Who pour their bounty on her; and her gain   10
> She gives the cursed bawd. Here we her place,
> And to her father turn our thoughts again,
> Where we left him on the sea. We there him lost,
> Whence, driven before the winds, he is arriv'd
> Here where his daughter dwells; and on this coast   15
> Suppose him now at anchor. The city striv'd
> God Neptune's annual feast to keep; from whence
> Lysimachus our Tyrian ship espies,
> His banners sable, trimm'd with rich expense;
> And to him in his barge with fervour hies.   20
> In your supposing once more put your sight;
> Of heavy Pericles, think this his bark,
> Where what is done in action, more, if might,
> Shall be discover'd; please you sit and hark.

(*Pericles*, V. Chorus 1–24)

Here, the speaker is clearly telling a story, rather than revealing an idiosyncratic mental state. He recounts the transference of Marina from the brothel to an 'honest house' (1–2), informs the spectators that Pericles has arrived in Mytilene (12–16), and that Lysimachus (the governor of the city) has put out in his barge to meet him (16–20). At the same time, Gower directs the responses of the audience towards the stage spectacle. He draws attention to the 'goddess-like' (4) properties of Marina, the iniquity of the bawd (11), and the continuing grief of Pericles (19 and 22). Far from breaking down the barrier between the play world and the spectator, the speaker here continually enforces it. His very appearance disrupts the process of enactment, reminding the members of the audience that they are watching a dramatized 'story' (2), while he constantly exhorts the onlookers to bring their imaginations into play (16 and 21–2), and stresses the fact that those he is addressing are spectators (24).

Gower's speech is obviously at a very considerable distance from the passages of introspection that are juxtaposed in *Hamlet* against the exaction of vengeance by the hero's fellow revengers, and the contrasting functions of the two kinds of utterance are readily apparent. In some cases, however, the long speeches Shakespeare assigns his characters are not as easily classified as these examples might suggest. In a number of plays characters who form an integral part of the play world and do not, like Gower, overtly mediate between the audience and the dramatic action, voice comments upon events that demonstrate an awareness of the spectator's presence. Petruchio's survey of his taming of Kate in *The Taming of the Shrew* illustrates the point:

> Thus have I politicly begun my reign,   175
> And 'tis my hope to end successfully.
> My falcon now is sharp and passing empty,
> And till she stoop she must not be full-gorg'd,
> For then she never looks upon her lure.
> Another way I have to man my haggard,   180
> To make her come and know her keeper's call,
> That is, to watch her, as we watch these kites
> That bate and beat and will not be obedient.
> She ate no meat today, nor none shall eat;
> Last night she slept not, nor tonight she shall not.   185
> As with the meat, some undeserved fault

I'll find about the making of the bed,
And here I'll fling the pillow, there the bolster,
This way the coverlet, another way the sheets.
Ay, and amid this hurly I intend   190
That all is done in reverend care of her.
And in conclusion she shall watch all night,
And if she chance to nod I'll rail and brawl,
And with the clamour keep her still awake.
This is a way to kill a wife with kindness,   195
And thus I'll curb her mad and headstrong humour.
He that knows better how to tame a shrew,
Now let him speak: 'tis charity to show.

(IV.i.175–98)

In this instance Petruchio is clearly not exploring his own
predicament or expressing his feelings in a manner that involves the
audience in his mental state. He is announcing his intentions to
those outside the play world in a highly non-naturalistic way, and
his awareness of the theatre audience is made plain by his direct
challenge to its male members in his concluding lines.

Even those speeches that are not overtly addressed to the
audience, and which are soliloquies in the commonly accepted
sense of the term, differ sharply in the ways in which they function
and the kind of information which they convey. Richard of
Gloucester's opening lines in *Richard III*, Macbeth's famous
soliloquies on the implications of the murder of Duncan and the
futility of human life (I.vii.1–28 and V.v.19–28), and Imogen's
lament in *Cymbeline* over the decapitated body she believes to be that
of her husband (IV.ii.291–332) are all, superficially, monologues of
the self-communing kind, yet they engage very different responses
in a theatre audience. Richard's wittily vicious lines merit quotation
in full:

Now is the winter of our discontent
Made glorious summer by this son of York;
And all the clouds that lour'd upon our House
In the deep bosom of the ocean buried.
Now are our brows bound with victorious wreaths,   5
Our bruised arms hung up for monuments,
Our stern alarums chang'd to merry meetings,

Our dreadful marches to delightful measures.
Grim-visag'd War hath smooth'd his wrinkled front:
And now, instead of mounting barbed steeds   10
To fright the souls of fearful adversaries,
He capers nimbly in a lady's chamber,
To the lascivious pleasing of a lute.
But I, that am not shap'd for sportive tricks,
Nor made to court an amorous looking-glass;   15
I, that am rudely stamp'd, and want love's majesty
To strut before a wanton ambling nymph:
I, that am curtail'd of this fair proportion,
Cheated of feature by dissembling Nature,
Deform'd, unfinish'd, sent before my time   20
Into this breathing world scarce half made up –
And that so lamely and unfashionable
That dogs bark at me, as I halt by them –
Why, I, in this weak piping time of peace,
Have no delight to pass away the time,   25
Unless to spy my shadow in the sun,
And descant on mine own deformity.
And therefore, since I cannot prove a lover
To entertain these fair well-spoken days,
I am determined to prove a villain,   30
And hate the idle pleasures of these days.
Plots have I laid, inductions dangerous,
By drunken prophecies, libels, and dreams,
To set my brother Clarence and the King
In deadly hate, the one against the other: 35
And if King Edward be as true and just
As I am subtle, false, and treacherous,
This day should Clarence closely be mew'd up
About a prophecy, which says that 'G'
Of Edward's heirs the murderer shall be –   40
Dive, thoughts, down to my soul: here Clarence comes.

(I.i.1–41)

It would be easy to be misled here into accepting this speech as a
piece of honest self-appraisal that initiates the audience into the
psychological causes of Richard's villainy, and thus promotes a high
degree of intimacy with, and understanding of, the speaker.

Richard comments, seemingly bitterly, upon his lack of aptitude for the arts of peace, and 'descants' (27) upon the deformity that bars him from normal human relationships. He appears, unlike Gower or Petruchio, to be addressing himself rather than the spectators, and he refers to his utterance as 'thoughts' (41) that must be concealed from others. Nevertheless, for all its introspective trappings, this speech is far from being a straightforward enactment of a thought process. In the first place, the mode in which Richard expresses himself is highly non-naturalistic. The syntax of the passage does not capture the ebb and flow of thought; it is formal, ordered – even patterned. The speech begins, for instance, with 'Now is'. This phrase is caught up in the 'Now are' of line 5, and re-echoed in the 'And now' of line 10. The recurring 'now' is then replaced by 'I'. Line 14 begins 'But I'; line 16 opens with 'I, that'; line 18 with 'I, that' again; and line 24 with 'Why, I'. In addition, lines 14, 16 and 18 follow the same syntactic pattern. Each begins with a pronoun, which is followed by a dependent clause consisting of a relative pronoun, a verbal phrase suggesting deficiency, an adjective (or modifier) and a noun, cf.

I, that am not shap'd for sportive tricks

(14)

I, that am rudely stamp'd, and want love's majesty

(16)

I, that am curtail'd of this fair proportion.

(18)

This kind of linguistic patterning is characteristic of the passage as a whole. Lines 6, 7, and 8, for example, begin with a possessive adjective, which is followed by an adjective, a noun, a verb (or implied verb as in line 8) and a prepositional phrase, cf.

Our bruised arms hung up for monuments

(6)

Our stern alarums chang'd to merry meetings

(7)

Our dreadful marches to delightful measures.

(8)

Not only do these lines match one another, but each is highly structured within itself. A strong sense of balance is produced in lines 7 and 8, for example, by the positioning of an adjective followed by a noun in both halves of the line, while the symmetry of the construction is enhanced by the use of alliteration – cf. 'dreadful marches/delightful measures' (8). Sounds are echoed, too, between, as well as within, lines. 'Arms' in line 6 is caught up in 'alarums' in the same position in line 7, while the concluding word of all three lines starts with the letter 'm' and is di- or polysyllabic. And these devices are not confined to this passage. Alliteration is rife throughout the speech – cf. 'lascivious pleasing of a lute' (13), 'piping time of peace' (24), 'descant on mine own deformity' (27) – and a high degree of syntactic patterning is evident to the close – cf. 'To entertain these fair well-spoken days' (29) / 'And hate the idle pleasures of these days' (31).

Richard, then, appears to be, or is superficially presented as, a specific individual engaged in talking to himself, but he does not talk in the way in which a man would naturally talk (or think) when alone. His soliloquy is far too structured to create the illusion of natural speech, and it keeps the reader or theatre-goer remote from the psychology of the speaker by the formality of its execution. Moreover, the things which Richard says are themselves surprising if this soliloquy is to be taken as a naturalistic representation of a mind at work. Rather than pondering his situation, for example, he repeatedly informs himself of things which he already knows. His opening lines –

Now is the winter of our discontent
Made glorious summer by this son of York;
And all the clouds that lour'd upon our House
In the deep bosom of the ocean buried –

(1–4)

could conceivably be accounted for naturalistically as a mental survey of the political scene, but such lines as 'I am determined to prove a villain' (30) and 'Plots have I laid, inductions dangerous' (32) are non-naturalistic in the extreme. Richard has no need to inform himself of his own resolutions, they are part of his mental equipment, and though he might mull over his plots with satisfaction, he is unlikely to have to remind himself of their drift. These lines cannot be said to create the illusion of an individual communing with himself, nor do they oblige the spectator to deduce the situation as the speaker's mind revolves around a specific predicament. It is the members of the audience who are addressed here, and they are being engineered into the position of confidants, to whom all Richard's projects are to be disclosed.

It is not only the superfluous nature of much of what Richard says, however, that militates against the psychological credibility of his pronouncements; his self-conscious dedication to evil is equally significant. Evil is generally embraced as a personal good, rather than as outright iniquity, yet Richard makes no attempt to convince himself of the inherent propriety of his conduct. Instead, such statements as 'I am determined to prove a *villain*' (30) and '*Plots* have I laid, *inductions* dangerous' (32) suggest that he is engaged, not in justifying his actions, but in defining, or, more appropriately perhaps, casting himself as a familiar dramatic type – the stage villain – whose activity is analogous to that of the dramatist himself. This emphasis upon the mechanics of play-acting heightens the audience's awareness of the stage spectacle as art, rather than life, while Richard's presentation of his character in terms of a role subverts his portrayal as a complex human being. These references thus serve to establish the speaker not as a rounded human being locked in the exploration of his own motives, but as a dramatic type, engaged in enunciating the credo appropriate to an embodiment of one pole of a stylized opposition between good and evil – cf.

And if King Edward be as true and just
As I am subtle, false, and treacherous.

(36–7)

Even the evolution of ideas in the course of the soliloquy works against the illusion that the audience is witnessing a mind at work. The speech does not follow the ebb and flow of thought; it functions as a reasoned argument, and everything within it is logical and orderly. It begins with the present situation ('Now'), contrasts the behaviour implied by that situation with the nature of the speaker ('But' (14)), draws a conclusion from the opposition between the two ('therefore' (28)), and closes with a course of action derived from the initial premise ('Plots have I laid, inductions dangerous' (32)). This kind of structuring of ideas could not be further removed from the compressions and omissions, the short-hand leaps and tangental starts of the human mind. Rather than initiating the audience into the unique workings of an idiosyncratic psychology by its associative development or unusual imagery, the speech distances the reader or listener by its rationality, intriguing the intellect rather than engaging the emotions. At the close of the passage, it is Richard's glib immorality upon which the attention of the audience is focused, not the mentality from which that immortality has sprung.

The total effect of this soliloquy is a complex one. On the one hand, since Richard sets the scene, describes his own character and motives, and outlines the first stage of his plans, it promotes a high degree of intimacy between speaker and listener, establishing the former as the stage manager of the play's events, and the latter as his fellow conspirator, or confidant. On the other hand, the highly organized nature of the utterance ensures that the spectator remains aloof from the inner world of the speaker, though formally apprised of his motivation. The patterned nature of the dramatic language establishes an idiom that distances the play world from that of the spectator, initiating a style of speech that is to build in subsequent scenes towards a ritual chanting that robs the individual of distinctive personality (cf. IV.iv.35–45). The imagery of the speech, too, directs the attention of the audience towards a cyclical process rather than towards an idiosyncratic mentality. The opening lines –

Now is the winter of our discontent
Made glorious summer by this son of York –

(1–2)

evoke the rhythmic alternation of the seasons, suggesting that the summer sun shining at the outset of the play on the house of York will inevitably give place to winter. Even the final lines of the speech, with their gnomic prophecy (38–40) point to the operation of forces outside the will of the protagonist, directing the attention of the audience away from the personality of Richard towards the process in which he is caught up. In short, for all the proximity between speaker and listener that these lines engineer, they do not serve to usher those outside the play world into a unique psychology. They set up a conspiratorial relationship between the central figure and the spectator, while initiating an awareness of the retributive pattern into which that figure's existence is ultimately subsumed.

Superficially, Richard's opening lines and Macbeth's long speech prior to the murder of Duncan have much in common. Both speakers are trusted kinsmen of the reigning monarch, both have aspirations to the throne, and both are engaged in pondering an immoral course of conduct. In execution, however, and hence in effect, the two speeches are strikingly different:

Macb[eth]. If it were done, when 'tis done, then 'twere well
  It were done quickly: if th'assassination
  Could trammel up the consequence, and catch
  With his surcease success; that but this blow
  Might be the be-all and the end-all – here,   5
  But here, upon this bank and shoal of time,
  We'd jump the life to come. – But in these cases,
  We still have judgment here; that we but teach
  Bloody instructions, which, being taught, return
  To plague th'inventor: this even-handed Justice   10
  Commends th'ingredience of our poison'd chalice
  To our own lips. He's here in double trust:
  First, as I am his kinsman and his subject,
  Strong both against the deed; then, as his host,
  Who should against his murtherer shut the door,   15
  Not bear the knife myself. Besides, this Duncan
  Hath borne his faculties so meek, hath been
  So clear in his great office, that his virtues
  Will plead like angels, trumpet-tongu'd, against
  The deep damnation of his taking-off;   20
  And Pity, like a naked new-born babe,
  Striding the blast, or heaven's Cherubin's, hors'd
  Upon the sightless couriers of the air,
  Shall blow the horrid deed in every eye,
  That tears shall drown the wind. – I have no spur   25

> To prick the sides of my intent, but only
> Vaulting ambition, which o'erleaps itself
> And falls on th'other –

                                              (I.vii.1–28)

There is no sign in this speech of the elaborate patterning at work throughout the opening lines of *Richard III*. Instead, the movement of the passage approximates to the rhythms of the speaking voice, with the regularity and balance of the blank verse line under-cut by the use of enjambement (cf. 1–5, 16–20, 25–7), variation in the position of the caesura (cf. 2, 13, 21, 26), and metrical inversion (cf. 9, 13, 14). Light and prepositional endings help to thrust the reader on from one line to the next (cf. 17, 19), creating the illusion that the speaker's mind is racing faster than he can speak, while the unobtrusive alliteration suggests the mind grappling with related ideas (cf. 'surcease success' (4)) rather than reinforcing a sense of design.

The very movement of this passage, then, unlike that of previous examples, together with its lack of overtly decorative or 'poetic' features, is designed to convince those outside the play world that they are witnessing the enactment of a thought process rather than listening to the enunciation of a position. And the naturalism of the passage is not confined to its verse structure. From Macbeth's opening words it is clear that the speaker is talking, not to the audience, but to himself, and considerable mental agility is required on the part of the spectator in order to keep pace with him. Where Richard spells out the situation that forms the back-drop to his decisions –

> Now is the winter of our discontent
> Made glorious summer by this son of York –

                                              (1–2)

Macbeth enters already engaged in the process of thinking, obliging the reader or spectator to deduce what it is that he is thinking about, rather than listening passively to what he has to say. The lines 'If it were done, when 'tis done, then 'twere well / It were done quickly' (1–2) involve a series of deductions or mental leaps on the part of the audience that must be performed in an instant if the significance of what follows is to be grasped. The initial 'it' has to be expanded into the murder of Duncan; the implied doubt over whether or not the deed would be 'done' (i.e. completed) when it is 'done' (i.e. performed) has to be interpreted in pragmatic or metaphysical terms (i.e. will there be repercussions in the political sphere, or after death?), while the need for speed, ("twere well / It were done quickly') has to be explained in terms of expediency or wavering resolution. There is no question here of Macbeth talking to himself about things which he already knows. He is able to refer to Duncan's death as 'it' (1) because his mind is already running upon the murder, while the phrase 'If it were done, when 'tis done' (1) has all the compression of a mind engaged in fusing a number of complex ideas in a single perception.

It is not merely the compressed allusiveness of the passage, however, that convinces the members of the audience that they are in the presence of a unique individual involved in grappling with a specific problem. The evolution of the speaker's ideas is also highly idiosyncratic and at a considerable remove from the rationality of *Richard III*. Where Richard of Gloucester's speech takes the form of a logical disquisition, Macbeth's consists of a series of intensely realized visual images, and it is the association between one mental picture and the next which gives the passage its cohesiveness, not its dialectical structure. The lines

> if th'assassination
> Could trammel up the consequence, and catch
> With his surcease success

(2–4)

have all the tautness of 1–2 discussed above, and their density of meaning is heightened by the ambiguity of 'his surcease' (4) which could apply equally to the consequences of Duncan's death or the murder itself. But Macbeth's mind is not working in terms of concepts; it is visualizing images, and the pictures which he conjures up draw together all the possible implications of the lines and communicate them simultaneously. He is imagining the act of murder as a huntsman trapping his prey in the folds of a net and thus encompassing all his desires by means of a single action. What is significant about the image is that in the moment that it forms in Macbeth's imagination it evolves into another, as the mental picture itself triggers further ideas associated with the deed. Thus, the act of assassination becomes first a huntsman entrammelling his prey – and then a fisherman killing it:

> that but this blow
> Might be the be-all and the end-all – here,   5
> But here, upon this bank and shoal of time.

(4–6)

This development is logically fallacious – the act of murder cannot perform a blow – but the linked images have an imaginative truth, in that they convey the ability of the mind to envisage a deed as both performed and being performed simultaneously. The reader or spectator is allowed no time, in any case, to ponder the rationality of the utterance. By line 5 the speaker's mind has already begun to focus, not upon the fisherman/huntsman's actions, but upon his location. The 'banks' (6) upon which the blow is struck emerge, in his imagination, as the sands of time – pushing his mind towards ideas of death, and to the temporal judgement which generates the images of the succeeding lines.

The kind of associative development at work in this passage is evident throughout the entire soliloquy. Whereas it is possible to predict the tenor of Richard's argument from the moment that he announces his antipathy to the present age, it is impossible to anticipate the point towards which Macbeth's deliberations tend, since the route by which that point is reached is highly personal and tangental. In order to understand the progress from 'If it were done' (1) to 'And falls on th'other' (28), the reader or spectator is obliged to live through the process of thinking with the protagonist, filling out the gaps in his utterance, and visualizing that which he visualizes. As a result, those outside the play world are drawn into the experience of the speaker, inhabiting his imaginative world with him, rather than merely listening, passively, to the information he conveys. Where Richard *tells* the members of the audience that he is 'determined to prove a villain' (30), Macbeth allows them to experience the agony of becoming one.

The kinds of information that the two soliloquies convey is also radically different. Richard's speech, as noted above, is designed to establish a particular kind of intimacy between the protagonist and the spectator, and the communication of factual information is an essential element in this process. The relationship between the central figure and the audience is a conspiratorial one, and it is towards the sharing of knowledge that the opening speech is geared. Richard confides his motives, his character, and the steps he has already taken towards his goal, enabling those outside the play world to view his subsequent actions from a position of awareness superior to that of those within it. Macbeth's speech, by contrast, is designed to initiate the audience into the workings of a specific mind, and the information that emerges in the course of the speech consequently relates, not to the political situation, but to the speaker himself. While Macbeth believes himself to be engaged in trying to decide whether to commit a murder, the means by which he thinks, and the images which he employs, are revealing the kind of man that he is, to an audience of which he isn't aware. For example, although as a soldier, he is accustomed to the sight of death and inured to physical violence, his attitude to the murder of Duncan is far from casual. Instead of concentrating, as one might expect, upon the practical problems attendant upon the deed, he focuses almost exclusively upon its moral, and ultimately metaphysical, implications. His proposed victim takes shape in his imagination, not as a human obstacle in his path to the crown, but as the embodiment of the bonds that bind society together – the bond between monarch and subject, kinsman and kinsman, host and guest. Even more significantly, he sees the repercussions of his proposed rupture of those bonds as extending far beyond the human framework of reference. For him, the murder of a virtuous king is an action that plunges the whole universe into turmoil and perturbation. Where Richard's survey of his position concludes with a cool appraisal of the events he has set in train, Macbeth's thought journey reaches a climax in an apocalyptic vision of an entire cosmos ringing with the knowledge of his deed and engulfed in grief by it:

> Besides, this Duncan
> Hath borne his faculties so meek, hath been
> So clear in his great office, that his virtues
> Will plead like angels, trumpet-tongu'd, against
> The deep damnation of his taking-off;   20
> And Pity, like a naked new-born babe,
> Striding the blast, or heaven's Cherubins, hors'd
> Upon the sightless couriers of the air,

Shall blow the horrid deed in every eye,
That tears shall drown the wind.   25

(16–25)

The nature of Macbeth's response is crucial to an understanding
of his tragedy. His soliloquy reveals that he is a highly imaginative
man – one prone to think in terms of visual images – and his feverish
creation of mental pictures prepares the audience for his vision of
the air-borne dagger, and his susceptibility to Banquo's ghost. At
the same time the reader or spectator is made aware that the
psychology of the speaker is at a considerable remove from that of
the conventional stage villain. He has a highly developed moral
nature, and is agonizingly aware of the implications of his actions in
the spiritual realm. For Macbeth, the arena in which the action is
played out is not Scotland but the entire cosmos, and the terms in
which he envisages the consequences of his deed bear witness to
the extent to which he is violating his own moral nature in
contemplating the murder of Duncan.

The very different relationships between speaker and audience
that the opening lines of *Richard III* and Macbeth's soliloquy in I.vii
promote are fundamental to the contrasting experiences offered by
the two dramas, and the very different kinds of tragedy that they
represent. *Richard III* is concerned with a historical process and its
focus is upon cause and effect, while *Macbeth* traces the destruction
of a human soul and centres upon the inner life of individuals. A
comparison between the speeches discussed above and the
soliloquies that occur towards the close of the two plays highlights
this difference. Both central characters encounter ill-omens before
their defeat in battle and are led to consider the nature of their lives.
Richard's speech is too long to quote in full, but the opening lines are
typical of the passage as a whole. He has been visited, while asleep,
by the ghosts of his victims and wakens uncharacteristically fearful
and self-questioning:

Give me another horse! Bind up my wounds!
Have mercy, Jesu! – Soft, I did but dream.
O coward conscience, how dost thou afflict me!   180
The light burns blue; it is now dead midnight.
Cold fearful drops stand on my trembling flesh.
What do I fear? Myself? There's none else by;

Richard loves Richard, that is, I and I.
Is there a murderer here? No. Yes, I am!   185
Then fly. What, from myself? Great reason why,
Lest I revenge? What, myself upon myself?
Alack, I love myself. Wherefore? For any good
That I myself have done unto myself?
O no, alas, I rather hate myself   190
For hateful deeds committed by myself.
I am a villain – yet I lie, I am not!
Fool, of thyself speak well! Fool, do not flatter.
My conscience hath a thousand several tongues,
And every tongue brings in a several tale,   195
And every tale condemns me for a villain.

(V.iii.178–96)

Like the soliloquy which opens the play, this speech has some of the
trappings of a naturalistic response to experience. The broken
rhythm of the opening lines suggests a moment of confusion on
emerging from sleep, while the succession of exclamations creates
the illusion of the speaking voice. But after the first five lines the
highly organized nature of the utterance becomes apparent. There is
considerable play on the words 'I' and 'myself' (cf. 183–7), for
example; antithetical balance occurs within the line (cf. 'Fool, of
thyself speak well! Fool, do not flatter' (193)); while syntactic
patterning becomes increasingly marked, cf.

And every tongue brings in a several tale,
And every tale condemns me for a villain.

(195–6)

At the same time, the representation of conflicting impulses within
the human personality by means of a debate, together with the
speaker's awareness of himself as a 'villain' (192), work against the
superficial naturalism of the passage, distancing the spectator from
the inner life of the protagonist, who emerges as a being engaged in
talking *of* rather than *to* himself. In short, for all the perturbation that
it evinces, this speech does not initiate the audience into a mind
contaminated by the performance of bloody deeds. It sustains the
intimacy between the central figure and the spectator established at

the outset, but its interest lies, not in the psychological progress of the protagonist, but in the possible repercussions of Richard's loss of resolution in the forthcoming battle.

In *Macbeth* exactly the opposite is the case; the inner life of the character is all-important, and the outcome of the battle almost an irrelevance. In this instance it is the death of the protagonist's wife that provides the impetus to soliloquize:

> She should have died hereafter:
> There would have been a time for such a word. –
> To-morrow, and to-morrow, and to-morrow,
> Creeps in this petty pace from day to day,   20
> To the last syllable of recorded time;
> And all our yesterdays have lighted fools
> The way to dusty death. Out, out, brief candle!
> Life's but a walking shadow; a poor player,
> That struts and frets his hour upon the stage,   25
> And then is heard no more: it is a tale
> Told by an idiot, full of sound and fury,
> Signifying nothing.

> (V.v.17–28)

The internal organization of this speech clearly aligns it with the soliloquy in I.vii discussed above. The use of enjambement (26–7), variation in the position of the caesura (cf. 19, 23, 25), and departures from the regular iambic pattern (cf. 20, 23, etc.), all help to suggest the speaking voice as against a poetic set-piece, while the utterance evolves once again through a series of vividly realized visual images, rather than through reasoned argument – suggesting the same kind of mind at work as in I.vii. The images themselves, however, contrast forcibly with those of the earlier speech, and it is in the distance between them that Macbeth's tragedy lies. The similes and metaphors employed are uniformly reductive. The succession of days that go to make up a life are seen in terms of slow movement without consequence (19–20); time has become a written account with a clearly defined end (21); existence is conceived as an uncomprehending progress towards a death that is perceived only in terms of dissolution (22–3); life is brief, insubstantial, illusory – a matter of candles and shadows – (24–5); a man's role in the world is analogous to that of an actor in a play, and he ceases to exist when he leaves the temporal stage (24–6); while human actuality is devoid of design, meaning, or purpose, a mere 'tale / Told by an idiot' rather than a product of the divine (26–8).

The contrast between these images and those of I.vii could hardly be more striking. In the earlier speech the figures in Macbeth's mental drama are dynamic, and their movements are positive. His actors are engaged in catching (3), jumping (7), pleading (19), striding (22), blowing (24). By contrast, the little movement that takes place in V.v is feeble and pointless – cf. 'creeps' (20), 'struts' (25), 'frets' (25). A similar pattern is evident in terms of sound. In I.vii Macbeth's imaginative universe rings with angel-like voices, pleading 'trumpet-tongu'd' (19) against the murder of Duncan, while in V.v human existence as a whole has become the inconsequential babble of an idiot (26–8). Above all, the actions performed in the inner world of the Macbeth of I.vii have consequences in a vast cosmic arena. To bear a knife against an anointed monarch is to set in motion a train of events that will send cherubim coursing to every corner of a universe in which heaven and hell are ultimate realities. In V.v human action has no significance in cosmic terms. The arena in which man acts out his life has dwindled from a boundless metaphysical universe to an earthly stage, and no existence beyond the temporal is envisaged.

The part played by the soliloquy in the structure of this drama is clearly very different from that played by the comparable passages of *Richard III*. As noted above, Richard's solo performances are designed to establish a conspiratorial relationship between villain and spectator and to direct the attention of those watching the play to the speaker's role as instigator, and ultimately victim, of events. In *Macbeth*, by contrast, the protagonist's moments of introspection encourage the members of the audience to participate in his situation, and they thus enable those outside the play world both to chart and to experience the progressive dereliction of his inner life – a dereliction that bears witness to the moral atrophy that he suffers as a consequence of his deed. Where the tragedy of Richard of Gloucester lies in worldly failure and death, the tragedy of Macbeth lies in the dichotomy between what he is and what he does, and between what he was and what he becomes, and it is this dichotomy which the soliloquy enables the spectator to comprehend.

The passages from *Richard III* and *Macbeth* quoted above exemplify two very different kinds of dramatic set-piece in that they differ markedly in the species of intimacy between speaker and listener that they engineer. In one respect, however, the two are similar, in that they represent a kind of dramaturgy in which the members of the audience and the protagonist share a common level of perception. In a number of Shakespeare's plays, the information possessed by the spectator does not accord with that possessed by the dramatis personae, and this discrepancy produces a type of soliloquy that, once again, is much more complex in its effect than the 'rules' outlined at the start of this chapter allow. Imogen's lines in *Cymbeline* on waking from a drugged sleep and finding a headless body she takes to be that of her husband afford a particularly interesting example of this class of utterance:

> *Imo.* [*Awakes*] Yes sir, to Milford-Haven, which is the way?
>   I thank you: by yond bush? pray, how far thither?
>   'Ods pittikins: can it be six mile yet?
>   I have gone all night: faith, I'll lie down and sleep.
>   But, soft! no bedfellow! O gods and goddesses!   295
>   [*Seeing the body of Cloten.*]
>   These flowers are like the pleasures of the world;
>   This bloody man, the care on't. I hope I dream:
>   For so I thought I was a cave-keeper,
>   And cook to honest creatures. But 'tis not so:
>   'Twas but a bolt of nothing, shot at nothing,   300
>   Which the brain makes of fumes. Our very eyes
>   Are sometimes like our judgements, blind. Good faith,
>   I tremble still with fear: but if there be
>   Yet left in heaven as small a drop of pity
>   As a wren's eye, fear'd gods, a part of it!   305
>   The dream's here still: even when I wake it is
>   Without me, as within me: not imagin'd, felt.
>   A headless man? The garments of Posthumus?
>   I know the shape of's leg: this is his hand:
>   His foot Mercurial: his Martial thigh: 310
>   The brawns of Hercules: but his Jovial face –
>   Murder in heaven! How – ? 'Tis gone. Pisanio,
>   All curses madded Hecuba gave the Greeks,
>   And mine to boot, be darted on thee! Thou,
>   Conspir'd with that irregulous devil, Cloten,   315
>   Hast here cut off my lord. To write, and read
>   Be henceforth treacherous! Damn'd Pisanio
>   Hath with his forged letters (damn'd Pisanio)

From this most bravest vessel of the world
Struck the main-top! O Posthumus, alas,   320
Where is thy head? where's that? Ay me! where's that?
Pisanio might have kill'd thee at the heart,
And left this head on. How should this be, Pisanio?
'Tis he, and Cloten: malice and lucre in them
Have laid this woe here. O, 'tis pregnant, pregnant!   325
The drug he gave me, which he said was precious
And cordial to me, have I not found it
Murd'rous to th'senses? That confirms it home:
This is Pisanio's deed, and Cloten – O!
Give colour to my pale cheek with thy blood,   330
That we the horrider may seem to those
Which chance to find us. O, my lord! my lord!

(*Cymbeline*, IV.ii.291–332)

From the start of this scene, the members of the audience are
predisposed to respond positively to the plight of the speaker. She is
a loyal and virtuous wife, who has been unjustly repudiated by the
husband she loves, and she has given convincing proof in the course
of the play of her capacity for action and powers of endurance. Both
the immediate context and subject matter of her speech are moving.
She has been left for dead by those with whom she had found
shelter; her only companion is a headless corpse; and in the course
of her soliloquy she becomes convinced that the body beside her is
that of her husband. The stage spectacle itself invites compassion,
and the pathos of the situation is heightened by the heroine's youth
and her isolation.

At first sight the soliloquy also appears to promote a process of
identification with the speaker. The lines are clearly designed to
create the illusion of natural speech, and to convince those outside
the play world that the heroine is talking to herself rather than
addressing an onlooker. Enjambement is frequent and insistent (cf.
303–4, and 306–7); variation in the position of the caesura makes it
very hard for the listener to be sure where the lines begin and end
(cf. 301–7); while metrical irregularities (cf. 307, 320, 327), feminine
endings (cf. 323, 325) and light endings (cf. 327, 331) abound.
Sentences are short, frequently exclamatory, and strikingly simple
(cf. 'But, soft! no bedfellow!' (295), 'A headless man?' (308), 'How
should this be, Pisanio?' (323)), while the vocabulary throughout is

familiar, with mild oaths (e.g. "Ods pittikins' (293)) and occasional elisions (e.g. 'The dream's here still' (306), and 'I know the shape of's leg' (309)) stressing the informality of the utterance. In short, in terms of its organization, the passage is manifestly dramatic rather than poetic, designed to enact experience as in *Macbeth* rather than to expatiate upon it as in *Richard III*.

The evolution of ideas in the course of the speech also works to create the illusion of a spontaneous response to experience, drawing the reader or listener into the inner world of the speaker, rather than imposing dramatic distance. Imogen wakes from her drugged sleep slowly, and her perception of the full horror of her situation is far from instantaneous. Her opening words are spoken before she is fully awake, and a full understanding of them is dependent upon the audience's readiness to enter imaginatively her dream. It is not until line 295 that she becomes aware of the body of Cloten, and her subsequent lines show her struggling to distinguish between dream and substance rather than responding at once to the corpse itself. Her initial awareness of the dead man is revealed, not by an explicit statement, but by an exclamation suggesting first surprise, and then horror – 'But, soft! no bedfellow! O gods and goddesses!' (295) – while her physical responses are implied in 'The dream's here still' (306), which suggests that her initial reaction to the corpse had been to close her eyes. Her 'recognition' of the dead man comes only after this second and fuller awakening, and once again, dawning understanding and stage action are charted simultaneously. Her first impression is a general one. She recognizes that the body beside her is that of a man, and it is the fact that he has been decapitated that – naturally enough – impresses itself upon her first. Unable to identify the corpse by its face, she turns to its clothes, and it is only at this point that fear and horror give place to more active concern, grief, and finally anger. Recognizing the garments of Posthumus, she begins a hectic examination of the corpse, the urgency of which is suggested by the increasing brevity of her exclamations as her conviction that the body is that of her husband grows:

> I know the shape of's leg: this is his hand:
> His foot Mercurial: his Martial thigh: 310
> The brawns of Hercules: but his Jovial face –
> Murder in heaven! How – ? 'Tis gone. Pisanio –'

(309–12)

The tumult of emotion that follows the recognition of the corpse is also enacted rather than stated. A succession of short phrases and tangental starts (cf. 'To write, and read / Be henceforth treacherous' (316–17)) convey the wild racing of the mind as it attempts to come to terms with a situation, while the abrupt shifts of thought and emphasis (cf. 'How should this be, Pisanio? / 'Tis he, and Cloten: malice and lucre in them / Have laid this woe here' (323–5)) compel the reader or listener to fill in the gaps of the utterance, and thus implicate those outside the play world in the speaker's experience.

Up to this point, it would appear that Imogen's lament over 'Posthumus' constitutes a further example of the kind of soliloquy exemplified by *Macbeth*, I.vii.1–28. The speaker is clearly communing with herself rather than the audience, and is engaged in grappling with a specific, and peculiarly painful, event. She speaks the truth as far as she knows it, and the reader or listener is drawn into her experience by sharing the process of thinking with her. The rhythm of her utterance is governed by the tempo of the emotions rather than the poetic form, while her ideas are organized in a way that convinces the spectator that he or she is witnessing a mind at work. Nevertheless, the total effect of the speech is very different from that of the superficially similar lines already discussed. As noted above, throughout Macbeth's agonized exploration of the implications of murdering Duncan the spectator's level of awareness is identical with that of the speaker. The plan to kill the King is an objective reality, and the immorality of the deed beyond dispute. The concern that acts may have repercussions on a metaphysical, as well as a physical, plane is a universal one, and has immediate relevance to Macbeth's tragedy. In *Cymbeline*, by contrast, there is a considerable discrepancy between the audience's level of awareness and the speaker's. Whereas, taken out of context, the speech appears to invite total identification with the central figure, returned to its place within the dramatic structure its effect becomes much more complex. Prior to this scene, the audience has not viewed the events of the play world exclusively through Imogen's eyes. Her appearances have been relatively few, and the spectators have been presented with a series of events of which the heroine herself has no knowledge. Among these is an encounter between Pisanio and Cloten (III.v.81–163) establishing the absolute fidelity of the former, and revealing the latter's intention to ravish Imogen while dressed in her husband's clothes; and a quarrel between Cloten and Guiderius (IV.ii.70–100) resulting in the former's death and decapitation. Thus, from the moment that Cloten's body is brought to the place where Imogen has been laid out for dead, the members of the audience anticipate the mistake that is to ensue and the suffering that will be caused by it.

On one level, the superior knowledge of the audience serves both to heighten the tension generated by the opening lines of the speech, and to increase the pathos of the scene as a whole. The spectator is painfully aware of Cloten's body throughout Imogen's slow awakening, and responds sympathetically to the agony of mind that recognition brings. At the same time, however, the information possessed by the audience imposes a considerable distance between speaker and listener. Throughout the scene, those outside the play world see more, both literally and figuratively, than those within it, and their fuller understanding generates a degree of objectivity towards the dramatis personae. Whereas in *Macbeth* the spectator had no doubt that the situation faced by the protagonist was a real one, in *Cymbeline* he or she is continually aware that Imogen's predicament is hypothetical, and that her responses, for all their emotional truth, are based on a false premise. While responding sympathetically to the heroine's suffering, the reader or listener can thus take comfort in the knowledge that she is wrong and look forward to a time when her error will be revealed. In short, whereas in *Macbeth* the parameters of the spectator's experience are defined by the speaker's consciousness, in *Cymbeline* the audience enjoys a play of mind independent of the mental activity of the central figure.

The discrepancy between the audience's level of awareness and that of the heroine allows for a considerable element of dramatic irony, which itself contributes to the distance between those inside and outside the play world. Not only does Imogen mistake Cloten's body for that of her husband, but she asserts that she recognizes the dead man's leg, hand, foot, etc. (309–11). She blames the loyal Pisanio and the slaughtered Cloten for the deed, supplying them with motives for their crime ('malice and lucre' (324)) and adducing 'evidence' of their guilt ('The drug he gave me / . . . have I not found it / Murd'rous to th'senses?' (326–8)). Though moved by the heroine's grief, the reader or listener cannot but be aware here that god-like properties are being assigned to an 'irregulous devil' (315), that a wife cannot distinguish physically between her husband and his enemy, and that the dead man is being accused of his own murder. Imogen's philosophical observations, too, heighten the dramatic irony. For example, when she first sees the body of Cloten she exclaims:

> Our very eyes
> Are sometimes like our judgements, blind.

(301–2)

The comment suggests that the heroine, as one might expect, is alert to the limitations of human perception and is prepared for the possibility of error or misjudgement. Her subsequent actions, however, betray her incapacity to relate her abstract ideas to her experience. Though aware, in theory, how readily the eye may be deceived by false appearance, she leaps instantly to the conclusion that the corpse before her is that of Posthumus, and is quick to convince herself that the visual evidence supports her supposition ('I know the shape of's leg' (309)).

The insistent dramatic irony at work throughout the speech lends an otherwise painful situation an unexpectedly comic aspect. Imogen's confident assertion that Cloten's leg has the unmistakeable proportions of her husband's is ludicrous as well as pathetic, while her misdirected curses (cf. 'To write, and read / Be henceforth treacherous' (316–17)) amuse by their extravagance, even while suggesting the speaker's distraction. The heroine's pained insistence upon the decapitation of the body can also be seen as comic by an audience secure in the knowledge that Posthumus is alive. The exclamations –

> O Posthumus, alas,
> Where is thy head? where's that? Ay me! where's that?
> Pisanio might have kill'd thee at the heart,
> And left this head on –

(320–3)

are grotesque rather than tragic, and they enable the reader or listener to hug the knowledge that the missing head holds the key to the situation. In all these instances it is notable that those outside the play world are smiling at, rather than with, the speaker. Unlike the heroines of the major comedies (e.g. Rosalind in *As You Like It*, or Viola in *Twelfth Night*) Imogen has no knowledge of the humorous aspect of her situation and is not therefore in a position to laugh with the members of the audience at the world around her. Though the amusement of the spectator is profoundly sympathetic, it is a product of superiority, and it thus contributes to the objective relationship between the reader or theatre-goer and the protagonist.

The discrepancy between Imogen's level of awareness and that of the spectator allows those outside the play world a play of mind that is not available to the heroine herself. For example, while Imogen is feverishly examining the corpse, and asserting that the limbs of the dead man are clearly those of her husband, the reader or theatre-goer is led, not simply to share the horror of the speaker's experience, but to ponder the implications of it. Throughout the play, considerable emphasis has been placed on the fact that, in terms of character, the rivals for Imogen's affections, Posthumus and Cloten, are polar opposites, the former an object of universal admiration, the latter of contempt. Yet, decapitated, and dressed in Posthumus' clothes, Cloten is sufficiently like his enemy to be mistaken for him by the person least likely to be deceived – his wife. The confusion between the two men inevitably leads the audience to reflect upon what constitutes the human personality. Posthumus and Cloten are clearly not as unlike each other as had initially appeared. They are physically indistinguishable, while Posthumus, like Cloten, has proved himself capable of ignoble action. For the first time, the spectator is in a position to perceive an aspect of Cloten that has hitherto been obscured by his viciousness – his physical beauty – while the real worth of Posthumus – his moral awareness and capacity for repentance – is effectively differentiated from his appearance. In short, while participating in the nightmare experience of the heroine as she first perceives and then recognizes the body, the members of the audience are simultaneously engaged in exploring the wider implications of her situation – implications of which Imogen herself is unaware, and which are a product of her lack of awareness. And once again, this divergency between the preoccupations of the heroine and the larger concerns of the audience frustrates that process of identification which is so often regarded as the hallmark of the Shakespearian soliloquy.

The total effect of Imogen's speech is plainly very different from that of either Richard of Gloucester in *Richard III* I.i, or Macbeth in *Macbeth* I.vii. Richard's soliloquy is designed to establish an intimate relationship between the central figure and his audience, but it allows relatively little insight into the workings of the human mind.

Macbeth's lines, by contrast, involve the reader or listener in the speaker's experience, allowing those outside the play world to share the mental turmoil of the protagonist at a moment of crisis. Imogen's speech has affinities with Macbeth's while being the reverse of Richard's: it promotes emotional involvement and intellectual detachment simultaneously, allowing the spectator to participate in the heroine's suffering while remaining aloof from her judgements. In each of these cases, the nature of the soliloquy is determined, not by a set of rules, but by the nature of the structure in which it occurs. Richard's lines are designed to focus the attention of the spectator upon the role of the speaker in relation to a significant sequence of events, while Macbeth's speech lays bare the consciousness which is to be the principal arena of the action. Similarly the extraordinary combination of proximity and distance in Imogen's soliloquy is an integral part of the drama as a whole. *Cymbeline* is concerned with individual experience set in the context of universal processes extending over considerable expanses of time and space (see above pp. 79–80), and the dual stance of the audience towards the heroine permits both the intimacy and the objectivity that the total structure requires. The members of the audience know what it is like to be Imogen, but they are also aware of patterns of behaviour and abstract issues lying beyond the heroine's perceptions.

It will be apparent from the above that Shakespeare's soliloquies cannot be approached via a set of 'conventions'. The boundary between monologue and soliloquy is an uncertain one, while the kinds of audience/actor relationships that the speeches set up vary from play to play. Petruchio's speech on the taming of Kate overturns the 'rule' that the speaker is addressing himself rather than the spectators; Richard of Gloucester violates the tenet that the soliloquy is an enactment of a thought process; while Imogen's reaction to the body of Cloten reveals the gulf that can exist between the consciousness of the speaker and the experience of the theatre audience. In each of these cases an attempt to interpret the relevant lines as if they were designed to function in the same way as Macbeth's meditation upon the murder of Duncan results in confusion and a sense of disappointment. Extrapolated from their context Petruchio's lines appear clumsy, Richard's psychologically unconvincing, and Imogen's ludicrous. Seen in relation to the structures in which they occur, however, these speeches emerge as dramatically effective. Petruchio's lines form one element of a composition that constantly transforms players into spectators (see above, pp. 89ff.), and they thus contribute to the game with audience/actor relationships that is played throughout; Richard's soliloquy establishes Gloucester's role as stage manager of events; while Imogen's exclamations over the murdered Cloten typify *Cymbeline*'s extraordinary fusion of contrasting dramatic modes. The range of theatrical experience these speeches represent demonstrates, once again, that the quest for Shakespeare's meaning is furthered more effectually by propounding questions than by attempting to apply critical formulae. The student or theatre-goer, confronted by a Shakespearian hero or heroine ostensibly bound on a voyage of self-discovery, should consider whether he or she is talking to him or her self; whether the organization of ideas is highly structured or associative; whether the members of the audience are implicated in the speaker's experience by being obliged to fill out the gaps in the utterance; whether the spectator's awareness is superior or inferior to that of the protagonist; and whether the speaker's lines have the same force for those inside and outside the play world. Above all, the reader or play-goer should bear in mind that the hall-mark of Shakespearian drama is not its rigid adherence to fashion or convention, but its inventiveness, complexity, and 'infinite variety'.

8

Art and Artifice

It has been a constant theme of previous chapters that Shakespeare's plays do not hold up a mirror to the real world in all its disorder and incoherence, but are a structured representation of it, designed both to delight the spectator and to illuminate some facet of human life. Even in those instances where the dramatist is concerned to project a vision of progressive disintegration (cf. *Troilus and Cressida*), or the loosening of the bonds of nature and the breakdown of order (cf. *King Lear*), the structures that act as a vehicle for the dramatist's vision are highly organized, involving multiple plots, contrasting characters and styles of discourse, and the use of significant spectacle. Shakespearian drama, in short, is highly artificial, and much of the pleasure that it affords derives from the order (and hence the meaningfulness) that it imposes on the flux of life. Nevertheless, the degree to which the attention of the theatre audience is drawn to the artificiality of the stage spectacle varies considerably from play to play. At one extreme Shakespeare may create the illusion of simply presenting the spectator with a 'slice of life', ungoverned by artistic intervention. In the Eastcheap scenes of *Henry IV, Part I*, for example, the tavern setting, prose dialogue, colloquial diction, and abundance of imagery drawn from daily life combine to suggest an ordinary conversation, recorded in a familiar location:

> *Prince.* What say'st thou, Jack?
> *Fal[staff].* The other night I fell asleep here, behind the arras,   95
>   and had my pocket picked: this house is turned
>   bawdy-house, they pick pockets.
> *Prince.* What didst thou lose, Jack?
> *Fal.* Wilt thou believe me, Hal, three or four bonds of
>   forty pound apiece, and a seal-ring of my grand-   100
>   father's.
> *Prince.* A trifle, some eightpenny matter.
> *Host[ess].* So I told him, my lord, and I said I heard your
>   Grace say so: and, my lord, he speaks most vilely of

you, like a foul-mouthed man as he is, and said he   105
would cudgel you.
Prince. What! he did not?
Host. There's neither faith, truth, nor womanhood in
me else.
Fal. There's no more faith in thee than in a stewed   110
prune, nor no more truth in thee than in a drawn
fox – and for womanhood, Maid Marian may be
the deputy's wife of the ward to thee. Go, you thing,
go!   (III.iii.94–114)

Here the members of the audience are placed in the position of
parties at an adjoining table, or observers looking in through a
window. The stage spectacle is self-contained, and the world that
the action projects is a version of that which lies outside the theatre
door. Launcelot Gobbo's comic monologue in *The Merchant of Venice*
represents one step away from this kind of realism. While the kind
of language that is used, the situation that is presented, and the
attitudes of the speaker all serve to convince those outside the play
world that they are watching a credible human being functioning in
a universe not unlike their own, the use of a dramatic convention
heightens the spectator's awareness of artifice:

Certainly, my conscience will serve me to run from
this Jew my master: the fiend is at mine elbow, and
tempts me, saying to me, "Gobbo, Launcelot Gobbo,
good Launcelot," or "good Gobbo," or "good
Launcelot Gobbo, use your legs, take the start, run   5
away." My conscience says "No; take heed honest
Launcelot, take heed honest Gobbo," or as aforesaid
"honest Launcelot Gobbo, do not run, scorn running
with thy heels." Well, the most courageous fiend
bids me pack, "Fia!" says the fiend, "away!" says   10
the fiend, "for the heavens rouse up a brave mind"
says the fiend, "and run." Well, my conscience
hanging about the neck of my heart, says very wisely
to me . . . .
. . . . "Launcelot budge not!" – "Budge!"
says the fiend, – "Budge not!" says my conscience.
"Conscience" say I, "you counsel well, – Fiend" say   20
I, "you counsel well," – to be rul'd by my conscience,

I should stay with the Jew my master, who (God
bless the mark) is a kind of devil; and to run away
from the Jew I should be ruled by the fiend, who
(saving your reverence) is the devil himself: certainly   25
the Jew is the very devil incarnation, and in my conscience, my conscience is but a kind of hard conscience, to offer to counsel me to stay with the Jew;
the fiend gives the more friendly counsel: I will run
fiend, my heels are at your commandment, I will run.   30

(II.ii.1–30)

In this instance, information is communicated to the spectators,
not by means of a naturalistic conversation, but through a soliloquy
– a device which requires the audience to accept that human beings
commonly express their thoughts aloud when they find themselves
alone. Moreover, the kind of soliloquy Launcelot is assigned is itself
non-naturalistic. He constantly informs himself of things which he
already knows, and gives the impression of addressing the
spectator rather than himself. The speech sets up a rapprochement
between speaker and listeners that is exploited in the remainder of
the scene, breaking down the 'fourth wall' or plate glass window
that separates the play world from the theatre audience, while
(paradoxically) heightening the spectator's awareness of the play as
play.

Tyrrel's account of the murder of the Princes in the Tower in
Richard III represents a further step away from the naturalistic
presentation of experience. Once again, as in the two previous
examples, the scene involves an element of narration, but the
immediacy and familiarity of the previous extracts is nowhere in
evidence. Whereas in *Henry IV, Part I* Falstaff addresses his account
of the loss of his ring to Hal, and is overheard by the spectators,
while Launcelot in *The Merchant of Venice* re-enacts the contrary
speeches of his two advisers to himself and the audience
simultaneously, Tyrrel narrates an incident that has been recounted
to him by others, distancing the deed from the spectators, and
transforming event into 'story':

The tyrannous and bloody act is done;
The most arch deed of piteous massacre
That ever yet this land was guilty of.
Dighton and Forrest, who I did suborn

To do this piece of ruthless butchery –   5
Albeit they were flesh'd villains, bloody dogs –
Melted with tenderness and mild compassion,
Wept like two children, in their deaths' sad story.
'O thus', quoth Dighton, 'lay the gentle babes';
'Thus, thus', quoth Forrest, 'girdling one another   10
Within their alabaster innocent arms;
Their lips were four red roses on a stalk,
And in their summer beauty kiss'd each other.
A book of prayers on their pillow lay,
Which once', quoth Forrest, 'almost chang'd my mind.   15
But O, the Devil – ' There the villain stopp'd,
When Dighton thus told on: 'We smothered
The most replenished sweet work of Nature,
That from the prime creation e'er she fram'd.'
Hence both are gone with conscience and remorse   20
They could not speak, and so I left them both
To bear this tidings to the bloody King.

                                                                    (IV.iii.1–22)

A host of factors contribute to the non-naturalistic nature of this scene. Once again, as in *The Merchant of Venice*, the members of the audience are asked to accept the conventions governing the use of the soliloquy, but in this instance the soliloquy itself is of a highly formal kind. The speaker is engaged, not in making up his mind, like Launcelot, but in relating a sequence of events with which he is already familiar, and no motive is supplied to justify his doing so. He thus functions, not as a participant in an evolving situation, like Falstaff and Hal, but as a narrator – a role which his faithful repetition of the murderers' words helps to sustain. At the same time, the vocabulary which he employs contributes to the treatment of the Princes' deaths in terms of a 'story' (8). The villains of the piece, Dighton and Forrest, are far from credible human beings. Though they are described as 'flesh'd villains' and 'bloody dogs' (6), they are capable of highly lyrical speech, and are totally overwhelmed by a deed that should be part of their stock in trade. The victims of the King's tyranny, the young Princes, are wholly unlike the two boys that the members of the audience have encountered in earlier scenes. They are described as 'gentle babes' (9), a phrase which at once reduces their age and heightens their innocence, while the hyperbole of Dighton's closing lines elevates them into embodiments of pre-lapsarian perfection. At the same time, Forrest's account of them 'girdling' (10) one another within their 'alabaster innocent arms' (11), together with the mention of the prayer book on their pillow (14), translates flesh and blood into monumental statuary, defusing the horror of the struggle for life implicit in death by smothering. The reference to the boys' lips as 'roses' (12) also contributes to the depersonalizing process at work throughout the passage. The term reminds the spectators of the emblems of the two branches of the Plantagenet family, assimilating the youths to the succession of roses cut down in the struggle between York and Lancaster.

The highly stylized treatment of the deaths of the Princes serves a number of purposes. The two boys have been vividly realized in previous scenes, and their on-stage murder would be a deeply shocking event. Though Shakespeare did not shrink from the presentation of such incidents where necessary (cf. *Macbeth*, IV.ii), in this instance the degree of audience sympathy the scene would attract would be detrimental to the structure of the drama as a whole. *Richard III* does not turn on the fate of the Princes in the Tower. In the total scheme of the drama the two youths constitute merely one more Edward in a succession of Edwards, and one more Richard in a succession of Richards, who fall victim to the power struggle within the house of Plantagenet, and the distanced treatment of the children's deaths ensures that their murder does not assume a disproportionate importance. At the same time, by translating the deaths of the Princes into a 'story', isolated from the flow of the action, Shakespeare is freed from the restrictions of realism, and thus able to present the event in terms of its significance, rather than as a literal happening. The boys are described, not as potential contenders for political power, but as embodiments of beauty, youth, and innocence, and their statuesque sleep consequently anticipates, not merely their own demise, but that of the virtues they represent in Richard's England.

The formal execution of Tyrrel's soliloquy is thus a deliberate strategy on the part of the dramatist designed to frustrate audience involvement in a particular event, and to highlight one aspect of the play's meaning. In some instances, however, the heightening of the spectator's awareness of artifice may have much more far reaching implications. V.iv of *Cymbeline*, for example, turns upon one of the most striking stage spectacles in the entire Shakespearian corpus, and is representative of a kind of dramaturgy at a very considerable distance from that exemplified by the conversation between Falstaff, the Hostess, and Prince Hal which formed the strarting point for this discussion. The scene opens with the entrance of the hero, Posthumus, between two jailers, and the first few lines establish a prison setting in the day-to-day world:

> *First Gaol.* You shall not now be stol'n, you have locks
>   upon you:
>   So graze, as you find pasture.
> *Sec. Gaol.*   Ay, or a stomach.   [*Exeunt*]

(V.iv.1–2)

The departure of the jailers is followed by a soliloquy from Posthumus that modulates into a prayer to the gods. This speech represents a movement away from the 'realism' of the opening exchange in that it involves the use of a dramatic convention, but in terms of execution, it is highly naturalistic – not least in its difficulty. The blank verse Shakespeare employs here is of an extremely flexible kind, with insistent enjambement, considerable variation of stress patterns, and an abundance of feminine endings, all contributing to the enactment, rather than the statement of emotion. The field of reference is familiar, while the elliptical style creates the illusion of the speaker wrestling with his thoughts rather than telling a story or announcing a position. The speech is too long to quote in full but the opening lines are typical of the whole:

> Most welcome bondage; for thou art a way,
> I think to liberty: yet am I better
> Than one that's sick o'th'gout, since he had rather   5
> Groan so in perpetuity than be cur'd
> By th' sure physician, Death; who is the key
> T'unbar these locks. My conscience, thou art fetter'd
> More than my shanks and wrists: you good gods, give me
> The penitent instrument to pick that bolt,   10
> Then free for ever.

(V.iv.3–11)

The passage concludes with Posthumus addressing his mind to his supposedly dead wife and falling asleep, whereupon the dramatic idiom once again changes. The sequence that follows enacts the prisoner's dream, or vision, and the otherworldly quality of the experience is indicated by an emphatic use of visual and aural effects. The opening stage direction calls for music and ritualistic movement appropriate to apparitions:

> *Solemn music. Enter (as in an apparition)* SICILIUS LEONATUS, *father to Posthumus, an old man, attired like a warrior, leading in his hand an ancient matron (his wife, and mother to Posthumus) with music before them. Then, after other music, follow the two young* LEONATI *(brothers to Posthumus) with wounds as they died in the wars. They circle Posthumus round as he lies sleeping.*

The closing direction is followed by a series of speeches by the spirits which sustain the ritual nature of the scene. Whereas Posthumus and the jailers were assigned blank verse, the apparitions employ a more overtly poetic medium, with alternating tetrameters and trimeters and insistent rhyme. Rather than addressing the sleeping man or one another, they combine in a choric lament to Jupiter, their unusual vocabulary, particularly their latinate diction, enhancing their remoteness from flesh and blood:

Sici.	Hath my poor boy done aught but well,	35
	whose face I never saw?	
	I died whilst in the womb he stay'd,	
	attending Nature's law.	
	. . . .	
First Bro.	When once he was mature for man,	
	in Britain where was he	
	That could stand up his parallel,	
	or fruitful object be	55
	In eye of Imogen, that best	
	could deem his dignity?	
	. . . .	
Sici.	Why did you suffer Iachimo,	
	slight thing of Italy,	
	To taint his nobler heart and brain	65
	with needless jealousy?	
	. . . .	

Sec. Bro.   For this, from stiller seats we came,
                 our parents and us twain,   70
                 That striking in our country's cause
                 fell bravely and were slain,
                 Our fealty, and Tenantius' right,
                 with honour to maintain.

First Bro.   75
                 Like hardiment Posthumus hath
                 to Cymbeline perform'd:
                 Then, Jupiter, thou king of gods
                 why hast thou thus adjourn'd
                 The graces for his merits due,
                 being all to dolours turn'd?   80

Sici.   Thy crystal window ope; look out;
                 no longer exercise
                 Upon a valiant race thy harsh
                 and potent injuries.
                 . . . .
                 Peep through thy marble mansion, help,
                 or we poor ghosts will cry
                 To th'shining synod of the rest
                 against thy deity.   90
                                        (V.iv.35–90)

The appeal of the apparitions is followed by a yet more spectacular
effect that serves to transport the spectator still further from the
world beyond the theatre door:

*Jupiter descends in thunder and lightning, sitting upon an eagle: he
throws a thunderbolt. The Ghosts fall on their knees.*

Here, all the resources of the theatre are called into play to generate a
sense of wonder, rather than to convince the members of the
audience that they are watching a documentary record of an event.
Meaning is communicated, not by 'overheard' dialogue, but
through the use of significant action, sound effects, and emblem.
The response of the apparitions to Jupiter's appearance – '*The Ghosts
fall on their knees*' – is indicative of the relative status of the two kinds
of supernatural beings, while the god's descent on an eagle signals
both his kingship (the eagle is traditionally regarded as the king of

birds), and the 'higher' realm to which he belongs. The thunder and lightning that accompany his descent attest his power and the scale of his influence, while the thunderbolt that he hurls expresses the terror of his punitive wrath. The stage spectacle also calls for impressive costume and properties. The god himself would be magnificently apparelled, while the eagle on which he sits would enhance his splendour through both its size, and its majesty as a bird of prey. The style of speech Jupiter is assigned is also indicative of his status within the play world. Where the ghosts used alternating tetrameters and trimeters, the supreme deity employs a stately blank verse, that differs from the dramatic language assigned to Posthumus in its impersonality and field of reference:

> No more, you petty spirits of region low,
>   Offend our hearing: hush! How dare you ghosts
> Accuse the thunderer, whose bolt (you know)   95
>   Sky-planted, batters all rebelling coasts?
> Poor shadows of Elysium, hence, and rest
>   Upon your never-withering banks of flowers:
> Be not with mortal accidents opprest,
>   No care of yours it is, you know 'tis ours.   100
> . . . . Be content,
> Your low-laid son our godhead will uplift:
>   His comforts thrive, his trials well are spent:
> Our Jovial star reign'd at his birth, and in   105
>   Our temple was he married. Rise, and fade.

(V.iv.93–106)

Here, the insistent use of the royal plural (94, 100), the firm assumption of authority (100), and the potency implied through the vast arena that is evoked (cf. 96 and 105) all establish the supremacy of the god and suggest the distance between his field of vision and that of the lesser apparitions. The deity's impact upon the three levels of spectators – the apparitions, Posthumus, and the members of the theatre audience – is expressed in the exaltation and wonder voiced by Sicilius:

> He came in thunder; his celestial breath
> Was sulphurous to smell: the holy eagle   115
> Stoop'd, as to foot us: his ascension is

More sweet than our blest fields: his royal bird
Prunes the immortal wing, and cloys his beak,
As when his god is pleased.

(V.iv.114–19)

Jupiter's spectacular exit (116–17) is followed by the departure of
the ghosts, and Posthumus then wakes. His idiom contrasts forcibly
with that of the supernatural characters and is evocative of a world
very different from that which the spectator has just glimpsed. The
rhythms of his soliloquy are broken and irregular; his vocabulary is
negative; while the imagery he employs is everyday:

Sleep, thou hast been a grandsire, and begot
A father to me: and thou hast created
A mother, and two brothers: but, O scorn!   125
Gone! they went hence so soon as they were born:
And so I am awake. Poor wretches, that depend
On greatness' favour, dream as I have done,
Wake, and find nothing.

(V.iv.123–9)

This kind of utterance clearly represents a step away from the
sublimity of the preceding lines, and the return to a dramatic
language evocative of the spectator's own world is completed with
the re-entrance of the jailers. Once again, soliloquy gives place to
dialogue, rounding off the scene's pattern of dialogue, soliloquy,
declamation, soliloquy, dialogue. Now, however, the naturalism of
the scene is heightened by the use of prose, while the field of
reference enforces the familiarity of the world in which the action is
set:

First Gaol. Come, sir, are you ready for death?
Post. Over-roasted rather: ready long ago.
First Gaol. Hanging is the word, sir: if you be ready for
that, you are well cook'd.   155
Post. So, if I prove a good repast to the spectators, the
dish pays the shot.
First Gaol. A heavy reckoning for you, sir: but the com-
fort is you shall be called to no more payments, fear

no more tavern-bills, which are often the sadness of 160
parting, as the procuring of mirth: . . .
. . . . .O, the charity
of a penny cord! it sums up thousands in a trice: you
have no true debitor and creditor but it: of what's
past, is, and to come, the discharge: your neck, sir, 170
is pen, book, and counters; so the acquittance
follows.
Post. I am merrier to die than thou art to live.
First Gaol. Indeed sir, he that sleeps feels not the toothache. 175

(V.iv.152–75)

The tone of this passage also contributes to the mundane universe
which the references to eating and drinking, taverns, debts, and
hanging help to evoke. Grim punning replaces the exaltation of the
central section of the scene, while the world is perceived, not in
terms of the wonderful (cf. 'never-withering banks of flowers' (98),
'his royal bird' (117), 'immortal wing' (118)), but the sordid,
negative, and painful (cf. 'fear no more tavern-bills' (159-60), 'the
charity of a penny cord' (167–8), 'the toothache' (174–5)). The
exchange between prisoner and jailers thus serves to bring the scene
full circle. The kind of dialogue that the characters employ here is
designed, once again, to create the illusion that the members of the
audience are the mute witnesses of an ordinary conversation, taking
place in the dark, work-a-day world.

The heightening of the spectator's awareness of artifice from the
appearance of the apparitions to the re-awakening of Posthumus is
clearly not accidental. Artifice is used here as a means of defining
another realm, or order . of experience, lying beyond the
commonplace actuality of Cymbeline's court, and endowing the
sufferings of its members with meaning. Music, costume, ritualized
action, lyrical dialogue and the use of 'machines' (the flying bird)
combine to enforce a contrast between one kind of actuality and
another – Cymbeline's realm and Jupiter's – with the emphatic use
of a variety of art forms projecting the superior beauty, harmony,
and wonder of the world that Posthumus momentarily glimpses.
The shift from one level of artifice to another in this scene thus plays
a crucial part in the projection of meaning. The movement from
seemingly natural speech, through soliloquy, to a species of masque,

translates the reader or theatre-goer from the mundane to the visionary, while artifice becomes a metaphor for spirituality.

While the entrance of the apparitions opens a window for both Posthumus and the members of the theatre audience upon a more beautiful and meaningful universe, the heightened awareness of artifice that accompanies the appearance of the spirits is recognized only by those outside the play world. Posthumus himself does not think of what he has witnessed in terms of a masque, nor does he reflect on the difference in style between his own speeches and those of the apparitions. In a number of plays, however, Shakespeare's characters do display a lively awareness of a variety of art forms. As noted in Chapter 4 they are often involved in the performance of plays, while they frequently call for music appropriate to their moods. In *Twelfth Night*, for example, Orsino opens the play with an injunction to his musicians to repeat a 'strain' (4) that fosters his love melancholia, while Sir Toby Belch and his drinking companion, Sir Andrew Aguecheek, add zest to their evening carouse with a 'catch' (II.iii.59) that rouses the household from sleep in the middle of the night. These musical interludes are different in kind from the appearance of the apparitions in *Cymbeline*, and constitute a further step away from the kind of naturalism exemplified by the conversation between Falstaff and Hal, in that they involve a performance within a performance. Whereas in *Cymbeline* art is employed by the dramatist as a means of differentiating between different orders of reality, in *Twelfth Night* art is employed by the characters as a means of enhancing their own happiness or enjoyment. The dramatis personae thus function as either performers, or members of an audience, with the work of art they commission representing a different level of artifice from that of the framing action.

The function of such 'inset' art forms is much more complex than might appear at first sight. While the various songs that are performed in the course of *Twelfth Night*, for example, serve to entertain both their internal and external audiences, they also contribute to the meaning of the play as a whole. The song that Feste sings in II.iv affords a useful example here. It is sung at the request of the Duke Orsino, who has a particular regard for it:

> Duke. O, fellow, come, the song we had last night.
>   Mark it, Cesario, it is old and plain;
>   The spinsters and the knitters in the sun,

And the free maids that weave their thread with bones　　45
Do use to chant it: it is silly sooth,
And dallies with the innocence of love,
Like the old age.
Clown. Are you ready, sir?
Duke. Ay, prithee sing.　　　　　　　　　　　　　　*Music.* 50

> *The [Clown's] Song.*

> *Come away, come away death,*
> *And in sad cypress let me be laid.*
> *Fie away, fie away breath,*
> *I am slain by a fair cruel maid:*
> > *My shroud of white, stuck all with yew,*　　　　　55
> > *O prepare it.*
> > *My part of death no one so true*
> > *Did share it.*

> *Not a flower, not a flower sweet,*
> *On my black coffin let there be strewn:*　　　　　60
> *Not a friend, not a friend greet*
> *My poor corpse, where my bones shall be thrown:*
> > *A thousand thousand sighs to save,*
> > *Lay me, O where*
> > *Sad true lover never find my grave,*　　　　　65
> > *To weep there.*

(II.iv.42–66)

This song gives pleasure to Orsino because it harmonizes with his own nature, and it thus supplies its secondary audience with an insight into the mind of one of the play's principal characters. The Duke's lines introducing the performance are particularly important in this context. On a superficial level Orsino merely commends the song to his page on the grounds of its age and simplicity, but the imagery that he uses is indicative of his preoccupations. His reference to the 'spinsters' (i.e. spinners) and 'knitters' (44) by whom the song is traditionally sung, together with his mention of 'their thread' (45) evokes an image of the Fates, spinning the thread of human life, and this suggestion is heightened by the use of the term 'chant' (46), with its ritual connotations, and by the allusion to the lacemakers' bobbins as 'bones' (45). Ideas of fate, transience and mortality thus underlie the surface meaning of the words, generating a wistfulness that is augmented by the speaker's evocation of a pre-lapsarian golden age (cf. 'old and plain' (43); 'silly', i.e. innocent/happy (46); 'innocence' (47); 'old age' (48)) and by the lack of sexual fulfilment implicit in the choice of vocabulary (cf. 'spinsters' (44); 'maids' (45)). All these ideas, which constitute a substratum of meaning in Orsino's speech, are caught up and emphasized in Feste's song. The piece turns upon the death of a lover from unrequited love, and is steeped in references to mortality (cf. 'death' (51), 'slain' (54), 'shroud' (55), 'yew' (55), 'coffin' (60), 'corpse' (62), 'bones' (62), 'grave' (65)). Death is seen, not in terms of renewal, but of physical decay (cf. 'corpse' (62), 'bones' (62)) and sorrow (cf. 'weep' (66)), while lack of fulfilment in life is implied by 'maid' (54), and the virginal 'white' (55) that brings together ideas of sexual purity and death. The song, too, has an 'antique' quality. The lover embodies an exemplary fidelity, since his 'part of death no one so true / Did share it.' (57–8). The burden of the piece, for all its lyrical beauty, is therefore negative, and its tone wistful – and these qualities have direct relevance to the character of the Duke himself. For all his grace and charm, Orsino's attitudes are life-denying, and the negative nature of his postures is expressed through the work of art he applauds.

Sir Toby's 'catch' (II.iii.59) is similarly eloquent, though the words, 'Hold thy peace, thou knave' (II.iii.66), are not, in themselves, remarkable. Once again, the lines introducing the song are significant in that they are indicative of the attitudes that the round encapsulates:

> *Sir To.* But shall we make the welkin dance indeed?
> Shall we rouse the night-owl in a catch that will
> draw three souls out of one weaver? Shall we   60
> do that?
> *Sir And.* And you love me, let's do't: I am dog at a
> catch.   (II.iii.58–63)

Where Orsino's song is 'silly sooth' (II.iv.46) and 'dallies with the innocence of love' (47) Sir Toby's is a much more vigorous piece, designed to 'make the welkin dance' (II.iii.58). Noise and gusto are clearly implied here, and yet the imagery that the speaker employs, comic as it is, does not have the festive ring that the carnival atmosphere of 'welkin dance' would appear to warrant. Sir Toby proposes to rouse the 'night-owl' (59), a bird of ill-omen, traditionally associated with death; and to 'draw three souls out of one weaver' (60), a class of worker often associated with the singing of psalms. The nature of the catch itself is indicated by the effect that it has upon the household. Maria, a waiting gentlewoman favourable to Sir Toby, describes it as a 'caterwauling' (II.iii.73), while Malvolio, the steward, remonstrates with the singers in the following terms:

> My masters, are you mad? Or what are you?
> Have you no wit, manners, nor honesty, but to
> gabble like tinkers at this time of night? Do
> ye make an ale-house of my lady's house, that ye   90
> squeak out your coziers' catches without any
> mitigation or remorse of voice? Is there no respect
> of place, persons, nor time in you?   (II.iii.87–93)

The discord, and lack of decorum, to which both Maria and Malvolio attest reflect upon the nature of the catch's instigator, Sir Toby himself. The gusto that he displays is dangerously anarchic, and the riotous song encapsulates his subversive vigour. At the same time, the kind of music that he and Sir Andrew demand of the Clown contrasts forcibly with that requested by Orsino. Where the kind of art to which the Duke responds is elegant, but effete, that which Toby and his companions enjoy is dynamic but anti-social. Incidental music thus constitutes an expression of the conflicting, and flawed, value systems of the play's social groups, with the languor of one section of society and the riotousness of the other suggested to the spectator by aural means.

The significance of the songs with which *Twelfth Night* is interlarded extends, however, beyond the definition of character and the differentiation of social groups. The play's incidental music also contributes to the atmosphere or mood of the drama, in that, with the exception of the catches sung by Toby and his companions which themselves, as noted above, have dark undertones, it is uniformly melancholy. The play opens with a piece of music that has a 'dying fall' (I.i.4), and the first song that Feste sings places love in the context of the transience of life:

> *What is love? 'Tis not hereafter,*
> *Present mirth hath present laughter:*

What's to come is still unsure.   50
In delay there lies no plenty,
Then come kiss me, sweet and twenty:
   Youth's a stuff will not endure.

(II.iii.48–53)

This piece is sung for Sir Andrew and Sir Toby, and immediately precedes their catch, and its burden contributes to the audience's ambivalence towards the 'present laughter' (49) of these characters in that it generates an awareness of mortality. Feste's song '*Come away, come away death*', quoted above, is performed in the scene that immediately follows Toby's midnight carouse, while the play as a whole concludes with a song that emphasizes life's disappointments:

When that I was and a little tiny boy,
   With hey, ho, the wind and the rain,
A foolish thing was but a toy,   390
   For the rain it raineth every day.

But when I came to man's estate,
   With hey, ho, the wind and the rain,
'Gainst knaves and thieves men shut their gate,
   For the rain it raineth every day.   395

But when I came, alas, to wive,
   With hey, ho, the wind and the rain,
By swaggering could I never thrive,
   For the rain it raineth every day.

But when I came unto my beds,   400
   With hey, ho, the wind and the rain,
With toss-pots still 'had drunken heads,
   For the rain it raineth every day.

A great while ago the world begun,
   With hey, ho, the wind and the rain,   405
But that's all one, our play is done,
   And we'll strive to please you every day.

(V.i.388–407)

The stress upon failure and death in these songs, together with their lyrical beauty, contributes to the definition of the play world. The main plot characters – Orsino, Olivia, Viola – have considerable charm, but they have assumed roles (the pining lover, the mourning sister, the devoted page) that threaten them with emotional attrition, and their cast of mind is thus melancholic. Similarly the sub-plot characters – Sir Andrew and Sir Toby – disport themselves in the servants' hall, rather than comporting themselves in a manner appropriate to their station, and their buffoonery leads to pain and resentment in its final stages. The dramatic universe, in short, for all its superficial beauty and jollity, is touched by sadness and frustration, and it is this atmosphere that the musical interludes communicate to the audience. The songs thus function as a distillation of the essence of the play world: they reflect the frame of mind of the characters, express the differences between one social group and another, and create the late autumnal mood which is the hallmark of the drama.

The final stanza of the song with which Feste concludes the play is also important in another respect. It draws the attention of the theatre audience to the play as artifice, rather than as reality:

> *A great while ago the world begun,*
> *With hey, ho, the wind and the rain,*   405
> *But that's all one, our play is done,*
> *And we'll strive to please you every day.*

Up to this point in the action, the inhabitants of Illyria have shown no awareness of themselves as characters in a play. Though Viola, in particular, is assigned soliloquies and asides, these have not been directed explicitly towards the theatre audience, but have served to distinguish her private thoughts from her public utterances. Similarly, the songs and incidental music have been directed towards an internal, rather than an external, audience contributing to the illusion that the play world is self-contained. The line 'that's all one, our play is done' (406) abruptly alters this view of the action. Whereas in the main body of the drama those outside the play world had been encouraged to view the dramatis personae as 'real' people, functioning in a self-contained dramatic universe, the final lines of the song require them to think of the characters as players, interacting solely in order to entertain. In *Twelfth Night* this change of perspective comes too late to modify the spectator's response to the principal action. The lines serve merely to transfer the members of the audience back from Illyria to the playhouse, and to invite a positive response to the entire performance. The song as a whole thus emerges as a species of epilogue, mediating between the different realities of the playhouse and the play. Nevertheless, Feste's closing words exemplify a very different kind of dramaturgy from that at work in the preceding acts, and the spectator crosses a boundary in the course of them between artifice and self-conscious art.

It is in his last plays, as has often been noted in the course of this book, that Shakespeare experimented most daringly with the medium in which he worked, and this is particularly evident in his interest in *metadrama* – drama that actively promotes an awareness of the play as play, and hence is concerned, on one level, with the nature of drama itself. *Pericles*, for example, as demonstrated in Chapters 4 and 7, is presented by an on-stage narrator, who insists upon the fictional nature of the events that are enacted; while *Cymbeline*, as noted in Chapter 3, opens with an exchange between two gentlemen which places considerable emphasis upon the fairy tale nature of the events that are described. In both these instances, however, though the choric presenters heighten the spectator's awareness of artifice, the inhabitants of the worlds that these characters introduce endow their universes with a degree of authenticity by their unqualified acceptance of their own actuality. Pericles' lament, for example, over his supposedly dead wife, Thaisa, is a moving enactment of a deeply felt emotion that qualifies the spectator's awareness of the speaker as one component of a work of art (cf. *Pericles*, III.i.56–64), and the same point might be made with regard to Imogen's response to being parted from her husband, Posthumus (*Cymbeline*, I.iv.25–37). In *The Winter's Tale*, by contrast, not only is the non-naturalistic nature of the action drawn to the attention of the audience by means of a Chorus (in this case, Time), but the dramatis personae themselves constantly allude to their experience in literary terms, undermining, even at moments of greatest tension, any sustained illusion that those outside the play world are the unseen witnesses of a real event.

The title of the play, *The Winter's Tale*, immediately sets Shakespeare's penultimate play aside from such dramas as *Richard III* or *Julius Caesar*, which lay claim, at the very outset, to deal with actuality. The title suggests a folk tale or fairy story, replete with incredible happenings, remote from day-to-day experience, and these expectations are quickly borne out by the plot, which involves a child exposed at birth, a prince falling in love with a princess who is believed to be a shepherdess, and a statue which miraculously comes to life. What is remarkable about *The Winter's Tale*, however, is not the plot material itself, since Shakespeare's plays very frequently draw on folk tale motifs, but the fact that the drama constantly draws the attention of the audience towards the extravagancies of the fiction, rather than away from them. In V.ii, for example, one gentleman remarks to another

> This news,
> which is called true, is so like an old tale that the
> verity of it is in strong suspicion, (V.ii.27–9)

while the same gentleman, enquiring the fate of another chapter, is told,

> Like an old tale still, which will have matter
> to rehearse, though credit be asleep and not an ear
> open. He was torn to pieces with a bear. (V.ii.62–4)

The use of the word 'tale' in these contexts undermines the illusion of actuality in a number of ways. Not only does it draw attention to the improbability of the plot material, but it reminds the spectators of the play's title, prompting those outside the play world to reflect upon the relationship between the work of art and a literary tradition, rather than encouraging them to identify with the speakers. At the same time, the lines 'though credit be asleep and not an ear open' (63–4) are so blatantly directed by Shakespeare towards his own audience they totally subvert any illusion that the world of the drama is self-contained. They imply that the play itself is so improbable the entire audience has ceased to listen to it, and invite laughter on the part of the audience at the dramatist's expense.

The tale is not the only art form, however, upon which *The Winter's Tale* draws. Throughout the play one character after another turns to the arts as a means of defining an experience or evaluating a situation. Leontes, for example, obsessed with the idea of his wife's infidelity, employs a theatrical metaphor (see above p. 166) to express his sense of humiliation:

Go, play, boy, play: thy mother plays, and I
Play too; but so disgrac'd a part, whose issue
Will hiss me to my grave,

(I.ii.187–9)

while his wife Hermione, obliged to defend herself in public against
a charge of adultery, uses the dramatized sufferings of historical
personages as a measure of her misery:

You, my lord, best know
(Who least will seem to do so) my past life
Hath been as continent, as chaste, as true,
As I am now unhappy; which is more   35
Than history can pattern, though devis'd
And play'd to take spectators.

(III.ii.32–7)

Similarly, Camillo, required by Leontes to kill King Polixenes,
declares he would not commit the crime, even had literary
precedents suggested that he would prosper by it:

To do this deed,
Promotion follows. If I could find example
Of thousands that had struck anointed kings
And flourish'd after, I'd not do't; but since
Nor brass, nor stone, nor parchment bears not one,   360
Let villainy itself forswear't,

(I.ii.356–61)

while an unnamed gentleman, lost for words to describe the
discoveries of the play's final scenes, falls back on an art form noted
for its extraordinary subject matter:

such a deal of wonder
is broken out within this hour, that ballad-makers
cannot be able to express it.

(V.ii.23–5)

The constant recourse to the literary and performing arts as a means of throwing light on events taking place in the world of the play enforces an awareness on the part of the spectator of the fictional nature of the dramatic representation. Where the field of reference in Falstaff's exchange with the Hostess helps to create the illusion that the members of the audience are witnessing an event taking place in the real world, the literary analogies of *The Winter's Tale* contribute to the awareness of artifice generated by the non-naturalistic nature of the play's events, and by the insistence on the drama as a tale. Moreover, the inhabitants of Bohemia and Sicilia do not merely exhibit their literary awareness through their choice of imagery, they also discuss a number of art forms. In II.i, for example, Hermione asks her son, Mamillius, to tell her a story, and the following exchange takes place:

> *Mam.* Merry, or sad, shall't be?
> *Her.* As merry as you will.
> *Mam.* A sad tale's best for winter. 25

> (II.i.23–5)

Mamillius' final line is important in a number of ways. It catches up the title of the play, encouraging the members of the audience to speculate that it may be a version of the Shakespearian drama itself that the child is about to relate, and hence contributing to their perception of the play as a 'story'. At the same time, the boy's comment on artistic decorum has relevance to *The Winter's Tale* itself. It too is a winter's story, and Mamillius' reminder of the nature of the genre to which it belongs leads the spectator to anticipate sad events, and to consider the artistic principles governing the dramatist's choice of incident.

It is in Act V scene iii, however, that the various strands of self-conscious artifice outlined above are drawn most potently together. Here, the dramatis personae do not merely draw on, or discuss, the arts they come together to view a work of art in a scene which, in its fairy-tale quality, clearly aligns the drama with folk tale rather than with 'real' life. Hermione, presumed dead by Leontes, pretends to be a statue in order to be re-united with him, the resemblance between the artefact and the dead woman prompting a series of comments from the spectators that serve to probe the relationship between art and reality. The scene is a lengthy one but

two extracts from it give some indication of the range of issues
Shakespeare explores:

[*Paulina draws a curtain, and discovers Hermione*
standing like a statue]
Leon[*tes*].   Her natural posture!
　Chide me, dear stone, that I may say indeed
　Thou art Hermione; or rather, thou art she   25
　In thy not chiding; for she was as tender
　As infancy and grace. But yet, Paulina,
　Hermione was not so much wrinkled, nothing
　So aged as this seems.
Pol[*ixenes*].   O, not by much.
Paul[*ina*]. So much the more our carver's excellence,   30
　Which lets go by some sixteen years and makes her
　As she liv'd now.
Leon.   As now she might have done,
　So much to my good comfort as it is
　Now piercing to my soul. O, thus she stood,
　Even with such life of majesty, warm life,   35
　As now it coldly stands, when first I woo'd her!
　I am asham'd: does not the stone rebuke me
　For being more stone than it? O royal piece!
　There's magic in thy majesty, which has
　My evils conjur'd to remembrance, and   40
　From thy admiring daughter took the spirits,
　Standing like stone with thee.
. . . .
Leon.   Do not draw the curtain.
Paul. No longer shall you gaze on't, lest your fancy   60
　May think anon it moves.
Leon.   Let be, let be!
　Would I were dead, but that methinks already –
　What was he that did make it? – See, my lord,
　Would you not deem it breath'd? and that those veins
　Did verily bear blood?
Pol.   Masterly done: 65
　The very life seems warm upon her lip.
Leon. The fixture of her eye has motion in't,
　As we are mock'd with art.

Paul.   I'll draw the curtain:
  My lord's almost so far transported that
  He'll think anon it lives.
Leon.   O sweet Paulina,   70
  Make me to think so twenty years together!
  No settled senses of the world can match
  The pleasure of that madness. Let't alone.
Paul. I am sorry, sir, I have thus far stirr'd you! but
  I could afflict you farther.
Leon.   Do, Paulina;   75
  For this affliction has a taste as sweet
  As any cordial comfort. Still methinks
  There is an air comes from her. What fine chisel
  Could ever yet cut breath?

(V.iii.23–42 and 59–79)

Here, while in terms of plot a miraculous reunion is being effected between a faithful wife and an erring husband, a much more profound exploration is being conducted into the nature and function of art. The scene emphasizes the capacity of art to imitate life, but it also points to the differences between the two, and affirms the superiority of the latter. The first of Leontes' lines quoted above establishes the likeness between the 'statue' and the living woman, but the King's subsequent surprise at the wrinkled aspect of the subject (28–9), and Paulina's response that the carver has let 'go by some sixteen years' (31), highlights an essential difference between art and life – their relationship with the temporal process. Where the living woman changes and develops with the passage of time, the artefact can only encapsulate and 'freeze' the moment. Leontes' second speech also focuses upon similarity and difference. Even as he exclaims 'O, thus she stood' (34), he qualifies the statement with an adjective that points to a quality that the work of art lacks – human warmth (36). The second extract follows the same pattern. Again Leontes celebrates the truthfulness of the work – 'Would you not deem it breath'd? and that those veins / Did verily bear blood?' (64–5) – but the terms in which he does so suggest the movement and vitality that distinguish humanity from sculpture, while his final exclamation, 'What fine chisel / Could ever yet cut breath?' (78–9) is an affirmation of the wonder of life, and the inability of art to reproduce it.

Art is not seen here merely as an inferior version of actuality, however. Standing before the statue, Leontes exclaims that the stone rebukes him 'For being more stone than it' (37–8), and declares there is a 'magic' (39) in the composition that has 'conjur'd' his 'evils . . . to remembrance' (40). The lines indicate that the statue, while reminding Leontes of his lost wife, has also prompted a process of self-examination, and has therefore been instrumental in enlarging his moral understanding. The words 'magic' (39) and 'conjur'd' (40) are particularly important in this respect. They suggest the capacity of the work of art to work upon the imagination of the spectator, and to transform his or her level of awareness. Thus, while on the one hand this scene asserts the superiority of life to art, on the other it affirms the value of artifice as a means of commenting on, and illuminating, reality.

It will be evident from the above that the kind of dramaturgy at work in *The Winter's Tale* is very different from that exemplified by the passage from *Henry IV, Part I* quoted at the outset of this chapter. In the extract from the historical play the members of the audience are encouraged to view the dramatis personae as real people, engaged in an everyday conversation, taking place in a familiar but self-contained world. The spectator thus functions as an unacknowledged eye-witness of events that evolve in accordance with their own internal logic, and he or she becomes involved in the stage spectacle, not by being directly addressed, but through sympathetic engagement with the speakers. In *The Winter's Tale*, by contrast, the non-naturalistic nature of the action is enforced from the very outset. The drama is set, not in the familiar world to which the members of the audience belong, but in the never-never-land of romance, while insistent emphasis upon artifice serves to maintain the spectator's awareness of the play as play. Rather than being mute participants in an event, the members of the theatre audience are self-conscious observers of a spectacle overtly directed towards them, and they relate to the work as a construct, rather than as a 'slice of life'. Where Tyrrel's speech in *Richard III*, and the appearance of the apparitions in *Cymbeline*, heighten the audience's awareness of artifice for a specific effect, *The Winter's Tale* enforces its own artificiality throughout, delighting the spectators by its fairy tale quality, while simultaneously conducting an investigation into the nature and function of art. Shakespeare's penultimate play, in short, is a highly self-conscious work. It calls upon the spectator to recognize the distance between art and life, rather than seeking to convince him of the reality of the stage spectacle, and is concerned, on its deepest level, not with a specific situation, but the relationship between art and the natural world.

All drama is artificial. It involves the impersonation of one person by another, and the pretence that the playing area is a place other than a stage. All performances are governed by a series of conventions, which vary from one society to another, but which the members of an audience implicitly accept when they take their places in an open-air arena or in front of a proscenium arch. Nevertheless, within the universal pretence which is the condition of drama, a limitless series of options exists for the dramatist at the moment he begins to write. However unconsciously the decision is made, each playwright must select a point on the sliding scale between ritual and documentary most appropriate for the statement he wishes to make, and must manipulate the conventions governing his form in order to project his meaning. Between his first appearance in London, and his retirement to Stratford following *The Tempest*, Shakespeare moved up and down that sliding scale with remarkable freedom, devising an extraordinary range of structures that create the illusion of psychological realism at one extreme, and invite an appreciation of artistic design at the other. The meaning of a Shakespearian play, as preceding chapters have attempted to illustrate, derives not simply from the story that is told, but from the way in which the play tells it, and the degree to which artifice is foregrounded by the dramatist is a major element in the process of telling. The more the conventions governing the drama are highlighted, the greater the distance between the dramatis personae and the spectator, the more acute the audience's appreciation of pattern, and the less their involvement with the specific. The reader or theatre-goer approaching a Shakespearian play for the first time should attempt to rid himself of the preconception that realism is the goal to which all drama aspires, and should seek to explore the relationship between play and spectator that the work before him engineers. Though he may not recognize, on first reading, the games that Shakespeare plays with his medium, he should have no difficulty in recognizing whether the dramatist is drawing attention towards the mechanics of his craft or away from them, and whether he frames one work of art within another. The Shakespearian corpus is not merely·an image of life, it is also a celebration of art, and the student attuned to this aspect of the dramatist's work will discover that Shakespeare's meaning is far more complex, and his plays far more intellectually satisfying, than a critical method rooted in twentieth-century assumptions about 'realism' suggests.

9

Conclusion: Discovering Shakespeare's Meaning

Shakespeare's plays enact stories and may be reduced to 'tales', but the stories that they enact are not the sole repositories of the dramatist's meaning. The significance of a Shakespearian play, as this book has attempted to show, is the sum of its parts, and derives from a complex pattern of contrast and analogy that emerges as the drama unfolds. Relationships are set up between linguistic modes, stage spectacles, strands of action, groups of characters, and levels of apprehension, while the degree of distance between play and spectator is exploited for specific effects. Shakespeare's method, in short, is essentially a poetic one, not simply because his principal medium is blank verse, but because the significance of his work is a product of a fusion between *vehicle* (or form) and *tenor* (statement), and is thus incapable of paraphrase. Though what happens to the central figure in a Shakespearian drama is obviously crucial, the disposition of characters around him is far from random, while the minor incidents that accompany his progress enlarge the significance of his experience. The quest for Shakespeare's meaning therefore involves an appreciation of *design*, and the student embarking upon it will find his progress facilitated by the cultivation of a heightened awareness of the *spatial structure* of drama (i.e. of the relationship between the elements that make up the composition).

The student or general reader should also bear in mind that Shakespeare's plays, though often encountered for the first time in the study or the classroom, were written for performance in a theatre and depend upon both visual and aural effects. Othello's first entrance amid flame and darkness, or Jupiter's descent from the heavens on an eagle, are designed to promote powerful – and diametrically opposed – responses in a theatre audience, and much of their impact is lost if they are not experienced as events. Similarly, the music accompanying a performance forms an integral part of the statement that the play makes. The 'dying fall' of the strains with which *Twelfth Night* opens conveys the wistfulness and languor of the play world, while Sir Toby's boisterous drinking songs are expressive of his disruptive effect upon Illyrian society. The student confronted with a text on a printed page is divorced from this aspect of the dramatist's art, and will find his understanding enriched by a close attention to stage directions (stated or implied) and by an attempt to act out the drama in the theatre of the mind. The music of Shakespeare's lines is also important in this context, in that it too contributes to the projection of meaning. The progressive disintegration of the rich harmony of Othello's distinctive idiom is expressive of the chaos into which the Moor descends following his temptation by Iago, while the trochaic rhythms of *Macbeth*'s Witches enact the perversity of their world. Whereas the spectator responds involuntarily to such effects in the playhouse, the reader is again at a disadvantage, and will lose some element of the playwright's purpose unless he banishes his inhibitions and reads the text aloud.

Shakespearian drama was not simply written to be performed; it was designed for a particular theatrical context, and some knowledge of the conditions that gave rise to it is also useful in removing barriers to understanding. Ben Jonson's famous pronouncement that Shakespeare was not 'of an age but for all time' can be misleading if it is taken to imply contemporaneity of form, as well as universality of content. Though the Shakespearian corpus is as 'relevant' today as it was in the Elizabethan–Jacobean period, the conventions which govern it are not identical with those governing twentieth-century drama, and an attempt to impose modern concepts of 'realism' or 'consistency' upon the products of the Renaissance stage can obscure, rather than illuminate their meaning. Just as an understanding of the work of Aeschylus entails some knowledge of the function of a Greek chorus, so the understanding of a Shakespearian play is promoted by an appreciation of sixteenth-century dramatic devices – the use of the prologue, soliloquy, or multiple plot. The theatrical context from which the plays sprang is also significant. Shakespeare was a highly self-conscious writer, living in an age when playhouses flourished, major dramatists abounded, and all sections of society flocked to see plays. Innovation, in such a period, is a condition of survival, and Shakespeare continued to delight his contemporaries, not only because of his profundity, but because he was continually engaged in pushing back the frontiers of his art. Part of the pleasure afforded by the Shakespearian corpus thus arises from the continual process of experimentation that takes place from play to play, and the probing of the nature and function of the dramatist's art to which this gives rise. Though a Shakespearian comedy or tragedy is undoubtedly accessible, on one level, to the reader or spectator with very little knowledge of the corpus, it will offer a much more rewarding experience to those attuned, by wider reading, to the innovatory and self-referential aspects of the playwright's work. In this respect an understanding of one play or group of plays within the canon may be said to enhance the appreciation of others.

Hamlet's exclamation, 'the play's the thing' might well have been adopted as the motto of this book in that it sums up the three principal points upon which its argument rests. In the first place, it is the total construct – the play – which expresses the dramatist's vision, not one particular aspect of it, however prominent that aspect in the design. In the second place, the meaning is fully realized in the playhouse, not the study, and is the product of the variety of effects that cohere in the course of a performance. And thirdly, the art form itself – the dramatic vehicle – is the means by which the playwright communicates, and the nature of that form must be understood if communication is to take place. It seems fitting that the world's most celebrated drama critic should have the last word on the discovery of Shakespeare's meaning.

Further Reading

The corpus of Shakespearian criticism is too vast and the multiplicity of approaches too varied to be adequately represented by a brief bibliography. The following items either relate specifically to topics covered in this book or offer a different starting point from which to approach the plays. Those seeking a more detailed bibliography should consult Stanley Wells (1990) *Shakespeare: A Bibliographical Guide*, Oxford University Press, which presents a survey of the major critical contributions to each of the principal areas of Shakespeare scholarship, and is an indispensible tool for anyone embarking on the study of the plays.

As a working dramatist, Shakespeare was writing with a specific set of theatrical conditions in mind, and an understanding of his work is enriched by a knowledge of the nature of the playhouses for which he wrote and the composition of their audiences. Andrew Gurr (1970) *The Shakespearean Stage, 1574–1642* and (1987) *Playgoing in Shakespeare's London*, both Cambridge University Press, offer valuable introductions to this aspect of Shakespeare studies. A knowledge of the sources on which the dramatist drew in constructing his plays also contributes to an appreciation of his art. G. Bullough (1957–75) *Narrative and Dramatic Sources of Shakespeare*, Routledge and Kegan Paul, represents the most significant contribution to this field, while Leah Scragg (1992) *Shakespeare's Mouldy Tales*, Longman, discusses Shakespeare's repetitive use of inherited plot motifs in the light of Renaissance attitudes to the creative process. For a more wide-ranging discussion of Shakespeare's literary experience see G.K. Hunter (1971) 'Shakespeare's Reading', in K. Muir and S. Schoenbaum (eds) *A New Companion to Shakespeare Studies*, Cambridge University Press, pp. 55–66.

The language of Shakespeare's plays may represent a barrier to the modern reader, and those seeking help in this area should consult S.S. Hussey (1982, rev. edn 1992) *The Literary Language of Shakespeare*, Longman, which expands on some of the issues raised in Chapters 1, 2 and 7 of this book. Study of the imagery of the plays (that aspect of the dramatist's language which has received most critical attention) begins with Caroline Spurgeon's pioneering work (1935) *Shakespeare's Imagery and What It Tells Us*, Cambridge University Press, while some indication of the light this kind of approach can shed on specific plays may be gained from R.B. Heilman (1948) *This Great Stage*, Louisiana State University Press, Baton Rouge (a study of the imagery of *King Lear*), or (1956) *Magic in the Web*, Kentucky University Press, Lexington (which explores the imagery of *Othello*). As noted in Chapter 2, visual and verbal imagery overlap in Shakespeare's work, and J.L. Styan (1967) *Shakespeare's Stagecraft*, Cambridge University Press, offers a useful introduction to the study of the text as a blueprint for performance, while expanding on some of the issues raised in Chapter 7. Shakespeare's use of inset actions and parallel plots is set in the larger context of Elizabethan-Jacobean attitudes to plot construction in Richard Levin (1971) *The Multiple Plot in English Renaissance Drama*, University of Chicago Press, while the varieties of interaction between play and audience, considered here in Chapters 4, 6, 7 and 8, are explored more fully in Anne Richter (1962) *Shakespeare and the Idea of the Play*, Chatto and Windus. Works concerned more broadly with aspects of the projection of meaning through form include Madelaine Doran (1954) *Endeavours of Art: A Study of Form in Elizabethan Drama*, University of Wisconsin Press, Madison, and Anthony Brennan (1986) *Shakespeare's Dramatic Structures*, Routledge.

Shakespeare's art of characterization has attracted the attention of a large number of scholars and any recommendation in this field must necessarily be arbitrary. However, an essential starting point for anyone embarking on the study of Shakespeare's tragedies is A.C. Bradley (1904) *Shakespearean Tragedy*, Macmillan, which includes major character studies. The use of the soliloquy is another topic that has been widely discussed, and explorations of specific speeches may be found in the introductions to most major critical editions. A broader investigation of the subject may be found, however, in Wolfgang Clemen (1987) *Shakespeare's Soliloquies*, translated by Charity Scott Stokes, Methuen.

It has been stressed throughout this book that the meaning of a play is fully realized not on the printed page but in performance, and it is in performance that the levels of artifice at work in the plays are most clearly apparent. A seminal work in this field is Harley Granville-Barker (1927 onwards) *Prefaces to Shakespeare*, Sidgwick and Jackson, while a number of studies have been concerned with the stage history of specific items in the corpus, including Marvin Rosenberg (1961) *The Masks of Othello*, (1972) *The Masks of King Lear*, (1978) *The Masks of Macbeth*, all University of California Press, Berkeley; Joseph Price (1968) *The Unfortunate Comedy (All's Well That Ends Well)*, Liverpool University Press; and Dennis Bartholomeusz (1982) *The Winter's Tale in Performance in England and America 1611–1976*, Cambridge University Press; while the volumes in Macmillan's Text and Performance series (ongoing), examine the projection of theme in modern productions. Students interested in the performance aspects of the plays should also consult the New Cambridge editions which place more emphasis on this aspect of Shakespeare studies than comparable critical editions.

Of the many 'new approaches' to the Shakespearian corpus, the one most relevant to the concerns of this book is that which challenges the concept that the plays 'mean'. For an introduction to the concept that 'Shakespeare doesn't mean: *we* mean *by* Shakespeare' see Terence Hawkes (1992) *Meaning By Shakespeare*, Routledge.

Index

Aeschylus, 230
Alliteration, 31
Alternate rhyme, 3
Art
  compared with life, 224–6
  educative function of, 102–12, 226
  self-conscious, 220–7
Artifice
  as a metaphor for spirituality, 209–14
  degree of emphasis on in Shakespeare's plays, 203–31

Background music, twentieth-century, 1, 2, 10, 16, 22, 31
Blank verse, 4; see also Dramatic language

Caesura, 4
Character
  defined through imagery, 35–7
  Shakespeare's treatment of, 143–75
Complementary action, see Parallel action
Couplets, 3

Donne, John, 60
Dramatic language, 1–30, 230

Elizabethan stage, physical structure of, 34, 42, 61
Emblem, 33–4, 120
End-stopped lines, 4
Enjambement, 6
Exposition, 61–85

Feminine caesura, 12
Feminine ending, 14
Foot, metrical, 4; see also Reversed foot
Frame plot, 88–91
Free verse, 4

Functional shift, 76

Greene Robert
  James IV, 88

Heilman, Robert B.
  Magic in the Web, 41n
  This Great Stage, 41n

Iambic foot, 4, 28
  pentameter, 4
  tetrameter, 3, 27
Imagery, 31–60
  figurative, 32
  iterative, 37
  literal, 32
Induction, 88–91
Inverted foot, see Reversed foot

Jonson, Ben, 230
  Bartholomew Fair, 91–2
  Cynthia's Revels, 88
  Volpone, 86

Kyd, Thomas
  The Spanish Tragedy, 88, 91, 116

Light endings, 14
Lighting, twentieth-century, 1–2
Lyly, John
  Campaspe, 86

Marlowe, Christopher
  Dr Faustus, 86
Marston, John
  Antonio and Mellida, 88
  Antonio's Revenge, 116
Masque, 213–14
Metadrama, 220–7
Metaphor, 31–3
Monologue, 176–9
Morality play, 61
Multiple plots, see Parallel action

235